In the Vineyard

In the Vineyard

Working in African American Studies

Perry A. Hall

The University of Tennessee Press • Knoxville

Armstead L. Robinson, Craig C. Foster, and Donald H. Ogilvie, eds., *Black Studies in the University: A Symposium* (New Haven: Yale University Press, 1969). Copyright © 1969 by Yale University. Used by permission.

James B. Stewart, "Reaching for Higher Ground: Toward an Understanding of Black/ Africana Studies," *The Afrocentric Scholar* 1, no. 1 (May 1992): 1–63. Used by permission.

The paper used in this book meets the minimum requirements of ANSI/NISO Z39.48-1992 (R 1997) (Permanence of Paper). The binding materials have been chosen for strength and durability. Printed on recycled paper.

Library of Congress Cataloging-in-Publication Data
Hall, Perry A., 1947–
In the vineyard : working in African American studies / Perry A. Hall. — 1st ed.
    p. cm.
Includes bibliographical references (p.) and index.
ISBN 1-57233-054-6 (cl.: alk. paper)
1. Afro-Americans—Study and teaching—History—20th century. 2. Afro-Americans—Historiography. I. Title.
E184.7 .H24 1999
305.896073'071—dc21   99-6025

For Omari and Pat
Who have been the rest of my life

Contents

Tables

Acknowledgments

The first acknowledgment must go to my former colleague Jon Michael Spencer, who first convinced me this book was possible; indeed that it already existed—in my thoughts, in my experiences, and in a few fragments already written but in need of refinement. I am also grateful for the valuable feedback he gave to the earliest drafts. For those fragments, thoughts, and experiences I am indebted to a host of colleagues with whom I interacted earlier in my career, beginning with Geneva Smitherman, who encouraged and, through spirited dialogue, helped to develop the central frameworks on which the book is based. Among others who made early contributions to my thought and practice, with lucid observations in animated conversations, were Alida D. Quick; Robert G. Newby; Larry Taylor; Norman Harris at Wayne State University; and Gerald McWorter (Abdul Alkalimat), Mary Emma Graham, and Ronald W. Bailey, among others from Peoples College; and the National Council for Black Studies. Professor Smitherman also read the first completed draft and gave valuable feedback. James Stewart and Delores Aldridge, who reviewed the first draft submitted, provided many helpful comments and suggestions that have considerably improved the product. Others to whom I am indebted for their suggestions, contributions, and responses to drafts of the manuscript in whole or in part at different stages include Edward Simpkins, Anne Rawls, Carlene Young, Ruth Iyob, and current colleagues Valerie Johnson, Kenneth Janken, and Robin Vander. When I needed them most, I was most gratefully aided by the sharp proofreading skills of Debby Crowder, Dineane Buttram, and Katherine Neer.

In the final stages I found it helpful to consult with members of my family of origin, particularly my brother, Charles J. Hall, and my mother, Phyllis L. Hall, as I struggled to articulate formally some of the common insight that had buttressed the lives we have shared together. Much earlier in the project, indeed much earlier in my life in the wider, metropolitan world, I came to appreciate the value of wisdom derived from the informal southern-based African American cultural tradition (some would call it oral, indigenous, or vernacular culture) that nurtured us, and which recurs as a reference frame throughout this text. Families are the vital channels through which these sensibilities flow and continually vitalize the living cultures of black folks, passing by intimate communion through the generations. Mine is a large, gregarious example of the black extended family form. The entire teeming clan of parents, brothers, sisters, aunts, uncles, cousins, nephews, nieces, and augmented members has organized itself largely around the love and spiritual power of one soul. To my maternal grandmother, Ms. Emma Beard, who brought cultural light from Clarksdale, Mississippi, during the Great Migration, goes the final acknowledgment. Before recently passing after her ninety-sixth birthday she gave a century of grace to this loving family and to an appreciative community. The most complete human being I have ever known, she expressed at the most sublime level the values and sensibilities that give traditional culture its power to transform and redeem. May she rest with the peace she deserves for a life well lived.

Introduction

Confessions of an African American Studies Professional

I like to say (and it is true) that I am one who grew up a poor boy from the Brewster Projects in postwar Detroit—whose grandparents from southern origins met there in 1921, during the Great Migration, answering Henry Ford's call to come to the city to make five dollars a day. I am a member of that postwar "baby-boom generation" that experienced childhood in the fifties, adolescence and early adulthood in the sixties, the Paying of Dues in the seventies, real Coming of Age (or the coming of Real Age) in the eighties, and the "Comin' 'Round of Things Gon' 'Round" in the nineties. My very life has developed its meaning, socially and culturally, in a significantly broad context of major transformation in the overall black experience. Entering college in 1965 I was in one of the first large classes of African Americans—the quantum increase in the presence of blacks in predominantly white colleges and universities that resulted from the previous decade of social mobilization and change following the momentous events of 1954 and 1955. (The very first class of the Opportunity Award program, under which my education was financed, entered in 1964.)

Prior to this period, the black presence in the mainstream of American higher education was mostly a matter of individual experiences, scattered and isolated, in which black individuals struggled to maintain body and soul under the most adverse circumstances. They prevailed when their individual will proved strong enough to enable them to overcome the myriad obstacles they faced. In the context of the awakened sense of black consciousness and the social protest movement then unfolding in the larger society, the increased presence of African Americans on U.S. college campuses resulted in a critical mass, creating the conditions in which private hurts could be linked to social experience. In his 1985 report to the Ford Foundation on the state of African American Studies, Nathan Huggins put it this way: "In earlier years, the handful of black students managed to fit in, badly or well, nursing as private matters any hurts they felt. With larger numbers it became possible (indeed, almost inevitable) to consider being black on a white campus a collective condition. Private hurts became public grievances."[1]

African American Studies (called Black Studies, Pan-African Studies, Africana Studies, and various other names) is one result of this period of social struggle and institutional change. The inauguration of Black Studies in the academy served to expose and transform institutional, methodological, and pedagogical blindnesses and shortcomings in the arena of higher education. As a student in the formative period of Black Studies, and a scholar at present in a degree-granting department, my entire postsecondary educational and professional life has been involved with the emergence and progress of African American Studies. On many levels, then, this book is intended to contribute to an understanding of the significance of African American Studies as an academic enterprise. It offers, first of all, a personal reflection on how and why the discipline evolved within the context of the wider social revolution changing the face of America—how the presence of blacks in the academy, in effect, uncovered the need for new insights and perspectives in the higher education curricula. These reflections help illuminate the urgency of our need for an educational experience that acknowledged our visibility and validated us as human beings.

The intellectual issues developed in this book constitute an analysis of how various perspectives, approaches, or schools of thought have evolved to constitute African American Studies, and how they interact within the field and interface with other areas of knowledge. Here my efforts are intended to conjoin and complement other recent work in a project to assess the development of what is now a well-established but still-developing field.[2] Furthermore, in illustrating various applications of my proposed analytic approach I hope to demonstrate how the insights and perspectives of African American Studies can be made "relevant"—a term from the founding era of the field—in a variety of contexts.

The years of my undergraduate education, 1965–69, were among the most tumultuous in the history of higher education—indeed, in American society as a whole. In my life these years brought the first visible manifestations of structural change, visible evidence of an ongoing black movement or revolution. A very short list of important and startling events occurring during those brief years includes the March on Selma; the Voting Rights Act; the assassinations of Malcolm X, Martin King, and Robert Kennedy; the emergence of the Black Power and Black Arts movements; major civil uprisings in Watts, Detroit, and more than a hundred other American cities; and the escalation of the Vietnam War as a military event, as a highly divisive social issue, and as a phenomenon affecting the course of the black experience.

To state that the surrounding sociohistorical environment profoundly affected, and in some ways overshadowed, the *institutional* process of undergraduate higher education is to understate the obvious. The need for a "relevant" education so insistently demanded by blacks on American campuses then, when our strongest guide was the authority of our own experience, seems even more pressing in retrospect. Before discovering a language to express it, we objected to the bias, the chauvinism, the cultural imperialism inherent in the concepts like "cultural deprivation," under which some liberal minds proposed to address the needs of "disadvantaged" blacks.[3] "*I'm* not culturally deprived," I remember amiably telling some whites on my undergraduate campus "*you* are!"[4] (The pride in "being who you are," ingrained by parents and elders in my life, was just one aspect of a rich foundation provided by the urban, working-class black culture that had nurtured me. Without being completely aware of its significance, I nonetheless became heir to a cultural tradition that was a critical anchor for my sense of self and crucial to my survival.)

In my first-semester speech class all but one of my presentations focused on race issues. Both the instructor and students in this otherwise all-white class made it abundantly clear they had heard more than they wanted about my subject choice in their final critiques. Though all my prior assignments had been A's and B's, my course grade was C. Dispossessed of a newly found voice, I was, along with others, an easy recruit to the notion that something especially important to us as African Americans was missing in this environment.

Discovery of the legacies left by the personal—and often isolated—struggles of previous generations of black scholars was crucial to our ability to survive as students in this alien intellectual environment. One of my first important discoveries was W. E. B. Du Bois's *The Souls of Black Folk*. Especially relevant to me was his concept of duality or "double-consciousness." This idea helped me articulate, if not necessarily resolve, the tensions and contradictions I was experiencing as I moved between the world of my lower-class urban origins and the new and strange world of a major, predominantly white university.

Du Bois is, of course, only one among many from previous generations of black scholars and intellectuals who left their personal, intellectual, and historical legacy to us, a highly fragmented body of literature inscribing their often obscure struggles to affirm their humanity and self, and, in turn, ours as well. Typically, in those days these journeys of discovery occurred totally outside of normal curricular activities. Indeed, it was precisely the absences of these voices in the curriculum that fueled the Black Studies movement on campuses across the nation. The institutionalization of African American Studies has been the struggle to make these voices heard in the curriculum and in the academy.

On many campuses undergraduate courses like the one on black literature I took during my senior year started to emerge slowly as a result of pressures brought to bear in conjunction with the increased presence of African Americans. Without such a course, the general idea that literature was connected to the cultural expression of a people was hardly meaningful to me, since so little of my world was reflected in so-called "American" and "world" literature. Neither were courses in sociology and history, as traditionally conceived, conducive to illuminating and addressing issues relevant to the experiences of African Americans in those tumultuous times. Most of these courses demonstrably failed in their ability to encompass our realities.

As African American courses and curricula appeared, many in the academy expressed skepticism, which lingers even today, regarding "legitimacy" of these areas of study. However, as I shall argue, the fact that a body of texts defining black historical and literary perspectives already existed at the time we launched the Black Studies movement is itself solid evidence of the "validity" and "legitimacy" of the field.

The early 1970s found me and my cohorts in a variety of postcollegiate experiences, in political movements and organizations or in graduate studies. In some fashion or other most of us were attempting to resolve the dilemma of "double-consciousness" and the "contradiction of double aims"—fundamentally, the contradictions between our experiences, needs, and imperatives as an oppressed community and the institutional environments to which we were being exposed. Ultimately, the duality of which Du Bois wrote would require us to transform and adapt the consciousness and energy of the previous collective mobilization to new settings. Among itinerant professional, political, and cultural experiences immediately following my graduation were those of part-time schoolteacher, journalist, political activist, war protester, writer-poet, philosopher, motorcyclic commuter, and general wanderer-seeker. Settling into graduate school after two years of these experiences, I, like my cohorts, had imperatives, objectives, perspectives, and methods shaped significantly outside of what at that time might have been called "conventional" intellectual and professional concerns.

Like many students, I perceived a need for transformation of perspective in graduate studies parallel to that which had been evident during undergraduate education. On the one hand, we had to acknowledge and analyze our status as outsiders (individually as well as collectively) in these "mainstream" institutions. On the other hand, the structure, content, and process of the institution itself had to be changed, reshaped, and transformed to incorporate the legitimacy of our experiences and those of our communities (that is, acknowledging the reality that we were *not* "outsiders"). Without such validation we were still like the nameless protagonist in Ralph Ellison's celebrated novel, *Invisible Man*—our dark faces seen but our humanity invisible.[5]

For those of us meeting in this graduate setting, representing various fronts, constituencies, and communities in the ongoing "revolution," the desired objective was to formulate the role of the black intellectual—namely, to learn to use knowledge to inform activism, and activism to vitalize knowledge. What we came to know as "praxis" was a strategy that would not just analyze but help change conditions and realities relevant to our individual and community experiences.[6] The issue of whether to work within or outside of "the system," intensely debated among militants and activists in the 1960s, resolved in the 1970s to a commitment to change from the "inside." Our aim was to make the system work *for* us rather than *against* us—that is, to make it function more legitimately by broadening its foundations to include African Americans.

A key insight informing our activism was an understanding of how race, as a historical and social construction, had shaped our contemporary world. Again, as we were to discover, Du Bois characteristically said it best: "The problem of the twentieth century is the problem of the color line."[7] It was critically helpful in this regard that my particular graduate experience was privileged by the presence of fellow students, along with a few teachers, representing diverse groups and nationalities among the world's peoples of color. We were brown, red, yellow, and black (and white), and the sharing of our collective experiences pointed to the global significance of race issues and to connections among our various peoples. In classroom interactions and in friendship groupings we learned to recognize our common oppression, to link the diverse threads of a common story plotted along Du Bois's global "color line." But it went much deeper.

In that time and place the particularities of our different race/ethnic/nationalities actually helped bond rather than divide us. We saw that what the system oppressed and denied in each of us was that which was most human, or humane, about us: our languages, our histories, our musics, which we shared freely and affectionately among ourselves in that setting. We came to understand that we were confronting a particular construction of knowledge that marginalized the histories and experiences of our peoples and marginalized us as individual scholars if we attempted to focus, or "center," our studies and inquiries on those experiences and histories. (It was this marginalization that had obscured and fragmented the previous documentation of an African American scholarly legacy). It was "knowledge" construed in a way that ironically allowed white intellectuals to insist that people of color who focused on understanding their own communities and experiences lacked a general, or so-called "universal," perspective, when our common humanity and common oppression told us it was most assuredly *they* who lacked this perspective. This curious dynamic was clearly captured at the important 1968 Yale Symposium on Black Studies in the University (discussed in chapter 2), which debated key issues relative to the initial emergence of Black Studies.[8] Our confrontation in the early seventies with "European particularisms . . . [which] translated into absolute standards for human achievement, norms, and aspirations" presaged the widespread public debates around the issues of multiculturalism and cultural pluralism that have peaked in the nineties.[9]

Activism to vitalize insight in this setting invariably involved developing an academic discourse aimed at redirecting, challenging, and refuting those precepts of the established system of knowledge that marginalized our humanity. As students, inside and outside of class, we looked at this challenge analytically. We found in the common experience of oppression a language, a frame of reference, through which we could communicate beyond the superficial barriers of culture and language to address and affirm that which was most basic and most human. Our dissertations, which would qualify us to "profess" in our respective fields of knowledge, were, simultaneously, monuments to our spiritual liberation.

My own doctoral thesis, which looked at how established social science paradigms shaped policy responses to substance abuse, became an early exercise in critically examining established paradigms and proposing the construction of alternatives. Challenging established social science paradigms configuring the circumstances of blacks was for me a further step toward embracing African American Studies as an academic enterprise. My emergent scholarship paralleled that of numerous others among my cohort who felt that alternative approaches were needed to confront distortions of black humanity in relation to a broad range of social or intellectual issues. At the Yale conference in 1968 some participants expressed the emergent view that the "normative" models and "systems" approaches dominating the social sciences at that time created distorted, "pathological" constructions of the black family and the black community.

With my first postgraduate position in the Black Studies "center" of a large state university, my mission was defined. From that point on, my career has been spent on the project of establishing that fledgling field as a legitimate component of the academy. For eight years I was acting director of the center. It was a position that allowed me ample opportunity to observe, and it compelled me to work through the various levels of obstacles—structural, institutional, intellectual—in the task of legitimizing the field.

During the late sixties the students and community wanted to install a legitimate academic enterprise called Black Studies at that institution. Although the institution in many ways encouraged those constituencies to believe that that was what they were doing, it is not in fact what they created. Its structure from the very beginning was clearly something far different from such a legitimized academic enterprise. My own experience bears witness to the truth of Robert L Harris's description, in the Ford Foundation publication *Black Studies in the United States: Three Essays,* of a typical scenario during the period:

> Although some colleges and universities were willing to establish Africana studies programs, they were less willing to organize Africana studies departments. Faculty within the traditional departments were reluctant to give up their prerogative of determining what constituted a course in history, literature, or government; who would take such courses; and how the professors teaching them would be evaluated for employment, promotion, and tenure. Advocates of Africana studies departments questioned how members of traditional departments that had not offered courses on the black experience or hired black faculty could sit in judgment on the nature and quality of work being done in this newly emerging field of study.[10]

The bottom line was that the established faculty denied the center the ability to grant tenure to its own faculty. Structurally it was neither a *real* department nor a *real* field of study in institutional terms. As a result, the realities of the university tenure system reified the dilemma of "double-consciousness" and the "contradiction of double aims" and professional objectives. Later it presented serious career problems for those who became more than nominally involved with the development of African American Studies. The competing interests created by the "contradiction of double aims" presented the alternatives of either marginalizing oneself within an established discipline or ignoring, deferring, or subordinating the objectives of the new academic enterprise.

In our case the program had makeshift arrangements and no solid fiscal support, as was typical in those days. The task of making our enterprise work was daunting. While there was sometimes an appearance of chaos, attributable largely to the temporary nature of the structure, there were nonetheless undeniable achievements and indicators of progress. To give structure and focus to our curriculum we developed an introductory survey course, several intermediate and special courses, and strategies that successfully increased and stabilized student enrollment. Attempting to bridge the double-consciousness, the duality, of our existence as blacks in the academy, we also cultivated connections with the black community, whose insistence had led, in the first instance, to our place in the academy.

Significantly, we developed and documented concepts, frameworks, and models that have since contributed to the institutionalization of African American Studies as a legitimate field of study. One document, for which I was principal author, developed the background and rationale and summarized the conceptual structure of a full degree-granting curriculum in Black Studies, with courses, taxonomies, and subfield areas. The curriculum proscribed cognate studies in other areas that would address the question of future skills and career areas for graduates, or research skills for graduate study. It described the value, "relevance," and necessity of Black Studies in the curricula of non–Black Studies majors and nonblacks. Although, this concept was not enacted during my tenure in the program, ten years later, in 1989, in response to a student-initiated movement, the university agreed to upgrade the Center for Black Studies to a full department, with tenure and degree-granting capability. This very document was then resurrected and became a "founding text" for guiding the university's first attempt to define that commitment. Whether or not always directly or officially recognized, such early efforts often helped define this new field.

Meanwhile, channels and venues linking activities and experiences among various institutions and locations—the formation of professional networks, associations, and forums for organization and discourse among Black Studies scholars at regional and national levels—promoted key activities in the ongoing project of building and developing an academic discipline. From professional organizations like the National Council for Black Studies authority was derived and voices developed to speak to the important issues that would define and constitute African American Studies. Among issues addressed in such discourse were the development of statements of shared curricular objectives that defined the academic substance and the theoretical and methodological issues of Black Studies, and the identification and development of existing and emerging scholarship as appropriate text materials for teaching and sources for research. As noted in the forthcoming chapters, vigorous debate has often been a feature of these associative activities; dialogue or discourse generated in such debates is key to the dialectical process of defining the Black Studies movement.

The late seventies to early eighties was a period when the dialogue was particularly dynamic and intense among activist elements in the Black Studies movement. The unity of the participants—based on their rejection of traditional academic modes and approaches to Black Studies then sanctioned by powers in the academic world—sometimes appeared threatened in the intense debate over what should replace the traditional modes and approaches.[11] The most polarized form of this dialogue involved a raging debate between Nationalist and Marxist factions or "tendencies" in the movement. One of the earliest introductory texts, *Introduction to Afro-American Studies,* was produced by a well-known Marxist collective in 1977.[12] Among nationalist productions, Maulana Karenga's *Introduction to Black Studies* (first published in 1982) was probably the most widely circulated introductory text to appear in this period.[13] The emergence of black women's studies during this period injected yet another element into the discourse. A pioneering women's studies anthology, *All the Women Are White, All the Blacks Are Men, but Some of Us Are Brave: Black Women's Studies* (Gloria T. Hull et al.) also appeared during this period (1982) of debate and contention.[14]

Under the auspices of the National Council for Black Studies this writer chaired a committee on curriculum standards and was principal author of its report outlining a Black Studies core curriculum.[15] Although the threat of political polarization posed a continual challenge to these collaborative efforts, it nevertheless ensured that the full spectrum of views in the field was represented in constructing this model. Adopted in 1980, the core curriculum outlined in the National Council for Black Studies Curriculum Committee Report was an effective guide for several programs in the development and expansion of their curricular offerings during the eighties.

This period in my own career was often occupied with matters other than finished scholarship, matters such as those mentioned above. Indeed, I did feel very much like the object of Robert L. Harris's description in the following passage:

> during the early days of organizing when the focus was on the quest for legitimacy and institutionalization . . . Africana studies was to provide the black presence, to supply role models for students, to have an active advising and counseling function, to organize film series, lectures, and symposia, and to influence traditional departments in the composition of their faculty and curriculum. This was a tall order that exhausted many Africana studies faculty. Having expended their energy on getting the new field off the ground, many faculty had not devoted sufficient time to research and publication and thus were caught short when evaluated for promotion and tenure.[16]

In spite of the haunting familiarity of that career trajectory, I have managed periodically to produce articles and other scholarship to intellectually document my experience as it connects with the overall development of African American Studies. In its first draft this book represented an opportunity for me to organize and reshape some of those earlier efforts into a unified statement. As it has turned out, augmentation, revision, and refinement of those pieces has produced a significantly original, integrated text. In three parts, summarized below, the present text documents the development of the analytical reference frame which has informed virtually all my efforts—institutional, instructional, and scholarly—as a Black Studies professional. In addition, I suggest how this frame of reference might be applied to study and analysis of several cultural, social, and political issues and problems that are pivotal in the field.

Part I: The Struggle for Black Studies

Chapters 1 and 2 reflect on elements of political struggle involved with the emergence of African American Studies: a consideration of how Black Studies programs emerged as institutional expressions of a "Black Studies movement." Chapter 1, "Struggle Outward: Barricades and

Ivory Towers," focuses on the struggle between the movement and the academy, the struggle to get the academy to accept the mission to create Black Studies. Chapter 2, "Struggle Inward: Whither, Then, and How?" focuses on the struggle among elements within the Black Studies movement to establish and define the character of the enterprise as institutional space was established for it in the academic world.

Part II: Theorizing African American Studies

Chapters 3, 4, and 5 address textual, academic, and theoretical issues that have developed as part of the maturation of the field. Chapter 3, "Afrocentrism: More or Less," focuses on the emergence of Afrocentrism as a widely recognized paradigm associated with Black Studies. Following the debate described above, Afrocentrism, as an orientation and as an intellectual framework, gained currency in the Black Studies movement during the mid-eighties. Established principally in work by Molefi Asante and his "Temple school" of Afrocentric thinkers, Afrocentricity seemed to become, for a time, nearly synonymous with African American Studies as a discipline or field of study. My discussion incorporates both its insights and achievements, and its limitations and critiques.

The concept of multiple viewpoints is developed in chapter 4, "Alternative Approaches in African American Studies." This chapter constructs African American Studies as a field or discipline containing several tendencies, schools, or streams of thought, each contributing to an ongoing discourse regarding salient issues in the field. Building on concepts developed by James B. Stewart, chapter 4 discusses African American studies as a "disciplinary matrix" that incorporates multiple theoretical perspectives, frameworks, or reference points.[17] In addition to conventional ("integrationist" or "inclusionist") and Afrocentric perspectives, an alternative framework, identified as "transformationist," is introduced.

Having situated my efforts among the various schools of thought, chapter 5 features a fuller treatment of the transformationist approach as it has developed to inform my own work in the field. Entitled "Systematic and Thematic Principles," this chapter describes my particular approach and presents its basic analytical terms, concepts, and premises. The paradigm is built around a perspective of "dynamic duality," which focuses on the constant, transformative interaction of an "Afrocentric strain" of African American experience (thematic and internal) with

Westernized, mainstream social structures (systematic and external) to create, shape, and transform black communities. A valid examination of any given aspect of black life, I propose, must address this interaction in multiple, sometimes complex, ways. An approach to conceptualizing this complex interaction is developed in this chapter.

Part III: In the Vineyard

Chapters 6, 7, and 8 demonstrate the application of the principles of this transformationist framework to intellectual tasks in three different areas. Chapter 6, "Conceptualizing Black Identity," looks at theoretical formulations and survey data related to studies of black identity. The discussion here draws on my earlier study of data, collected by the University of Michigan's Institute for Social Research, from the first nationally representative cross-sectional sample of black Americans ever assembled for the purposes of an academic survey. My study of this data illustrates how the paradigm developed from my previous efforts can be applied to the interpretation of so-called "objective" data and contribute new insights to interpret such studies.

Chapter 7 is titled "The Songs of Black Folks." This chapter applies the precepts of the paradigm outlined in "Systematic and Thematic Principles" to an examination of cultural transformation in the black experience, as reflected in popular music. In addition, I also point to the importance of folk, popular, or traditional forms of expressive culture in understanding the overall context of black life in any given historical moment. The core of African-based orality on which folk/popular culture is based suggests that oral forms such as music can tell about more aspects of the story of black people than customary literary sources alone.

Chapter 8, "Crisis, Culture, and Literacy in the Community," looks at how ideas associated with African American Studies have influenced public policy discourses, especially in education, and suggests how insights associated with the paradigm previously developed might be used to inform other processes of policy formation. In addition to uncovering historical clues to black identity, culture, and history, African American Studies must direct its insights to problems current in the black community: violence, drug use, high dropout rates, early parenthood, so-called "family dysfunction," and a long list of other conditions symptomatic of the deepening crisis in the African American community. This chapter attempts to propose programmatic steps in that direction.

The epilogue, "Working in African American Studies," concludes this work with a summary of the current status and direction of the African American Studies project. The current trends in the field's schools of thought are addressed. The discussion is framed in terms of challenges and opportunities confronting Black Studies in the United States, and elsewhere in the African diaspora, as a new millennium approaches.

Part 1

The Struggle for Black Studies

Chapter 1

Struggle Outward:
Barricades and Ivory Towers

The various stages through which Black Studies programs evolve tell us much about how academic institutions confer (or withhold) "legitimacy" regarding academic enterprises or fields of study such as Black Studies. In the case of my first program, Black Studies' entry as a "center" was a result of political forces that engulfed the university rather than intellectual engagement. The center's peculiar institutional placement (it was not in an academic college), lack of academic authority (the liberal arts college allowed courses and credit as "courtesy" under the "interdisciplinary" heading), and inability to grant rank and tenure indicate little if any sense of legitimacy on the part of the academy.

There are some indications that time and intervening events may have changed that institutional view somewhat. The program, along with others surviving into the nineties, eventually evolved into full departmental status. Ultimately, however, the center's acquisition of these tools of institutional legitimacy was still the result of extra-normal forces (a student movement in 1989) rather than internal intellectual or institutional initiative. This indicates that, despite the establishment of departmental structures, the view of Black Studies as interloper with no real "academic legitimacy" is probably unchanged among a significant sector in the academy.[1] Another way of framing the issue is to say that the achievement of legitimate institutional status, like the initial formation of the field itself, has depended more on the actions and initiatives of Black Studies activists and scholars themselves than on the largess or enlightenment of the academic establishment.

So, the question of legitimacy lingers still in the view of a significant portion of the academy; this in spite of the fact that, contrary to prediction, African American Studies has survived and, in effect, established its own legitimacy. The study of the historical and contemporary experiences, conditions, and aspirations of descendants of Africa is not only legitimate. It has, as historian Darlene Clark Hine noted, "opened up vast and exciting new areas of scholarship, especially in American history and literature, and has spurred intellectual inquiry into diverse social problems affecting the lives of significant portions of the total population."[2] Indeed, African American Studies has constituted itself as a legitimate, distinct, discrete field of study in most circumstances before, and independent of, being granted the tools (departmental status and academic authority).

Black Studies in the University: The Yale Symposium

The reconstruction of the period of Black Studies formation in the late 1960s illustrates how extra-academic forces, intellectual legitimacy, and institutional recognition have interacted in interdependent as well as sometimes independent ways. A sense of how issues of legitimacy have shaped, defined, and engaged the Black Studies project can be discerned by looking at some key events charting the formation of this fledgling enterprise. To that end I have utilized a singularly useful documentary aid. Published as *Black Studies in the University: A Symposium*,[3] this remarkable text documents the proceedings of a conference organized by the Black Student Alliance at Yale in spring 1968 as part of the process of establishing a Black Studies Program at the University. It is fascinating and instructive for two reasons: (1) the debates and discussions codified in this document are fairly representative of the manner in which these issues were engaged in academic settings across the country during that period; and (2) while the Yale program that eventually evolved was regarded by some to be "the strongest and most respected in the country,"[4] and while the model it represents was generally favored by administrators and establishment academics, this program model has not been embraced by activists in the field, who make up the Black Studies "movement."

The symposium was organized to bring pressure on the Yale faculty to install a Black Studies Program after students noted that their efforts to correct "the glaring inadequacies which then typified the intellectual treatment of the Afro-American experience" had produced little progress "in the struggle to convince the faculty at large of the validity and importance of our concerns."[5] Supported with funds from the Ford Foundation, and watched over by foundation president McGeorge Bundy, the symposium featured two days of papers, presentations, and discussions involving black and white scholars and activists representing a significant cross section of thought for and against various aspects of Black Studies.[6] The documented proceedings of this meeting are not only important in themselves but in the fact that they reflect, in a representative manner, the issues of a national discourse that was occurring at that time in a documented form that allows us to examine them from a contemporary perspective. In that regard, a good deal of the material relevant to my discussion here comes from discussions and questionand-answer sessions between presentations, rather than from presentations themselves.

The timing of the conference, May 1968, places it in an extremely urgent, microhistorical time bracket. By May, we had already seen the Tet offensive and the abdication of President Lyndon Baines Johnson, and the recent assassination of Dr. Martin Luther King Jr. The symposium was occurring at the same time, or shortly after, the student strike that shut down Columbia University. (During the same week the radical students and workers in France nearly toppled the government there.) Still to come in 1968 were the assassination of Robert F. Kennedy, the antiwar demonstrations at the Democratic convention in Chicago, and the violent uprising of Miami blacks during the Republican convention, among many other signs of the continuing social crises that then gripped the nation.

One can surmise that the symposium's participants, indeed the entire world, in some way felt the pressures signaled by those events. (I can say that I, along with those who shared my setting in that intense period, were all keenly in tune with events in the surrounding context.) It is clear, however, that those pressures and anxieties manifested themselves differently among students and activist scholars than they did among established scholars. The Yale students who precipitated the event, though restrained in tone in comparison with many student movements of that period, were still clearly manifesting a sense of urgency when they issued their challenge: "Fundamental inequities and incongruities infest the structure of the educational establishment. These tensions will be relieved. It is still not too late for educators to choose to assist the process of reforming their institutions; how long that option will remain theirs is any man's guess."[7] In comparison, Yale Provost Charles Taylor[8] seemed both timid and doubtful in defining the symposium's essential questions: "Is the special study of the black experience intellectually valid? Is it educationally responsible? And, is it socially constructive for both blacks and whites?"[9]

Noted cultural historian Harold Cruse, nationalist community activist Maulana Karenga, radical Marxist Gerald McWorter (Abdul Alkalimat), and Nathan Hare—who would all be visible in the ideological debates of the next period—participated. However, the ideological outlines that would divide them from one another at a later period were not readily apparent on this occasion. Maulana Karenga was later to become prominent as a leading nationalist, and is currently prominent in the development and spread of Afrocentric thought. (Indeed, he was already credited with creating the African American holiday Kwanza and the "Ngoza Saba," the seven principles Kwanza celebrates.) At the conference, however, his presentation was entirely that of a community radical: "The white university is not primarily an educational institution but a political one, and it seeks to maintain the power base of American society. All those people who go to work for the CIA, for the government at large, for big industry . . . come from the universities." At that time Karenga's nationalist ideology expressed the concept of community control in terms of national sovereignty. From that perspective he addressed the university as the agent of a foreign nation, stating that his description of "what the university could do for the community" was "non-intervention, foreign aid, and civilizing committees."[10]

While not brandishing Leninist rhetoric as he would later during the 1970s ideological debates, Gerald McWorter presented a nonetheless radical critique of academia: "white people who have performed as scientists and as academicians and scholars have indeed been apologists for whatever racist practices exist in society today." However, in that early period he still appeared to be associating himself with nationalist principles, referring to the concept of "a black university" and to elements of African American culture.[11] Nathan Hare—then in the midst of his rather short tenure as head of the nation's first Black Studies department at San Francisco State University—would later co-found *The Black Scholar*, arguably the first (modern) Black Studies academic journal, whose pages would be heated by the coming debates. At this meeting, however, he also projected community-based militancy in a performance that, along with Karenga's, earned the description "deeply anti-intellectual" from Nathan Huggins, who included a report on this event in his 1985 report to the Ford Foundation.[12]

What should be understood here is that Karenga, McWorter, Hare, along with Cruse, then writer in residence, and later professor of history at the University of Michigan, were among that group of participants who, along with the students, clearly maintained a direct conceptual link between the impetus for Black Studies in the university and the tumultuous events outside academia. Cruse, whose studious, conference-opening presentation won Huggins's scholarly approval, specifically linked the demand for Black Studies programs to a strain of cultural nationalism emerging from the earlier era in which integration had been emphasized in the broader black movement. He and the other radical voices, who later would delineate ideological differences among themselves, were confederated against "the system"; "the establishment," whose presence at this event was significant as eminent faculty from Yale and elsewhere; and the officials and funds of the Ford Foundation. (Among the other black participants were Alvin Pouissant and Martin Kilson, both Harvard faculty who represented the moderate-to-conservative current in black intellectual thought of that period.)

The Yale faculty must surely have also seen the potential linkages between the broader turmoil and their confrontation with the black student movement. Perhaps with equal urgency they were concerned, on one level, with keeping the linkages from forming. As evidenced in their comments and questions following presentations, they were immediately concerned with maintaining a separation between intellectual and ideological issues. One Yale faculty, responding to Cruse's presentation, put it this way: "One [thrust] would be to include in its curriculum studies of the Negro experience; another would be, also, preparation for some kind of public service work once a student left the university and went back into society. . . . Are you asking that the university accept these courses despite the fact that they contain a certain ideological bias?"[13] But of course the point being made by Cruse and by the students who called the conference was precisely that the curriculum was already ideologically biased in ways that negated and marginalized the sensibilities and realities of blacks. "[C]ultural nationalism," Cruse stated in response to this point, "is nothing but an attempt to prevent the cultural particularism of the dominant white group from continuing to overshadow and submerge the essence of the black experience in America."[14]

However, this was clearly a major problem for some white and black faculty members. The dialogue recorded at Yale seems fairly representative of how faculty persistently repeated the belief that knowledge, in order to be valid, had to be separate from politics or advocacy. One faculty member qualified his support for Black Studies in this way: "I suggest that we've created a viable basis for expanding the curriculum and inquiry without acquiescing in the notion that tied to such expanded inquiry has to be any particular programmatic notion of how our society should be changed."[15]

Another faculty discussant stated: "I am prepared to maintain that the educational validity of studying the black experience, when it is divorced from any specific black nationalist standpoint, is a study which might include an analysis of both the black nationalist standpoint and the critics of that standpoint."[16]

Speaking at the end of that conference, McGeorge Bundy, John F. Kennedy's former national security adviser and then Ford Foundation president, was careful to discern the various agendas at play: "It was made very clear by Maulana Karenga that his interest in these matters is a political interest. . . . That seems to me a first-class purpose and a proper target. It also seems to me *not* to be the way to define interesting topics in black history. . . . So there is a difference, to put it no more sharply, between the *political* view of a set of historical events and the *historical* view of those events."[17]

Bundy also pinpointed another theme that was a constant feature of dialogue around the country regarding these issues. "Another dividing line which seemed to me to be present but not sharply delineated, is the dividing line between the importance . . . of the subject in its own right and the picture of the subject as a *means* for providing a sense of purpose, identity, and direction for young black men and women, black students in the university . . . there is nothing *wrong* . . . but it is a very dangerous thing to start pushing the subject around for that purpose."[18]

In pressing his point, Bundy seemed to actually confuse the matter, badly: "If you undertake to study a subject because of the *subject's* importance, then at least you are doing something real. If you undertake to study a subject because of the importance of that act to *you*, then, in the long run what you are doing is unreal."[19] In cold print in 1998, this statement seems completely incongruous. It was precisely the importance of such study *to* African Americans that made it *real for* African Americans. Bundy's statement only makes sense when one factors in the information that the *you* to whom he referred were black students seeking to establish the Black Studies program (an "other"). "If you focus on the particularity of your blackness," your "otherness," he seemed to be saying, "then what you are doing is unreal."

Again, it seemed to students, activists, and some academics that this "establishment" view missed the point in at least two ways. First, a sense of purpose, identity, and direction (precisely the terms Karenga had used, and repeated by Bundy) was exactly what the university experience has always provided for many of its students, in accordance with the dictates of a white, middle-class, Anglo-American cultural framework. It was not a perversion for black students coming from a cultural nationalist perspective to expect similar forms of edification in curricula more attuned to their cultural background. Curriculum per se was only one way black students felt the "white" institution failed precisely to serve their needs to develop purpose, identity, and direction. According to Huggins, "The newly developing black student associations . . . pressed to make the [general] college environment congenial and hospitable to what they described as black values and culture. They wanted student activities for black students, black cultural centers. Sometimes they asked for separate dormitories (or black floors or sections of dormitories); they established black tables in dining halls."[20] All these domains in which the social and cultural needs of college students have traditionally been served were felt to be deficient in their ability to incorporate the increased presence of blacks in the university setting.

Second, the sense of major social crises in the world outside the halls of academia was what created the need for purpose and direction among the thousands of young blacks "caught up" in these crises at this very critical stage of their lives. The conditions of inequity and crises to which Yale student Armstead Robinson spoke were too stark, too immediate to be discarded, minimized, or even looked at with so-called "objectivity." For many, to study and pursue some kind of ivory tower abstract knowledge without concerning oneself with how that knowledge was related to understanding, changing, overcoming, or even just surviving such conditions would just be too "irrelevant." It was, then, simply impossible for them to disassociate the political and personal from the academic in this tumultuous setting. As one of the students wrote: "Students are demanding more "relevance" precisely because they are recognizing that most of what they have learned has no *revealing* relationship to the way the world functions. It is the rude shock that comes as a result of being made forcefully aware of the incongruity between life as it is described in school and *life* as it is in the streets that lies at the heart of most contemporary student unrest and ferment."[21]

Even the most supportive liberal whites found it necessary to pay homage to the principle of intellectual detachment, even when they partially admitted the existence of intellectual biases. David Brion Davis, for example, sounds alternately perplexed, sympathetic, and condescending in summing up the Yale symposium: "Despite the exaggerated rhetoric of the blacks, they have convinced many whites of the validity of their basic contention—namely, that the university, which has thought of itself as enlightened and objective, has in reality been a racist institution. We have assumed that we could admit increasing numbers of Negro students without modifying our traditional educational standards and our ideal of the educated man; we expected Negroes to assimilate our culture and to integrate on our terms."[22]

Davis concedes knowledge and ideology are not always separable, stating, "While the reputable scholar strives for objectivity, he knows that knowledge represents power and often serves an ideological function."[23] In fact, he seems to strike to the heart of the matter, observing that students "are understandably suspicious of trite claims to universality which have demonstrably been used to justify slavery, enforced segregation, exploitation, and effacement of nonwhite, non-Western identities."[24] However, he seems to patronize the idea of a "black perspective," with his remarks that, "It is understandable that for many blacks who are struggling for their own souls and for their own survival, the ideal of objective truth appears as an encumbrance or luxury they cannot afford."[25] Not understanding, apparently, how the terms of that proposition apply exactly to him, Davis, in the end, upholds the central concern of the mainstream academics, concluding: "Yet we must insist on maintaining the distinction between political ideology and education."[26]

With the added wisdom and perspective (and hopefully not the added baggage) that comes with age, experience, time, and distance it is possible to appreciate some legitimacy from both, or all, sides of this historical debate. Certainly it is not possible to dismiss the professors' concerns out of hand as merely racist apologism (though some of it surely was). In the world of 1968 (as, some would argue, in the world of 1998) politicization was a fact, and over-politicization to the detriment of any ostensible "educational" function was a danger, and a fact, in some instances. If the experiences of blacks were worthy of serious study, it is valid to suggest that they should be studied seriously. As Huggins pointed out in his report, some of the older black and white scholars whose work created an intellectual foundation for Black Studies were concerned their work would not be taken seriously and would become even more marginalized in this atmosphere.

On the other hand, it is not possible to dismiss the validity of the challenge presented to the educational establishment by students and activists (including some faculty and scholars) as to the establishment's legitimacy, or authority in matters involving the discernment of "objectivity," in the development of Black Studies. The initiative for the Yale conference, like most initiatives in the Black Studies movement, didn't come from the pursuit of "objective" truth by (mostly) white intellectuals pursuing established venues of scholarship. It came from the students, who themselves reflected the intrusion on campus of the broader movement of black assertion for equality. They made it clear that they called the conference after being unsuccessful in their attempts to persuade Yale faculty of the legitimacy of the proposed studies. (In the double-voiced rhetorical tradition of "signifyin"[27] they are telling us, "We tried to be nice, but then we saw we had to act up just a little.")

Those institutions that didn't have major disruptions (as San Francisco State did) or events as orderly as the Yale conference felt the pressure from reviewing the experiences of those that did. Black Studies was not instituted because the established professorate in American institutions of higher education came to determine, by any natural internal process of scholarly inquiry, any traditional venue of pursuit of "enlightenment," "objectivity," or "truth," that it constituted a field worthy of serious study. Given their history, the professorate could never legitimately claim that the established disciplines of this intellectual tradition would, of their own methods and devices, reverse their momentum and correct their own errors, redefine their "universal truths" to validly incorporate all the "others" that tradition has, in fact, created. One questioner at the Yale conference, who described himself only as a lawyer, and who I presume is white, projects an eloquent sense of this, pointing the specific significance, importance, and historicity of Yale itself in this tradition: "This university has produced extraordinary alumni, some men of great distinction, who have gone out to do a great deal of evil in the world—men like John Calhoun. We have had extraordinary men on the Yale faculty who have uttered the most appalling nonsense in the particular area we are now considering—I think of William Graham Sumner."[28]

The crises to which those who challenged this tradition were responding were, if not the result of this legacy, certainly the result of ongoing systems of oppression and dehumanization with which this intellectual tradition was clearly and devastatingly complicit.[29] If one result of the crises was that a void had been created for politicization, opportunism, charlatanism and all the other things they feared would taint their academic standards (especially if they insisted that the legacies of Calhoun and Sumner had not already tainted them), then it was a result "they" clearly had the major role in creating. Thus, for the Black Studies movement students, scholars, and activists, it was never enough for university representatives to suggest, "Now that we're apprised of our lack of inclusiveness, we will address our inadequacies appropriately, but we will also maintain authority to decide what is legitimate in this area." It is fairly clear from the proceedings at Yale which participants felt they were outsiders attacking this tradition, and which, however liberal and supportive (for example, David Brion Davis), felt compelled to defend and maintain it.

As one who has now spent more than twenty years in a Black Studies career—with the increased experience, knowledge, information, and skill to marshal reason, logic, evidence, and data—I say adequate intellectual treatment of the experiences, conditions, and aspirations of blacks cannot depend on the methods, approaches, and paradigms of that tradition of "established" disciplines. The professors' assertions were encapsulated in a Euro-American particularity they were unable to transcend, while we were forced to appreciate, assert, and transcend our own particularity by their systematic efforts to impose theirs. Our position, which has apparently been accepted in the interim by postmodernists and others, was that all knowledge was political, constructed around the legitimization of a point of view. The university, as then constructed, represented a truth that was alien to us. The political nature of the truth we represented was obvious only because we were the outsiders challenging the status quo. Conversely, it was clear the academic establishment's insistence that it represented "universal" intellectual truths served to conceal ideological forces that shaped and controlled academic institutions.

That we could have "known" this illustrates what Dr. Martin Luther King Jr. had called the "Zeitgeist of the times." He used that phrase to describe what had caught up with Rosa Parks when she refused to give up her bus seat in Montgomery. (As recently as August 12, 1995, Ms. Parks stated that she didn't do it because she was physically tired, as has sometimes been reported, but because she was tired of bad treatment.) It was a self-conscious recognition of us making our part of the history, which we were then discovering, of the black presence in this society and culture, and in the world. It was the combination of knowing "faith that the dark past has taught us" and "the hope that the present has brought us."

Discovering the Texts

The theme of faith provides a segue to another aspect of the question of Black Studies' legitimacy: the faith that there was some body of knowledge to which the term "Black Studies" could refer. Gerald McWorter, in his radical and articulate critique of the educational institution as "a set of powers," made a tactical error at the symposium when he stated, "I think that the black curriculum cannot be created today—not the black curriculum and the black university that I'm interested in being a part of. The simple fact is research does not exist, the findings do not exist, when it comes down to the black community." McWorter may have been attempting to parlay the urgency of the moment to create support for a proposal he made later in his presentation (which he later directly inquired of McGeorge Bundy): "a few million dollars—which is not a lot of money—could be made available to black social scientists to investigate the whole question of the black experience and the body of knowledge that must be amassed, knowledge that is authentically an extension and reflection of the black experience."

I call this a tactical error because it undermined the students' urgent assertion that changes could and should be made immediately. (Bundy later cited and embraced McWorter's assertion as a concern for slowing down the process.) The students themselves were quick to pick up and comment on this, as is made clear in the remarks of student organizer Donald H. Ogilvie: "Professor McWorter's proposal is necessary; indeed, it is crucial. However, we must also keep our eyes on . . . the kind of curriculum changes that students seek today."[30] Rejoining the issue of the "faith" of those times, Ogilvie went on to say: "Black students have thought about what we are missing in our university experience and we see a black curriculum as giving us the opportunity to find direction . . . no matter how poorly documented some of those areas within the social sciences and humanities that touch on the black perspective may be, or how limited in number and scope some of the analyses and interpretations are, an initial exposure to this existing material is possible now."[31]

Their (our) intuitive faith was on target. McWorter, whatever his rhetorical purpose, was too pessimistic. When we looked for material to give substance to our enterprise we did not find an empty void. Rather there was an already extant world of texts from which to constitute a body of knowledge pertaining to the objects of our study. Without these texts, both as primary documents and in many important compilations, there would indeed have been no intellectual content involved in the enterprise. They are remembered fondly by hands like mine, which thumbed their pages, sometimes in restless exhaustion, while creating and organizing courses in the early days.

These texts were largely in historical and literary areas. Sociology too, though burdened with a race-relations approach that always made the black experience "other," also was a source of some useful materials, insights, and information relative to the enterprise. History, or perhaps more accurately, historiography, can be considered the backbone of all African American Studies. It is the redrawn historical picture that includes these critical new viewpoints that anchor the various other aspects of the field. Through modern historians like John Hope Franklin, August Meier, Herbert Apthecker, and Lerone Bennett Jr. (his work, though snubbed by academic historians because it was built from secondary sources, is both eloquent and accessible) we were lead to the earlier reflections of Du Bois, Carter G. Woodson, Benjamin Quarles, and others; to the nineteenth-century experiences of free and enslaved blacks; to Frederick Douglas and Martin Delany; to the Negro convention movement; to the fabled Du Bois–Booker T. Washington split. Slave history itself was undergoing significant revision with work by Eugene Genovese, John Blassingame, Herbert Gutman, Sterling Stuckey, and others.

The area of literary studies was truly rich with works and compilations, traditions of black poetry, drama. This rich vein of materials included the later novels of Richard Wright, Ralph Ellison, and James Baldwin, and autobiographies and essays. (The existence of this literary tradition says much about the theme of "freedom and literacy," discussed in more detail in chapter 5.) Important literary compilations that aided immeasurably in carrying out the mission of the Black Studies movement in those days included Addison Gayle's *The Black Aesthetic* and *Black Expression,* the two-part *Amistad* series; Amiri Baraka's and Larry Neal's *Black Fire;* and Abraham Chapman's *Black Voices* anthology.

In the social science area, the classic studies of Du Bois, Charles Johnson, and St. Clair Drake availed themselves for our project.[32]

Again, the sardonic philosophy: If this isn't the substance, the palpable "stuff" of real intellectual inquiry into the human experience, then what is it? Or, in the immortal words of Sojourner Truth, "Ain't I a woman?" The project of creating a "usable past" and a usable intellectual tradition from the documents and remembrances of ancestors was, in fact, already underway when we joined it in the late sixties and early seventies. What we found were bodies of the normal products and artifacts involved with production of intellect, ideas, and culture. Histories, studies, novels, essays all were there awaiting us to unearth them. But in the milieu of the academy they were in the marginalized background, part of no discipline's "canon," fragmented among a multitude of disciplinary frameworks, unseen in their integral wholeness, invisible to the institution. They would be invisible to us, except for our restless ramblings outside the conventional structure of knowledge production, outside "Eurocentrism." In many ways the task of comprising Black Studies as a discipline has involved the creation of a "meta-narrative" that ties together the body of narratives and texts.

African American Studies in the University: Proliferation and Variation

From the Yale conference to the events leading to the creation of full academic departments,[33] the process of organizing the knowledge these materials embody signifies how Black Studies became a discipline independent of the institutional status that legitimized it. It was a process begun rapid fire, yet piecemeal, in the whirlwind of the sixties—in the bosom of individual and collective struggles to establish authenticity—and which continues to mediate itself in the present.

Thus, "[b]etween 1966 and 1970, most colleges and universities added to their curricula courses on Afro-American life and history, and most made efforts to include blacks on their faculties and administrative staffs."[34] The scope, depth, and form of these curriculum changes have varied greatly. Many institutions merely added a few courses in history or literature. Some formed programs by developing new courses and coordinating curricular activities in existing disciplines and departments. (The Yale model for this "program" approach has been cited as the most effective; but, in some cases the formation of a Black Studies

program consisted of little more than the publication of a brochure listing already extant courses, some of which bore little obvious or direct
relevance to Black Studies.)

University administrators and established academics favored this
program approach.[35] However, activists among students and scholars
who challenged the legitimacy of this approach were likely to press for
more autonomous structures, such as the Black Studies departments
formed at Harvard, Indiana and Ohio State universities, and the nearly
self-contained Institute for Africana Studies at Cornell. The circumstan-
tial contexts associated with these programmatic developments varied
dramatically. At one extreme was the nationally visualized spectacle of
armed, leather-jacketed, rifle-and-ammunition-belt-bearing black students at Cornell. Then, there were a host of situations that, while not
involving the showing of arms, were nearly as militant and bitter, such
as the movements at Harvard and San Francisco State. With the Yale
conference and similar situations defining a midpoint on the spectrum
of circumstances in which Black Studies entered the academic arena,
many institutions, especially small liberal arts colleges, instituted
courses in black history, literature, and other areas with little fanfare.[36]

In his 1985 report to the Ford Foundation, Huggins argued for a relationship between originating circumstances and subsequent program
stability: "The programs that survived naturally reflected the circumstances in which they were created. In the short run colleges like Yale
and Stanford, where programs were adopted in relative calm, seem to
be among the soundest and most stable." Huggins's evaluation also suggested that integrated programs were more successful in terms of interacting in the academic setting than those housed in administratively
autonomous structures: "Furthermore those that opted for programs—
avoiding faculty conflict over departmental status—have tended to en-
joy the easiest relationship in their academic communities. . . . At
schools like Berkeley, Cornell, Columbia, and Harvard, the events of
1968 through 1970 deeply divided the faculty; bitterness stemming from
those divisions still remains."[37]

Huggins also concluded that, "From an academic point of view the
"program" approach has been the most successful. It acknowledges the
interdisciplinary character of Afro-American Studies by using faculty from
established departments. . . . While a faculty member's appointment may
be principally to offer courses and service to Afro-American Studies, his
or her membership remains with the department of discipline."[38]

Departments and other autonomous structures tended to be the result of campaigns of an aggressive, militant character. From Huggins's perspective, they tended to be guided by "separatist" ideologies he termed "black power" and "cultural nationalist."[39] He also posed some negative concerns related to more supposedly autonomous structures, suggesting that "Departmental autonomy, it turns out, is not as absolute as some believed. . . . The department has the power and budget to make recommendations for appointment, but, lacking other arrangements, it must find scholars willing to take positions in Afro-Americans studies alone. In practice, most senior scholars with major reputations insist on joint appointments with the departments of their discipline. So, most often, an Afro-American Studies department's appointment is contingent on another department's approval of its candidate."[40]

At the time of Huggins's report, the field of African American Studies had been in a period of "shakeout" following a peak around 1973 of formational dynamics characteristic of the Black Studies movement. It is not surprising that Huggins's evaluation, commissioned by the Ford Foundation, who also funded the Yale conference, favored the program model of African American Studies that integrated Black Studies within (and subordinated it to) existing departmental disciplines. In 1974 Robert Allen suggested that "by selecting certain programs for funding while denying support to others" during this shakeout period, "government agencies and foundations could manipulate the political orientation of these programs and the direction of academic research."

Such tendencies and biases, however, cannot eclipse the activities of other groups of scholars in the field who augmented or implemented alternatives to this model. Contrary to Huggins's suggestion, at least some of the autonomously structured Black Studies units have also enjoyed stability, sometimes in spite of bitter originating circumstances. The Institute at Cornell, described by Huggins as "one of the most separatist and most political in the country,"[41] has also been one of the most long lived and stable. Indeed, an important text documenting the evolution of perspectives and issues in the field was produced under the auspices of that program on its tenth anniversary in 1980.[42]

Furthermore, Huggins's assessments do not anticipate how the view of Black Studies as a distinct field of study, and the view that the department comprises the most appropriate structure, have endured and actually grown in the most recent period. Programs that, whatever the circumstances of their origins, managed to survive through these periods of shakeout and transition have increasingly aspired to departmental status as the field continues to develop.[43]

The processes through which this differentiation evolved have involved both academic advancement and institutional politics. Increasingly, however, as I will attempt to show in the following section, the issues determining this continuing movement toward differentiation may be understood in epistemological terms—in terms of philosophies of knowledge. It is, I submit, on that level that the emergence of African American Studies must be understood and its substance and structure analyzed.

Chapter 2

Struggle Inward: Whither, Then, and How?

While recounting the development, current structure, and diversity of African American Studies, it becomes clear that several tendencies, approaches, and schools of thought emerged and interacted during the founding years. The participants in this discourse often construed the mission of Black Studies in different ways. As summarized by Robert Allen in 1974:

> One school of thought viewed Black Studies . . . [as] purely . . . concerned with researching black history and illuminating the contributions of blacks to American society. Others, such as Harold Cruse, considered Black Studies to be an instrument of cultural nationalism specifically concerned with critiquing the "integrationist ethic" and providing a counter-balance to the dominant Anglo-Saxon culture. Still a third viewpoint, best expressed by Nathan Hare, saw Black Studies as a vehicle for social change, with a functioning relationship to the black community, to break down the "ebony tower" syndrome of alienated black intellectuals.[1]

Among the first group are scholars who construct frames of reference to analyze and interpret black experiences and behavior from a revisionist standpoint, within the context of conventional disciplinary paradigms. As Ronald Taylor observes, this school did not favor "the wholesale abandonment of conventional theoretical constructs, but the reformulation of those conceptual frameworks with the greatest potential for illuminating various aspects of the Black experience."[2] The aims of this first group align with Allen's description of those viewing Black Studies as concerned primarily with researching and illuminating the experiences and contributions of blacks in a purely academic sense.

In this "contributionist," "inclusionist," or "integrationist" approach, knowledge about the experiences and contributions of blacks are included, or "integrated," into the traditional disciplines and departments. This approach is consistent with the integrated "program" concept, initially favored by administrations and establishment-oriented scholars. The Yale program that followed the 1968 symposium on Black Studies in the university was the best-known example of this approach. In the view of those who challenged this model, the inclusionist approach left the definition and determination of the Black Studies' subject matter still within the purview of established disciplines and usually did not require or result in a new departmental structure to house and administer the program.

As previously indicated, Black Studies proposals that did envision departmental or autonomous structures were likely to encounter more resistance from the university establishment, and succeeded only when considerable external pressure was brought to bear. Such outcomes were often the result of relatively militant confrontations. Given the charged times and circumstances in which African American Studies emerged in its midst, it is not surprising that the academy's resistance to departmental autonomy was expressed in terms of preservation of "intellectual standards" and "academic principles" in a charged political atmosphere. However, a fundamental source of resistance may be obscured by the preoccupation with scholarly "integrity." Specifically, the political struggles over structure, departmental control, tenure, academic credit, and other tools of academic legitimacy actually had a strong epistemological basis. In fact, the academy's resistance to the epistemological issues was a major cause of failed mediation between university values and the emergent interests of young black scholars and activists during the formational period of the Black Studies movement.

Relevance and Epistemology

The universalist contention of establishment academics that there was no "black perspective," or for that matter no "white perspective," was rejected by most Black Studies scholars. While a "black perspective" was manifest mostly at an intuitive, or experiential, level, it seemed clear that the academy represented a "white" or "establishment perspective" that held little truth value for a generation of students and scholars looking for a more useful, relevant perspective. Like the Yale students with whom David Brion Davis spoke, they questioned the "universality" claimed by establishment academics.[3]

As Russell Adams argues, the pseudo-universality of Euro-American particularism was eventually challenged by all who called their work "Black Studies," including even those who thought of this work in primarily disciplinary terms. Adams, long-time chair of the Afro-American Studies Department at Howard University, ably illuminates this attack on false notions of universality in a special 1984 issue of the *Journal of Negro Education* devoted to Black Studies. Adams indicated that even though most Black Studies scholars were trained in the traditional disciplines, they are "engaged in epistemic renovation."[4] He states that the almost inevitable differences in interpretations between white and black academicians on the fundamentals of race "suggests the existence of a difference in epistemological content [a] . . . 'fault-line' in the pre-analytical aspects of white / black intellectual interpretation . . . too consistent to be coincidental."[5]

Adams derives this epistemological "fault-line" from generations of nineteenth-century black scholars, suggesting that "the institutional presence of Afro-American / Black Studies offers the first collective opportunity to deal with basic epistemic problems." Up to the advent of the Black Studies movement there had been a tendency to marginalize and fragment aspects of the black experience, obscuring the "epistemic legacy" of Woodson, Du Bois, and others whose works make up the intellectual foundations of the movement.[6] These nineteenth- and early-twentieth-century precursors were determined to transcend the epistemic limits of their disciplines to better serve their efforts to illuminate and authenticate the lives of black folks.[7]

The discourse around African American Studies was often framed in terms of political ideology and / or organizational structure; but it was, in fact, a set of underlying epistemological issues—determining what (and who) constitutes valid knowledge about black people and black communities—that united the various groups of the Black Studies movement opposing the integrated, inclusionist model based on traditional disciplines and the epistemological framework they embodied. For them, the "epistemic renovation" that Russell spoke of required a totally restructured analytical framework. Mere inclusionism and contributionism regarding the experiences and achievements of blacks were insufficient for these purposes.

This radical element, then, unanimously rejected the possibility that knowledge relevant to "black liberation" could come from the culturally and politically biased disciplinary canons created from traditional Western epistemology. The systematic nature of the bias and exclusion suggested an entire system of knowledge likely only to repeat its pattern of neglect and distortion. Essentially, the very fabric with which knowledge was constructed and contextualized within these traditional epistemological modes tended to systematically negate, marginalize, and distort the lives, experiences, and humanity of blacks. The pervasive, systematic nature of this process of knowledge construction required an alternative approach to producing knowledge relevant to the exigencies and possibilities of black existence.

However, although rejection of the prevailing epistemological approaches of the established disciplines united these groups, there was no single alternative model around which they rallied. As vociferously as they rejected the traditional disciplinary approaches, they debated along a broad political, ideological, and cultural spectrum over the alternatives to "white studies": "Marxists vs. nationalists, reformers vs. revolutionaries, accommodationist institutional role players vs. political activists on social change projects."[8]

The differing ideological predispositions also reflected the broader political climate of discourse and debate among this activist element through the 1970s and into the 1980s. If unanimous rejection of traditional academic approaches often masked the degree of consensus among contentious elements, then the vigor of their debate sometimes masked the common ground among various camps as well. The approaches described in Allen's typology cited above were, in practice, not sharply delineated and mutually exclusive. Virtually all agreed that Black Studies was academically important, but few among the activist element in the field felt it was only of academic concern. Most incorporated an ethical imperative to "change the condition of black people." For some that imperative meant emphasizing change in material conditions; for others, it meant preserving and developing a black cultural ethos that would ultimately lead to such change.

The Marxists and the Nationalists: Divergence and Synthesis

During the 1970s these exchanges, which ran along a continuum from nationalist/Pan-Africanist to socialist/Marxist, were reflected in the pages of journals like the *Black Scholar, Journal of Black Studies,* and *Western Journal of Black Studies.* In addition, proceedings and reports of political events like the 1974 conference of the African Liberation Support Committee (a vehicle for much ideological activism in the 1970s) and the historical Sixth Pan-African Congress in Dar es Salaam, Tanzania, held that same year, also reflect the character of this ideological dialogue.

Maulana Karenga, visible among nationalistic and now Afrocentric thinkers in the Black Studies movement, addressed some limitations of nationalism in terms compatible with the Marxist critique in a 1974 *Black Scholar* article, "Which Road: Nationalism, Pan-Africanism, Socialism?" "Nationalists," he said, "tend to mystify the nature of our identity as a people, emphasizing its organic or racial character rather than stressing its social basis. . . . Joined to our racial identity, is our social or class position . . . nationalists tend to mask contradictions among blacks in pursuit of an elusive ideal unity . . . there are basic conflictual differences among blacks and those are class differences."[9]

Most who considered themselves nationalists agreed with Karenga, "It must be obvious to us by now that capitalism cannot and will not provide for us, that it is based on the ruthless and endless pursuit of profit, not on moral principles and that it couldn't care less about the scars and holes it leaves in our lives. . . . It is at this point . . . that we of necessity look further to the left to socialism."[10] And while a few nationalists found fault with capitalism only because it had not yet worked satisfactorily for *them,* most agreed with Marxist Tony Thomas's statement that "black liberation and socialism are directly linked, as are racism and capitalism."[11]

Imamu Amiri Baraka (previously LeRoi Jones), noted African American poet, playwright, cultural critic, and political activist, is also famous for having switched sides on the nationalist/Pan-Africanist vs. socialist/Marxist question. He appeared in *The Black Scholar* on both sides of the debate at different times; but his transformation to a black Marxist point of view is, perhaps, less baffling considering that his previous viewpoint combined nationalism, Pan-Africanism, and socialism ("African Scientific Socialism").[12] It was reported that Baraka, like many black nationalists and Pan-Africanists, developed pro-Marxist views out of his concrete experiences in the movement, namely his sense of betrayal stemming from his experiences with mayoral politics in Newark.[13]

In the intense context of this discourse among emerging schools of thought, however, fine points argued vociferously between ideological opponents, and even among ideological allies, were capable of producing significant division and of fracturing operational unities. Like Carlos

Brossard, many felt ideological tensions were both helpful and costly: "The ideological differences were healthy in bringing out background variances and dispelling myths of uncritical racial unification. . . . However, they came with acrimony, which further fragmented organizational consensus. Polarization and alienation from within delayed the tunnel vision which went with well-defined rationalizations of institutional purposes."[14]

James B. Stewart suggested that a lack of ideological synthesis was a serious barrier that threatened the further development of the field during this period,[15] and there were, in fact, significant efforts to operationalize such a synthesis. For example, the Black Studies Curriculum Project of the Institute of the Black World (IBW) involved the collection, compilation, analysis, and evaluation of Black Studies course syllabi then in use all over the country. Reporting on Black Studies social science syllabi to the IBW conference, Lloyd Hogan stressed the critical need for a political economy perspective consistent with class-based analysis to explain the emergence of slavery and racism. The lack of such a perspective in traditional social science disciplines, Hogan said, "expunges from the collective intellectual memory the major pathology of the American political economy as if it never existed. And the consequence has been a failure of ordinary social science disciplines to clarify the issues which embody the essential description and explanation of how the system of capitalist political economy works itself out in the real world."[16]

Cultural issues, on the other hand, had to be constructed, almost by definition, in terms of nationalist discourse. Marxists, for this reason, were continually forced to rethink and restructure their theoretical statements on cultural phenomenon. Their emphasis on materialist determinism included a tendency to subordinate cultural issues, often neglecting their importance in conceptualizing African American social cohesion. For many nationalists and their allies, materialist determinism failed to consider adequately the "African" and "black" spiritual, cultural, and aesthetic matrices shaping the African American experience. Not all sensibilities within the cultural nationalist framework could be dismissed as "pork chop politics," the derisive term some leftists applied to nationalist ideas. Furthermore, Marxism failed to satisfactorily address the issue of the formidable presence of racism among white workers who, theoretically, should be allied with blacks. In addition, Marxism seemed to struggle in vain with the "contradiction" that the Black Studies movement, in character and structure, was itself (as Cruse had noted earlier) a vehicle for cultural nationalist sentiment;

it was fundamentally a nationalist formation, though a nationalism that leaned to the left, in part because of the presence of Marxists.

While mediation of these and other issues became the basis for potential operational unity (as well as conflict) among the various elements, the alliance of the Black Studies movement with social and political struggle in the "real" world provided another such base. During the 1970s the ongoing African liberation support movements provided a means to link Black Studies academic and social missions. The movement led by Amical Cabral in liberating and building a new nation in Guinea provided a program that all sides could support in a way that illuminated principles and sensibilities emphasized by each. As noted by Phil Hutchings, reporting on the African Liberation Support Movement conference in 1974, "Cabral is supported by all tendencies in the black movement for their own reasons . . . cultural nationalists in the movement like the attention Cabral gave to culture and identity in the national liberation movement. Black Marxists admire his dialectical and historical materialist approach to the problems of Guinea and struggle in general. And then there are those who like Cabral because he was a black man leading a successful armed struggle against Western colonialism in Africa."[17]

Ideological and Conceptual Frameworks

In the course of debating various differences, the activists agreed that the overarching, white-dominated system, or superstructure, influenced and shaped reality for all people, including their mental processes and ways of knowing. It was a system of thought that conceived no alternatives to the marginalization, or "othering," of blacks, that allowed no possibility of new actualization, no expression of human potential. This shared view is significant in considering how the disparate factions forged a level of operational unity, and in understanding how ideological discourse among these elements translated into the competing intellectual frameworks of African American Studies today.

The need for an alternative but equally powerful and well-developed system of thought helps clarify the influence of Marxist and socialist approaches in this discourse. A new system of thought capable of unraveling the racist fabric of conventional Euro-American thought and ideology would have to be as forceful and compelling as the dominant Eurocentric mode. In addition to incorporating political ideology, Marxism is the basis of an established and well-formulated system of intellectual thought.

And, though Marx probably considered himself a historian, the influence of the system of thought associated with his name has not been limited by disciplinary boundaries. Indeed, Marxism, in one form or another, provides a framework of analysis for many social science and humanities disciplines. As an analytical framework it offered an approach to explaining racism and its relation to other forms of oppression informed by a vision of social transformation that allowed for the elevation of black humanity along with that of the downtrodden workers of the world.

Among the various streams of nationalist ideas flowing into the discourse of this early period, Harold Cruse's *The Crisis of the Negro Intellectual*—a cultural nationalist critique of the integrationist ethic that dominated the early movements for black equality—wielded great influence among those seeking to build an alternative, cultural nationalist paradigm. For many, this influential work set forth in nationalist terms a comprehensive, analytical, and scholarly approach capable of providing the conceptual muscle necessary to lift the study of black life from the disciplinary ghettoes in which such studies had been consistently fragmented and marginalized. Thus, Cruse's sharp rejection of integrationism struck a responsive chord among the youthful activist elements of the field, who never quite understood why the progress of blacks apparently had to be measured in terms of their visibility or acceptability in the "white world."

Over time, however, Cruse's conception of cultural creation and transformation, along with his prescription of an alternative ideological path along which black intellectuals were to lead the masses, was subjected to critique. As early as 1969, for example, Robert Chrisman challenged Cruse's conception of the relationships between culture, politics, and social change: "Cruse . . . maintains that culture precedes political and social change; that culture is created by intellectuals and artists and then shoveled to the masses who eventually grow politically and socially activist from the culture they have acquired."[18]

Like many nationalists, Cruse's concepts are based on imitation and appropriation of Euro-American concepts and constructs as much as they are based on their rejection. Thus, Chrisman's indictment suggests that Cruse's conception of culture is not only elitist but fails to account for the extant, living aspects of black culture; indeed, Cruse seemed disinclined to legitimate the very cultural reference frame that had allowed many of us to survive in the erstwhile hostile academic environment. Cruse's conceptually flawed elitism is perhaps most apparent when he decries the lack of a "black Gershwin" to give direction to a black "high culture." Chrisman writes, "In a peculiar sense, the book is blind. Sixty years of black culture are seen and not seen. Black achievement is not recognized nor is the full nature of white oppression. For both integration and separation are responses to white oppression; if one fails to see them in perspective to white oppression, then error occurs. . . . Who needs a black Gershwin when there is a black John Coltrane, a black Charlie Parker, a black Miles Davis. In crying for a black culture he ignores the black culture that exists—and his ignorance comes in the name of blackness."[19]

Regarding the quest for an alternative conceptual framework appropriate to the new approach manifest in the Black Studies movement, Cruse himself pointed to an existing void when he told the Yale symposium that "as a result of this failure [of "integrationist ethic"], at this present moment we have no viable black philosophy on which to base much-needed Black Studies programs."[20] It should not be surprising, then, that the value of the Marxist analytical framework, a system of thought capable of both illuminating issues of race and class while opposing the traditional Eurocentric tendency to marginalize and pathologize blackness, was often acknowledged, even admiringly, by the nationalist camp. Marxism provided a methodology, a "systematicity," a disciplined and "scientific" approach that might potentially organize and unify a system of thought that could be as effective in liberating black humanity as the dominant system was in negating it.

The lack of such a comparably systematic approach to organizing the sometimes hazy formulations of nationalist discourse was often acknowledged by nationalists themselves. Molefi Asante, who came to represent Afrocentrism in the eighties, addressed in 1978 the need for a "Systematic Nationalism": "The truth of the matter is that nationalist thought has not been as structured as it should have been. Thus, brothers and sisters looking for a unified approach to revolutionary struggle have found Marxism easier to argue."[21]

There has even been a tendency among nationalist and Pan-Africanists toward stylistic appropriation of Marxist rhetoric, symbols, and concepts. (There is, for example, an abiding, still-articulated notion that Pan-Africanism is the "highest form" of nationalism, mirroring the Marxist-Leninist assertion that imperialism is the "highest form" of capitalism.[22]) Asante's early form of "Systematic Nationalism," a notion that preceded his emergence as progenitor of Afrocentrism, also reveals this tendency: "As Marx and Engels had done for the economically oppressed, Garvey and Muhammad did for the racially oppressed. That is why the systematic nationalist says socialism to deal with class contradictions; nationalism to deal with race contradictions."[23]

On this subtextual level, then, the opposing sides in the Black Studies discourse were further united with regard to the constitution of a paradigmatic alternative to the Eurocentric elitism upon which traditional disciplines were based. The Marxist appeal, however, was temporary and somewhat limited. Despite the apparently superior theoretical and methodological weapons that Marxists brought to the ideological battles, the war turned to one of attrition. Piece by piece, tenets of Marxism itself were critiqued and rejected as racist and Eurocentric. The racial statements of Marx, Engels, and other theorists were denounced on the one hand, while, on the other hand, their concepts of social communion and cooperation were said to be derived from African concepts (for example, communalism). The validity of socialist ideas, so goes this reasoning, need not attach to a "white" and necessarily racist frame of reference.

While appropriating Marxist rhetoric to examine race and class, the terms were often reversed—race rather than class becoming the "fundamental contradiction" that "scientific socialism" should address in building black nationalism and Pan-Africanism. The power of race over class in nationalist discourse became manifest in other ways as well. For example, Ronald Walters, the Howard University political scientist who has been a key figure in the presidential campaigns of Jesse Jackson, wrote, perhaps disingenuously, in 1974, "it is not clear what the class formations are in the black community, what causes them, or even if it makes any difference in the larger struggle for black liberation (which I suspect it does not)."[24]

Walters goes on to reflect, accurately, on the ways in which race is maintained as the dominant concept in the thinking of many nationalists:

> although it is fashionable today to coequate the struggle against Capitalism and Imperialism, our analysis must clearly keep before us the centrality of the degradation of African peoples all over the world, not by "systems" but by peoples of a different civilization than ours. Race has been, is now, and will continue to be dominant over class for the foreseeable future as the key to the determination of oppressive behavior exercised by whites, especially in places like the United States, where blacks are an identifiable, powerless, minority of the entire population . . . . racism may be impervious to the structural composition of the state. That is to say, the socialist revolution can be accomplished nationally and internationally and the position of blacks still not be affected because of the dominance of racism.[25]

Marxism, to the degree that it gained a foothold in the Black Studies movement—and in black intellectual and political thought in general during the period—had appeal and legitimacy because of its utility as a tool and a model for deconstructing Eurocentric perspectives that distorted and marginalized black humanity. Ultimately, however, the powerful legacy of race rendered it insufficient as a means for achieving the real goal of the nationalist Black Studies agenda. The real goal, as described by Darlene Clark Hine, was "an intellectual and often overtly political commitment to black liberation from European, or more crassly white, categories of thought and analysis." Something as broad and pervasive as the dominant Euro-American modes of thought and discourse required a comparably broad and pervasive counterdiscourse that reflected images of black humanity (not another European-derived system of thought). Eventually that counterdiscourse would provide the grounding for an entirely new framework and interpretive context. This need for more complete deconstruction of oppressive modes of Eurocentric discourse would lead to a historiographical reconstruction involving all of Africa, and especially ancient dynastic Egypt.

So, although radical Marxist critiques were prominent in shaping the dialogue during those early periods of intense debate, the phoenix that rose from the ashes of those ideological battles was the form of cultural nationalism we now know as Afrocentrism. As a conceptual and analytical framework, Marxism was and remains valuable in illuminating the real nature of "race relations" in the modern world. Its limitations as an alternative to Eurocentric hegemony are suggested in a 1991 presentation by Darlene Clark Hine at the Wisconsin Conference on Afro-American Studies in Madison, subsequently published in *The Black Scholar*'s special issue on Afro-American Studies in the twenty-first century. Referring to scholars like Cheik Anta Diop, Ivan Van Sertima, and Yosef ben-Jochannan as "Originists," she suggests that they "provide African Americans with their own origin stories that lay claim to the credit for much of the knowledge that allegedly has been erroneously attributed to Greeks and Romans." She adds, "All groups and societies need origin stories. Taken collectively [these] works provide a sense of beginning and belonging."[26]

For these and other reasons, Afrocentrism emerged during the 1980s as the central theoretical perspective around which to organize the discipline and as the most visible alternative to the "integrationist" or "discipline-based" inclusionist paradigm. With broad support among Black Studies scholars, Afrocentrism has sprouted from the seeds originally sown by the movement's activist founders. Nowhere has the ascendancy of Afrocentrism been more evident than in its repeated incorporation in the theme of the National Council for Black Studies annual conference since the late 1980s. Further, it was the express epistemological orientation of the first and largest Black Studies Ph.D. program, a landmark for the Black Studies movement.

Various notions of Afrocentricity have also energized scholars in traditional disciplines like psychology, education, and even medical practice and architecture. Moreover, something like an Afrocentric movement has spilled over from the academy to the larger society in sometimes sharp engagement with newly defined notions of modern African American cultural identity. Popular culture has become infused with signs and symbols of "Africanity": kufi hats, kinte cloth, dreadlock hairstyles. Indeed, the "Afrocentric Idea" represents a "paradigm shift" not only in the academy but also among the populace. It is a shift based on the need for an alternative to Euro-American hegemony, articulated by scholars and activists in the academy but experienced and lived in the "real world."

With regard to African American Studies in the academy, Afrocentricity as a belief system, or theoretical perspective, became, for many, a synonym for Black Studies as a discipline or field of study. With this tumultuous historical backdrop as a reference point, the following chapter will examine the context in which Afrocentrism emerged as a major influence in African American Studies as the field reached a "stage of theoretical refinement and more sophisticated analysis and interpretation."[27]

Part 2

Theorizing African American Studies

Chapter 3

Afrocentrism: More or Less

Making the case for the most effective alternative approach to conceptualizing and organizing African American Studies became a major task for activist elements in the original Black Studies movement who strongly opposed the traditional approach. It was observed on many occasions that synthesis of text materials to introduce the field to students—as well as conceptually organize it—was critically important in this paradigm-forming period of African American Studies' history. Introductory texts, therefore, were important at this stage. Some texts, especially early ones like that of Carlene Young in 1972 were edited volumes that combined original and existing materials.[1] One of the earliest introductory texts written as a single, integral piece, *Introduction to Afro-American Studies*, was the work of Peoples College, a well-known Marxist collective.[2]

In textual terms *Intro*, which has endured now through six editions, demonstrated the effective way that black Marxists drew upon Marxist/Leninist analytical constructs to illuminate and examine black experiences. For example, the historical periodization of the black experience in North America conceptualized in *Intro* provided an extremely useful framework for depicting, assessing, and evaluating changes in social conditions, economic forces, cultural sensibility, and political orientation. However, overladen with Leninist language, and neglectful of continuities among black experiences before and beyond the North American situation, *Intro* also illustrated the areas of weakness or dissatisfaction with this approach.

Thus, in curricular practice it was often combined with other supplementary texts available at the time, such as Young or Bright et al.[3]

Reviewing available introductory texts in 1979, James B. Stewart posed the question as to "whether the existence of at least two schools of thought within the Black Studies movement" would be sustained. He was, in fact, anticipating "the production of a Black Studies text which embodies a nationalistic instrumentalist ideology. If this effort is successful, the foundation will have been laid for the serious examination of the issues which divide the adherents to the respective ideologies."[4]

The Afrocentric Idea

The work he anticipated, nationalist counterparts to the influential analytical work of Marxist Black Studies scholars, came first in the form of Maulana Karenga's *Introduction to Black Studies*, first published in 1982.[5] In the context of the struggle among participants in the Black Studies movement to formulate alternative frames of reference that opposed the established system of knowledge, the appearance of this text was a significant step. In the view of those activists, the tangle of Eurocentric bias and distortion, seminal in the historical construction of Western social science and aesthetic studies, made an adequate grasp of the actuality of race in the modern world virtually impossible. For them the need for development of paradigms free of this burden was clear. The infusion of the "idea" of Afrocentrism, in various forms and permutations, in the wider culture indicates that the perception of inadequacy as inherent in "Eurocentric" modes and modalities of style, beauty, and thought was widespread among African Americans. As expressed in the preface to *Introduction to Black Studies*:

> This enterprise is self-consciously Afro-centric, critical and corrective in response to the internal demands of the discipline itself, whose subject matter and academic and social mission clearly demand this approach. An Afro-centric approach is essentially intellectual inquiry and production centered on and in the image and interest of African peoples. This responds to the early and continuing demands for academic and social relevance of the educational process and its contents. The critical thrust is the advancing of severe and ongoing criticism of the established order of things in order to negate myths, mystifications and insubstantialities of traditional white studies on blacks, society and the world.[6]

Thus, this text represented a substantial step in the emergence of an Afrocentric paradigm (Kawaida theory) shaped to address the epistemological issues raised as Black Studies evolved from a movement to an institutionalized field of inquiry. The work of Karenga and his Kawaida associates laid foundation and much infrastructure for the emerging Afrocentric paradigm, which has emerged not only in the academic world but also in society. (For example, recognition of Kwanza, the African American holiday based originally on Kawaida's formulations, continues to grow each year.) However, as it spilled outside of Black Studies and outside of the academy itself, the discussion has come to focus more on the work of Molefi Kete Asante, who published several books exploring and defining "Afrocentricity" in the eighties. Moreover, after assuming the chair of the African American Studies department at Temple University, Asante presided over the development of the first bona fide Ph.D. program in African American Studies. The program was explicitly organized to reflect, develop, and further refine an Afrocentric paradigm. In that position Asante became a natural spokesperson for Afrocentrism, often representing the "Afrocentric perspective," for example, in various venues during the recent debates about multiculturalism in education.

In addition to that societywide dialogue on multiculturalism, the influence of Afrocentric ideas is increasingly seen in traditional disciplines as scholars in psychology, education, even medical practice, seek to apply the term to their approaches to studies of black life and community. In these educational settings, as well as in settings outside the academy, however, the definition, application, and execution of Afrocentricity has been anything but systematic or consistent. This makes it difficult to determine connections among the settings in which the term has been applied, as well as how academic Afrocentrism influences and is perceived in the wider culture. Within the field of African American Studies the works of Karenga and Asante have been at the core of a discourse addressing the development and application of Afrocentric thought. In terms of this examination of how Afrocentrism has emerged as a paradigm within the field, it is important to focus there.

Both Karenga's and Asante's approaches to defining Afrocentrism begin from the same point: the need to negate, or deconstruct, traditional bodies of knowledge and systems of thought that distorted black humanity. They also aim toward the same ambitious goal: the construction of a comprehensive system of thought reflecting and deriving from an African American epistemological standpoint. Using the seven principles of his Kawaida theory—the same principles that inform the African American holiday celebration of Kwanza—Karenga sets out to define the history, structure, substance, and thrust of Black Studies as an "interdisciplinary discipline." The seven subject areas defined by Karenga are black history, black religion, black social organization, black politics, black economics, creative production, and black psychology. Each of these core areas represent subjects that, in conventional terms, would be covered by various social science and humanities disciplines in the traditional structure: "These intradisciplinary foci which at first seem to be disciplines themselves are, in fact, separate disciplines when they are outside the discipline of Black Studies, but inside, they become and are essentially subject areas which contribute to a holistic picture and approach to the Black experience. Moreover, the qualifier Black, attached to each area in an explicit or implicit way, suggests a more specialized and delimited focus which of necessity transforms a broad discipline into a particular subject area."[7]

Following an introductory chapter that recounts the conditions in which the field of Black Studies emerged, each of the next seven chapters addresses one of the core subject areas Karenga defined. Each chapter includes a survey of historical material relevant to the subject area, and a summation of major issues and schools of thought relative to each subject. Thus, Karenga, whose Yale symposium presentation had been labeled "deeply anti-intellectual" by Huggins, presents a well-researched, cogently presented survey of important dimensions and subject areas constitutive of one vision, at least, of Black Studies as an academic field.

Structured specifically for classroom use, with study questions and extensive bibliographies supporting each chapter, this text, through several printings (and now a second edition), endures in present practice. Reviewing this text in 1983, Stewart, after suggestions that included incorporation of a periodization scheme to sharpen the text's historical focus, gave significant praise: "Karenga has fueled the dialectic of Black Studies conceptual development more systematically than any other scholar in recent years. The onus is now on other schools of thought to match his contribution to allow more rapid progress toward sustainable theoretical, methodological and ideological synthesis. But for now, Karenga's work can be said to be the standard bearer of the 'discipline.'"[8]

The Temple Afrocentric School

Though Karenga's *Introduction to Black Studies* remains in present practice after several printings, it was not updated from its original version for more than a decade. Over the years it has become clear—even in the revised, expanded 1993 version—that the ambitious breadth of the text entailed limitations on the depth of exploration and analysis. (His treatment of black music as a mode of "creative production" in the original edition, for example, was slightly more than seven pages.) Karenga's contribution is significant in breadth and structure, but Asante—who has published three major works on his conception of Afrocentricity—has become more associated with the concept of Afrocentricity from the mid-1980s and 1990s. The first of Asante's texts, *Afrocentricity: The Theory of Social Change,* was published in 1980. The ideas developed in that first volume have received their widest exposure in the third, enlarged edition of this work, entitled simply *Afrocentricity.* These conceptions are further explored in *The Afrocentric Idea.* The third text in this series, *Kemet, Afrocentricity, and Knowledge,* emphasizes the language, philosophy, and culture of ancient Egypt (Kemet) as the cornerstone in the construction of an Afrocentric system of thought.

As a body of thought, Asante's work reads, at some points, like ideology, sometimes like mysticism or theology, and sometimes like an intellectual paradigm. The conceptual thrust of Asante's Afrocentrism is probably clearest in *The Afrocentric Idea;* however, all the above named elements are present in each of the three works cited. In terms of intellectual discourse, two things stand out through the body of this work. First is a concern with language as a linchpin in the construction of knowledge, meaning, identity, and culture. Second is the continual reference to African ideas, cultures, and histories as backdrops for the alternative construction of knowledge that emerges as Afrocentrism. Ultimately this thrust focuses on the reclamation of the histories, philosophies, and monuments of dynastic Egypt as a cornerstone from which the project is to construct an Afrocentric worldview with as much historical depth and cultural legitimacy as Eurocentrism.

The primacy given to language that is apparent in all Asante's work focuses on language both as a limiting condition in the formation of knowledge and consciousness and as a tool in the reformation of knowledge and consciousness that locates frameworks and images derived from Africa at the foundation of any study involving the culture or behavior of descendants of Africa. In other words, through the body of his work Asante illustrates the use of language as a tool for deconstructing Eurocentric conceptions that marginalize black humanity, and for reconstructing an Afrocentric alternative from the inside out.

While language is used in many ways to aid this microlevel reconstruction process, the increasing focus on the historical anteriority and cultural unity of Africa in general, and on Egypt (Kemet) in particular, represent this paradigm-defining process in its macrohistorical dimensions. This focus reaches a crescendo in *Kemet, Afrocentricity, and Knowledge,* in which much of the text is devoted to establishing Egypt at the historical base of both classical Western civilization (through Greece) and to the rest of continental Africa.

From another angle of vision these different standpoints might be seen to reflect Asante's conception of "the two fundamental aspects of the Afrocentric project . . . *innovation* and *tradition.*"[9] Regarding innovation, he asserts, "The advancement of the African American Studies paradigm must begin with a codified Afrocentricity."[10] From such a centered perspective, he suggests, the Afrocentric scholars may then interrogate in every direction. In every field, every aspect of life or society, he states, "Afrocentric critical methods start with the primary measure! Does it place Africans in the center?"[11]

The process thus involves tradition as a reflective backdrop for innovation. As expressed by Asante, "there is nothing more correct, more innovative, more rooted in tradition, than the centrality of our own historical experiences."[12] At many points through the body of these texts Asante invokes the analogy that "Egypt will do for Africans what Greece and Rome do for Europeans." Ultimately, then, in the process of conceptualizing Afrocentrism, the search for meaning of tradition leads to the Nile Valley: "The Afrocentric analysis re-establishes the centrality of the ancient Kemetic (Egyptian) civilization and the Nile Valley cultural complex as points of reference for an African perspective in much the same way as Greece and Rome serve as reference points for the European World."[13]

The linguistic focus of Asante's work is not surprising considering Asante's previous training and work in communications. It is also relevant that the critique Asante and others in the Black Studies movement have pursued regarding the epistemological hegemony of Western traditions of knowledge has occurred in concert with the examination of others, among the postmodernists and poststructuralists, who, from within that tradition, have questioned and reexamined many of its basic presumptions. Asante's work exhibits considerable familiarity and significant engagement with this discourse among European and American philosophers and scholars of literary and rhetorical criticism. In some ways, Asante sees his task in terms analogous to those of other modern and postmodern critics. Like the phenomenologist, he says, the Afrocentrist's quest is to search for knowledge by "questioning all assumptions about reality that are rooted in a particularistic view of the universe."[14]

In any case, his approach to the deconstruction of Eurocentric bias often focuses on language and the context of discourse. In the following passage, for example, he suggests the symbolic connection between political structures and the context of discourse: "The rhetorical condition is symbolic of the political structure; it thrives on the same principle and it liberates or imprisons its interactants on the same philosophical grounds."[15] While examining the limiting conditions of discourse he notes that language, in a given context, takes its meaning from social structure in a manner reminiscent of Michel Foucault. Asante writes, "it does not matter if the language of the imperative is polite and gentle, so long as the imperative structure endures; a social environment has been created where one, for instance, gives orders and the other is expected to obey."[16]

What Asante appears to share with other participants in the postmodern discourse is an acknowledgment of fallacies inherent in the assumption that "objective" truth or knowledge exists at some so-called "universal" or "privileged exterior" level. He writes that "Universality can only be dreamed about when we have slept on truth based on specific cultural experiences."[17] Like many in this discursive critique of modernity, Asante is involved with the ideas of Enlightenment philosopher Georg Hegel. Looking at the recent theorists who have followed the philosophical trail from Hegel to postmodernity, Asante takes them to task for not adequately addressing Hegel's racial shortcomings.[18] Noting Hegel's assertion that Africans and other non-Europeans were peoples without history, Asante comments, "It is because of such formulations that the Livingston-Stanley duet in the African Forest becomes history while hundreds of thousands of people living in the same time and space are said to be without history. . . . In Hegelian terms Africans are an obscure people . . . because Europeans do not know them."[19]

Thus, on the one hand, Asante is not averse to drawing selectively from some participants in the postmodern conversation—such as Theodor Adorno, Herbert Marcuse, and Michel Foucault—who have questioned, challenged, and sought to revise the veritable foundations of Western thought.[20] On the other hand, he maintains that, since few of these scholars have avoided the previous neglect of Africa and its contributions to the world's intellectual history, their work "misrepresents much knowledge and perpetuates a narrow scholarship."[21] In fact, Asante suggests, the recent debate exacerbated rather than eliminated many of these critical errors.[22] Thus, although they develop useful premises for examining established frameworks, deconstructionists ultimately fall short in their relevance to Afrocentrism. He writes, "The deconstructionists come close to redesigning the critical framework, although much of what they do falls squarely within the context of the Eurocentric theoretical framework."[23]

Thus his linguistic semantic focus deconstructs limitations inherent in forms of Eurocentric discourse and dissertation, and also points the way toward reconstruction of discourse free of such dissonance and distortion. Namely, he states, Afrocentrism "identifies ways in which the black protester resists discourse limitations and creates new rhetorical ground."[24] Rather than looking to postmodern critical discourse, then, Asante insists on the need for discourse within an Afrocentric framework distinctly focused on the needs and experiences of black people. He states that the appropriate ideology cannot be imposed from without but must derive from blacks' particular experiences.[25]

The very precise concepts, terms, and even the words in which this discourse is conducted are, Asante insists, of vital importance. These discursive units are the important blocks, joints, and structures through which language and (spoken and written) discourse are employed in developing and applying Afrocentrism from the inside out. Asante states: "Our liberation from the captivity of racist language is the first order of the intellectual. *There can be no freedom until there is a freedom of the mind.*"[26] And language—that is, words, names, and terminology—in Asante's analysis is key in the ability to conceptualize freedom. Referencing Franz Fanon, he writes, "Always the protester must use different symbols, myths, and sounds than the established order." To do otherwise is always disadvantageous because "the oppressed can never use the language of the established order with as much skill as the establishment."[27]

Thus, as Asante observes, political constructs impose limits on how aspects of reality can be defined and expressed.[28] Looking at epistemological implications of certain usage of language and concepts, he seeks to examine and penetrate the instance and nature of such limits. In its most salient deconstructive thrusts, Asante's analysis of words and language is often effective in clarifying subtle, and not so subtle, distortions and limits represented in conventional discourse: "There were no 'warlike' people in Africa, at least, no more than the French or English or Germans were warlike when they invaded Africa. Normally, if an ethnic group or nation defended itself it was labeled by the invaders as 'warlike.'"[29]

Asante proposes that language be employed as a tool to erect and connect epistemological units or insights into a usable, alternative epistemological structure. In an Afrocentric sense, rhetoric for Asante is "the productive thrust of language into the unknown in an attempt to create harmony and balance in the midst of disharmony and indecision."[30] Language and discourse are tools to redefine the world as one encounters it "in its current and historical unfolding" (using a phrase often employed by Karenga). Asante's description of language in this context suggests a process in which, through purposeful shaping of language, one conceptually re-creates the world on a minute-to-minute basis.

The relationship of language to the process of ongoing conceptual "centering" of knowledge and inquiry is conveyed in the following passage in *Afrocentricity:* "To say that you are going to the continent must mean you are going to Africa. . . . The European who says 'I have just come from the continent' will find me asking, 'What were you doing in Africa?' . . . When someone says 'middle ages' you must ask, whose middle ages? When they say 'classical' you must ask, whose classical? Only in this way can you prevent Eurocentrism from imposing itself as universal."[31] Through such processes of discursive engagement, Asante believes, "The national idea, galvanized by Afrocentricity . . . will act in all directions of thought and action as it becomes ever present."[32]

Kemet: The Foundation

In all the works cited, Asante consistently refers to Egypt as the ultimate historical reference point for the Afrocentric paradigm. However, in *Afrocentricity* and *The Afrocentric Idea* he grounds himself historically by drawing on nationalist traditions of African American social thought and cultural practice: a kind of classic nationalist pantheon that includes Edward Blyden, Martin Delany, Henry McNeal Turner, Marcus Garvey, Elijah Muhammad, and, presumably, Malcolm X. (There is an argument to be made that the notion of "Afrocentricity," as implying the kind of sense of cultural continuity and affinity with Africa that Asante suggests, rests uneasily among the legacies of these early militants. But that is an argument for a later chapter.)

Asante, Karenga, Jacob Carruthers, and other major figures among the Afrocentrists have sought to further excavate the historical roots from which Afrocentrism derives. Increasingly, in this excavation they have focused on the project of reclaiming ancient, dynastic Egypt and Nubia. These "classical African Civilizations" are a connection to Africa, to black people, and to Afrocentric thought that provides an anchor and a legitimate basis, finally, for a way of constructing knowledge, for constructing a reality, securely based in history, that is as monumental in its impact on civilization as Greece and Rome. As mentioned above, the theme of Egypt as the Afrocentric counterpart to Greece and Rome runs strongly through the body of Asante's work. While focus on language and orality figures in the day-to-day microconstruction of the Afrocentric framework developed in the body of Asante's work, the focus on restoring Egypt as a macrolevel cultural monument and a historical reference point is intended to place Afrocentricty on a deeply rooted historical foundation.

On the relevance of such roots, Asante comments that a classical tradition "forms a part of the grand continuity of concepts, values, experiences, visions, and possibilities."[33] And, as deconstruction was involved in the microlevel reconstruction of an appropriately centered perspective, so was it necessary at the macrolevel of reconstruction of this "grand continuity of concepts." "Just as we had to throw off the yoke of oppression from our bodies and our lands," he writes, "we will have to liberate the study of the classical civilizations because the European colonization of geography, that is, land went hand-in-hand with the colonization of information and knowledge."[34]

In reclaiming Egypt as part of a history of "classical African civilizations," Afrocentric historiography connects the glory, wisdom, and knowledge of Egypt to the development of the rest of Africa. This counters, or deconstructs, ideologically distorted Western historiographies that either cut classical Egypt away from the roots of Western Civilization, and/or cut Egypt itself away from Africa, in terms of racial characteristics and cultural and historical ties. In this regard, Asante writes, "A fundamental position of my argument is that all African societies found Kemet a common source for intellectual and philosophical ideas. These manifestations are shown, for example, in: the conversations of the Dogon's blind philosopher Ogotommeli; Julu oral poetry, as brought to us by Masizi Kunene; Yoruba Ifa divination rights; Nsibidi texts, and in the practices and words of the Shona spirit mediums."[35]

In addition, Afrocentrists seem to have another agenda in the project of recovering Kemet. In this restored historiography it is Egypt, rather than Greece and Rome, that stands as the source of "high culture" and *of Western civilization itself.* In this regard, connections are uncovered between ancient Kemet and important philosophical, cultural, and religious ideas commonly attributed to Greek or otherwise "Western" origins.[36] In making the case for Egypt's position at the fountainhead of African history and culture, Afrocentrists stand on the firm foundation of the work of the Senegalese scholar Cheikh Anta Diop, among others. Diop's works—establishing, as their titles suggest, *The African Origin of Civilization*[37] and *The Cultural Unity of Black Africa*[38]—are widely respected even by those who express disagreement or strong reservations about some of his premises and conclusions.[39] In making a case for Africa's influence on Europe (through Egypt), they are aided, in addition to Diop, by the recent work of white Egyptologist Martin Bernal, whose *Black Athena* argues for the premise that the Greek culture borrowed heavily from the older Egyptian civilization.[40]

Finally, the primacy of Egyptian reclamation and the focus on the importance of language come together in *Kemet*, where Asante aligns himself with other Afrocentrists (Diop, Carruthers, and Karenga) who insist that the language of ancient Egypt must be the cornerstone of any real discussion of African Studies.[41] Moreover, the analogy and the connection between Greece and Egypt also comes into play around this "classical language" issue when he embraces Carruthers's assertion that "we should use that language as our classical language just as the Europeans use Greek and Latin today."[42] (Note that nothing in the context of this statement suggests what a "classical language" is "used" *for*. The important point seems to be to "have" something that can be called a "classical language" that cannot be claimed as European.)

From the ground up and from the beginning, then, Afrocentrists seem to want to argue, the historical picture of humanity must be redrawn to include Egypt as part of Africa's heritage, and to include Africa's heritage in the historical picture of humanity itself. From the very phonemes and morphemes of Kemet (according to Diop and Asante, the beginning of spoken and written discourse) through all the discourses that have accompanied the historical formations of modernity, processes of knowledge construction must be redesigned to acknowledge the primacy of Africa in the heritage of blacks, and of humankind itself. Asante sums it up this way: "We must begin from the perspective that sees post-Diopian Afrocentricity as the intellectual movement which restored the place of Africans in world history and reestablished the human project in terms consonant to a critique of knowledge from African-centeredness."[43]

Thus, the construction of Afrocentrism has been a vital element in the final, necessary deconstruction of Eurocentrism. Afrocentrism has been widely embraced, perhaps somewhat uncritically, because it represents this final deconstruction of the Eurocentric particularism the Black Studies movement has sought since its inception out of the transformational struggles of the 1960s; it provided a way of breaking out of the "strait-jackets of thought" cited by Du Bois half a century ago as a major obstacle seemingly designed to restrain those who reach for truth and clarity regarding the affairs of black folk.[44] Furthermore, the body of knowledge and information emphasized by Afrocentrism has been essential in the reconstruction of intellectual perspectives and cultural sensibilities that affirm the historical legitimacy of blacks while providing an anchor for their consciousness as a people; it offers a basis for unified theory construction relative to the study and analysis of black people and black communities.

For these reasons, perhaps, a presumption has developed, both inside and outside of the field, that Afrocentricity and African American Studies are synonymous. In Asante's summation of Black Studies' evolution toward maturity, it is clear that Afrocentricity views itself as the totalized form of that evolution. At the outset, he states:

> The absence of a comprehensive philosophical position, with attendant possibilities for a new logic, science, and rhetoric condemned us to experimentation with an Islamic base, a Marxist base, a civil service base, a reactionary nationalist base, a social service base, systematic nationalist base, or a historical-cultural base. Systematic nationalists tended to be grouped with the historical-cultural school because they, at least, understood that Black Studies implied a different perspective although they could never thoroughly articulate that perspective.
>
> Afrocentricity, *as that perspective* becomes indispensable to our understanding of Black Studies; otherwise, we have a series of intellectual adventures in Eurocentric perspectives about Africans and African-Americans. (Emphasis added.)[45]

While the deconstructive initiatives of the Afrocentric paradigm may be necessary, my argument is that its reconceptualizations cannot be considered sufficient in constituting a viable African American Studies disciplinary-matrix. Aside from acknowledged contributions, some aspects of Afrocentrism are controversial and questionable. Examination of a number of issues reveals arguable limitations, errors, and distortions associated with assertions of Afrocentrists.

As one stream of thought among several that interact synergistically within a self-refining "black/African disciplinary-matrix," such as that outlined by James B. Stewart, Afrocentrism's possible errors and distortions occur in context with a continuous stream of critical discourse, maximizing the possibility that useful insights will be produced in the process. In Stewart's words, "Ameliorating the collective weaknesses in the self-contained systems of thought under discussion is a strategy that can guide efforts to refine the collective disciplinary-matrix in a manner that can help Black/Africana Studies scholar/activists to reach higher ground."[46] In other words, the presence of alternative perspectives promotes dialogue, which in turn promotes clarity, within the discipline. Within a self-contained system of thought, however, these weaknesses become self-reifying barriers between Afrocentrists, other Black Studies scholars, and other fields of study and areas of praxis.

Afrocentrism is correct, in any meaningful sense, as a deconstructor of Eurocentric hegemonic mythology. In spite of elaborate protestations to the contrary, however, Afrocentrists seem to use similar methods to construct an Afrocentric hegemonic mythology. I remain unconvinced by the frequent and elaborate denials that say Afrocentrism does not replicate the very errors and limitations it criticizes. The overall intellectual aim of Afrocentrism is to develop a knowledge structure analogous in many ways to the Western traditions of thought called collectively "Eurocentrism."

This tendency is reflected in the many Afrocentrist assertions that make Egypt a "classical African civilization" that does for the African world what Greece and Rome do for the European world. Typical of such assertions is Asante's statement that "[t]he Afrocentric analysis reestablishes the centrality of the ancient Kemetic (Egyptian) civilization and the Nile Valley cultural complex as points of reference for an African perspective in much the same way as Greece and Rome serve as reference points for the European World."[47]

What exactly it is that ancient Greece and Rome "do for the European world" today, and whether it is desirable for the African world, are themselves issues that could benefit from more critical scrutiny. In any case, such statements reveal that, although Afrocentrists are concerned with resurrecting and raising African symbols and concepts, the subtextual model for this process is often based on Western Eurocentric models. For example, Asante, while discussing modernist critical theory, states, "I seek a critical method applicable to Africans, wherever they are, in much the same way Western scholars have set the procedures for criticizing Western discourse."[48]

The tendency is implicit in the numerous other assertions that reflect a wish to obliterate, or at least counterbalance, all reference frames, reference points, symbols, and symbol systems that have ostensibly European connections. For example, Asante demands that, "When you sit in classes and listen to lecturers speak of Keats, Yeats, Twain, Wordsworth, Frost, Eliot, and Goethe, you had better be able to call upon Baraka, Shange, Welsh, Guillen, Cesaire, Abiola, Ngugi, and Okai. Not to call upon these spirit voices when you are bombarded with alien shadows makes you a victim of the most detestable isolation and alienation from your own past and present."[49]

There is, thus, a kind of ambivalence, and ambiguity, which is laid bare as other "centrisms" are rejected as inapplicable to blacks while at the same time serving as models for alternatives. Afrocentrism, this logic says, is legitimate because it does what Eurocentrism does, but better because it does not. Consider, for example, Asante's statement in *Kemet, Afrocentricity, and Knowledge*: "Centrism, the groundedness of observation and behavior in one's own historical experiences, shapes the concepts, paradigms, theories, and methods of Africalogy. In this way Africalogy secures its place alongside the other centric pluralisms without hierarchy and by a commitment to centering the study of African Phenomenon and events in the particular cultural voice of the composite African people."[50]

In this passage Asante suggests that Africalogy has legitimacy "alongside the other centric pluralisms" based on its similarity to them ("groundedness of observation," etc.). It is different, however, in that it is "without hierarchy." The paradox, consistent in Asante's work, is in the continual legitimizing of "Eurocentrism," or the Western tradition that goes along with its continual rejection. In *Kemet*, Asante claims, "Africalogy . . . does not deny rationalism its historical place but neither does it deny other forms of human inquiry."[51]

Quite similarly, in *The Afrocentric Idea* he notes, "I do not castigate any other method, for all methods are valid within their contexts."[52] Referring to European "classical music" in *Afrocentricity* Asante states, "they may be classical to Europeans but not to us. . . . *I applaud their nationalism*" (emphasis added).[53] In that same work he states that rejection of non-Afrocentric thoughts, actions, behavior, and values "is not done because we have something against someone else's culture; it is just not ours."[54]

With statements such as these, Asante validates his own "centrist" approaches in context with his explicit validation of those approaches he opposes. At other points, however, Asante attends closely to the need to distinguish this particular kind of "centrism" from others. In addition to the claim that Africalogy's "centrism" is "without hierarchy," Asante claims that Afrocentrism embodies a greater sense of humanity. In *The Afrocentric Idea*, for example, his discussion of the role of rhetoric and discourse as "wholly committed to the propagation of a more humanistic vision of the world"[55] includes the assertion that "Afrocentric rhetoric, while it is in opposition to the negative in Western culture, allows other cultures to co-exist, and in that particular aspect is substantially different from Western rhetoric. It is neither imperialistic nor oppressive."[56]

In *Afrocentricity* his rejection of the inherent Eurocentrism of Marxist thought includes the argument that "both . . . [capitalism and Marxism] believe in utter destruction of aliens. This, of course, is contradictory to the Afrocentric value which respects difference and applauds pluralism."[57] In this same discussion he argues that progress in Eurocentric terms comes of dialectic conflict. "For us," he states, "life is culture, spirit, and harmony."[58]

Since Africalogy's "centrism" is grounded "alongside" other centrisms, the assessment that it is "without hierarchy" and has otherwise avoided the pitfalls of Europe's "centrism" is one that should not go without scrutiny. If the hierarchy is defined in terms of degree of embodiment of humanistic values, clearly Afrocentrism does place itself hierarchically above Eurocentrism. While this may appear to be a small point it represents one of the key criticisms Stewart identified with "strong claim" Afrocentrism, which "encourages racial chauvinism and inter-group conflict by asserting the superiority of peoples of African descent relative to other populations."[59] In that way, it is theoretically not different from the racial chauvinism associated with current racist domination of peoples of color.

The logic for the assurance that the Afrocentric way of life does not seek domination is not obvious. Indeed, its validation in connection with the actual record of African history is debatable. Even more problematic are statements that say "we accept no dictatorship of any kind,"[60] or that "We cannot be antagonistic to nature,"[61] or "Only in traditional western societies are there conflicts between classes; such is not the case when we operate from our traditional base of harmony."[62] With the truth of current realities in Nigeria, Rwanda, Somalia, and other places in Africa, these assertions are simply calamitous.

Thus, as noted even more sharply elsewhere,[63] Afrocentrism's focus on anteriority leads it away from critical contemporary issues for both African Americans and Africans. Asante would account for current crises on the African continent by insisting that "[t]he breakdown of our central political organizations from the disintegration of Egypt during the coming of the foreigners all the way to the enslavement of Africans represents one massive slide away from our center."[64] The current problems of Africa, it would seem, occur because African governments are no longer Afrocentric: "Since the colonial era, many [African] countries have adopted all of the symbols and behaviors of decadent Western societies . . . which have proved themselves neither in their native lands nor among us."[65]

Again, the proposition that all problems, disharmony, and inhumane tendencies among Afrocentric peoples are due to the "coming of foreigners" is debatable. Egypt, after all, was a class-differentiated society with slaves and an imperial history. Even if that proposition were correct, though, it could not be considered a sufficient response to the current crises of Egypt's or Africa's descendant, dispersed children in Africa or on any other continent. Three thousand years is a long time to slide. It is not at all clear how the calamitous effects can be undone either by reclaiming the past or renaming the present.

Stewart summarizes three kinds of critiques he says apply to the "strong claims" of Afrocentrism: "One criticism suggests that predetermined models of society and individual behavior are attached to the concept that adherents seek to impose on all peoples of African descent. A related criticism alleges that the models of society and individual behavior celebrated by Afrocentrists are drawn from epochs long past and are largely irrelevant to the modern world. A third criticism suggests that the concept encourages racial chauvinism and inter-group conflict by asserting the superiority of peoples of African descent relative to other populations."[66]

It seems to me, however, that the strongest of the strong claims are those that say African American Studies itself is Afrocentrism and nothing else. Indeed, in my view it is critical, both for Afrocentrism and for African American Studies, that the latter be understood as the larger domain in which Afrocentrists and others function and contribute as Black Studies scholars. Although Afrocentrism has clearly had an important role in the evolution of African American Studies, the African American Studies discipline is accurately conceptualized as a *set* of theoretical perspectives, rather than a single theoretical perspective, a set of perspectives that has developed out of a discourse about how to constitute knowledge of the historical and contemporary experiences, conditions, and aspirations of black people. Implicit in this view is that each perspective raises legitimate issues for other perspectives. In a previous article I argued, not quite tautologically, that any perspective was good for what it could show you, but not good for what it could not show you; that what one saw depended on what one looked for, and what one looked at.[67]

A mainstream discipline as an example: among sociologists structural functionalism is a theoretical perspective thought to be good for looking at how a given social group, organization, or society is structured and how it functions. The key word is *given*. Structural functionalism takes what is given as normative and concerns itself almost exclusively with how what is given functions and is structured at the time and point of inquiry. (For this reason, some say, it is especially compatible with the need to maintain an existing structure of social order.)

Structural functionalism reveals little or nothing at all about how what is given as normative comes to be accepted as "normal." To focus on social change and transformation rather than structure, one must go to (or "come from") the "conflict perspective," based on the premise that intergroup conflict is the key factor in social change and evolution. Along with those two perspectives is the "interactionist" perspective, which focuses primarily at the level of social interaction among individual members of social units to contextualize, explain, and predict social phenomenon. There are also sociologists who attempt to stand astride the margins and borders between the various viewpoints to merge and synthesize certain aspects of them. It is worth noting that none of these would say the other is not a sociologist.

While Afrocentrism has contributed important new ideas to the emerging discourse in African American Studies, in the view of some it has too often ignored or diminished the importance and legitimacy of other approaches. Thus, in discussing the emergence of Afrocentrism in this chapter I have endeavored to validate its contribution, as well as to lay bases for addressing its possible limitations. While acknowledging it as a useful point of reference, I have argued against the presumption that the Afrocentric perspective itself defined and delimited African American Studies and set it off from other areas of intellectual study.

Moreover, in view of the recent tendency of many to equate

Afrocentrism, the theoretical orientation, with African American Studies per se, I have placed Afrocentrism in a context that is normative for academic disciplines. Here differing schools of thought coexist that are in some ways competitive with and in some ways complementary to one another. In the following chapter I will further develop this view while outlining and summarizing several general approaches that have emerged in the discourse of African American Studies and are identifiable within the body of work constituting the field.

Chapter 4

Alternative Approaches in African American Studies

African American Studies, like all academic disciplines, has been constituted from several paradigms or schools of thought evolving historically in intellectual and social arenas. While respecting and incorporating much of what Afrocentrists have brought to the field, I argue that several perspectives or viewpoints are potentially valid in developing Black Studies as a focus of inquiry. In this chapter I will summarize several general approaches within African American Studies that reflect more comprehensively the diverse strains of its history. In that view, Afrocentrism is seen not as an end but rather as part and parcel of the ongoing project.

The increasing visibility and influence of Afrocentric ideas during the late eighties and nineties has led to a perception, both inside and outside the discipline, that Afrocentrism is synonymous with African American Studies per se. However, while adherents of particular schools of thought sometimes seek to define the discipline solely in terms of a single paradigm, the reality is that no theoretical perspective, approach, or point of view contains all the legitimate insights and contributions that make up the knowledge foundation of the field. In fact, the varied circumstances of its origin and development among various programs suggest that a good deal of what might be designated "Black Studies," from one perspective or another, is work by scholars primarily associated with traditional disciplines. In other words, a discussion of various approaches within African American Studies cannot, at this point, be separated from a continuing discussion of various conceptions of what Black Studies in fact is, and how Black Studies is distinct from and/or related to other areas of knowledge. Indeed, as James B. Stewart notes, "The debate has intensified recently, in part due to the visibility afforded to writings by literary critics and historians who, although they identify primarily with traditional disciplines, assert connections to Black Studies.... This turf battle has re-energized discussions about the nature of Black Studies, i.e., is it a self-contained and distinct body of knowledge or simply an adjunct to traditional disciplines?"[1]

Addressing the issue of point-of-view in an earlier article, I developed a categorization of general perspectives in the field that placed Afrocentrism in a broader disciplinary structure that included at least two other general approaches. I use the terms *integrationist* and *inclusionist* to describe the first perspective, in which the substance and content of an area of black life was integrated or included in the body of knowledge represented by an existing conventional discipline. Clearly, the Afrocentrist perspective has been most visible among those who sought to challenge the basic epistemological ground on which these conventional, integrationist approaches were based. *Transformationist* is the term I propose to refer to a range of alternative perspectives that maintain critical scrutiny of both conventional epistemological approaches and the emergent Afrocentrist alternative. From this perspective, relevant Afrocentric insights and sensibilities are seen through a lens that clarifies their interaction, or transformation, in the context of more traditional Western forms and structures.[2]

These terms also align closely with those employed in Manning Marable's recent analysis of ideological and intellectual trends among black leadership and intelligentsia. Here he uses the terms *inclusionist, nationalist/Afrocentrist* and *transformationist* to describe "three overlapping, strategic visions about the nature of the contemporary political economy, the meaning of 'race' in the post–Civil Rights era, and what is to be done in the next century to address the problems of black people and to construct a multicultural democracy."[3] Of course these terms are, in some sense, only labels of convenience that could, with overly rigid application, oversimplify the variations in approach and perspective that exist within the field. In reality each term surely refers to a set of perspectives rather than a single one. Here, the terms are intended to suggest a general level of delineation among various approaches for purposes of description and comparison.

In sifting through these descriptions it will be additionally helpful to refer to James B. Stewart's Black/Africana Studies disciplinary matrix, which conceptualizes the historical and contemporary variation among Black Studies scholars in terms of the rationale that have emerged in conjunction with successive conceptions of Black Studies. Stewart has drawn from the work of Thomas Kuhn to develop those rationale into the idea of a disciplinary matrix as a model useful for conceptualizing, analyzing, and further developing the field.[4]

Integrationism/Inclusionism

Stewart suggests that recently influential works from literary critics and historians embody conceptions of Black Studies based on the same *"value-added"* rationale that he associates with many early programs—a rationale that suggests "Black Studies has a legitimate role in academe because it extends the explanatory powers of traditional disciplines."[5] As indicated in the previous section, early formational dynamics tended to favor the production of programs that sought to involve traditional disciplines and departments as central conceptual and programmatic (that is, structural) components.[6] Such has been the context for the work of some Black Studies scholars and much of the work about blacks that comes from traditional disciplines in which the aim is to "integrate" the heretofore neglected studies black life into the theoretical and methodological frameworks of so-called "established" disciplines.

Implicitly, then, this rationale alone did nothing to distinguish whether Black Studies was "a subset of the knowledge base of traditional disciplines or a model identifying Black Studies as a self-contained and distinct body of knowledge";[7] nor did it incorporate the social and cultural missions inherent in the movement: the confrontation of conventional academic values with the emergent African American cultural consciousness and self-assertion. Far from seeking to define a new discipline or field, this approach views special courses on, say, black history and literature as temporary and provisional. This view in its extreme was typified by Nathan Huggins, who stated, "The question . . . is not whether English departments offer courses in Afro-American literature, but whether works by black authors are taught in courses on American literature."[8]

Criticism and rejection from Black Studies activists aside, this "integrationist" or "inclusionist" perspective is simply, as fait accompli if nothing else, a visible and influential aspect of the discourse. The program at Yale came to be considered the model for this approach and enjoyed support and prestige among academic establishment venues.

The Ford Foundation, involved with Black Studies since its inception, underwrote the conference at Yale in 1968 that accompanied the development of that school's program, a model apparently favored from the start.

The scholars cited by James B. Stewart who assert connections with Black Studies even though they "identify primarily with traditional disciplines" were historians Darlene Clark Hine, Robert L. Harris, and Nathan Huggins, and literary critics Nellie McKay, Houston Baker, and Henry Louis Gates Jr., all of whom have made substantial contributions to the body of literature upon which African American Studies draws in its continuing self-definitional discourse. Baker and Gates, both students in the Yale Afro-American Studies program at some point, have been especially influential in the current period. As Stewart suggests, the degree to which Gates (now chairing the Afro-American Studies department at Harvard) and other influential scholars are primarily identified with traditional disciplines is the degree to which differentiating Black Studies from a merely inclusionist approach to traditional studies remains an issue.

Anticipating epistemological issues subsequently engaged among Black Studies scholars, Stewart finds it significant that in most of these instances associated with *value-added* rationales "the issue of whether the theories and methods utilized in traditional disciplines are directly applicable without modification to the study of the experiences of peoples of African descent is not addressed."[9] In fact, the frequent criticism of the *value-added* perspective has been that—whether it calls itself Black Studies or a traditional discipline—it mirrors the approaches and methodological and theoretical frameworks, as well as some of the errors and distortions, of traditional disciplines in the study and analysis of the black experience.[10]

On the whole, Black Studies activists see the task of disentangling this fragmented knowledge from its mire of intradisciplinary biases and cross-disciplinary barriers as indeed great, and the results less than useful. Writing in a special issue of the *Journal of Negro Education* in 1984, Russell Adams, longtime chair of Afro-American Studies at Howard University, puts it this way: "professionals in the field . . . must understand how these disciplines came to be and to what extent their epistemological foundations complicate the creation of an alternative and perhaps more accurate epistemic for approaching the black experience."[11]

Stewart regards this issue in a similar manner, distinguishing between a "weak" and "strong multi/interdisciplinary rationale." According to Stewart, "weak" multi/interdisciplinary rationales tend to accept the existing disciplinary structure: "Most advocates of this position simply assume that because Black/Africana Studies examines aspects of life experience that cut across traditional disciplinary boundaries the resultant analyses are by definition interdisciplinary. However, virtually no attention is devoted to the examination of the underlying theoretical constructs necessary for 'interdisciplinary' or 'multidisciplinary' to be manifested."[12] Since this rationale takes the existing disciplinary structures as given, it involves no attempt to challenge or alter the epistemological processes that shape the legitimacy of knowledge in those respective areas. In programmatic terms the result is another version of an inclusionist/integrationist concept.

Afrocentrism

According to Stewart, Afrocentrist approaches have achieved great presence, visibility, and influence in this discourse by addressing a "strong multidisciplinary" rationale for underlying theoretical constructs that effectively erase disciplinary boundaries. Afrocentrism, as it appears in work by Karenga and Asante, seeks to challenge and reshape the basic epistemological premises through which conventional disciplinary methods are applied to studies of black lives and communities. It is this Afrocentric framework, according to Afrocentrists themselves, that locates their work in a different field—namely, "Black/Africana Studies," a field separate and distinct from the work of the integrationists/inclusionists.

In my view Afrocentrism's significant contribution is its deconstruction of prevailing Eurocentric bias; its basic challenge to the hegemony of conventional approaches to knowledge in framing, contextualizing, and studying the historical and contemporary experiences, conditions, and aspirations of blacks. Afrocentrism has been widely embraced as a species of "antidote" to the biases of Eurocentrism that are among the many odious legacies of Western imperialism. Arguably, Afrocentrists are at their best when engaged in the project of deconstruction. For example, Asante writes, "The ruling ideologies continue to abuse positions of power on questions of knowledge. That is why I have maintained that the Eurocentric West is trapped, even in its best intentions, by its concentration on itself, its selfishness, its inability to draw a wider picture."[13]

Eventually, however, the "inability to draw a wider picture" seems precisely the barrier Afrocentrism erects for itself. Framed in terms of the particulars of a Black/Africana Studies disciplinary matrix, Stewart's paradigm highlights both the validity and the limitations of Afrocentrism as one aspect of the matrix. Regarding the increasing emphasis that Afrocentrists are placing on "classical African civilizations," for example, Stewart offers extensive discussion as to why such studies are important to the Black/Africana Studies disciplinary matrix:

> The thrust of interest in this area in general has been to identify the African origins of Egyptian civilization and, more specifically, to document the extensive presence and impact of peoples of sub-Saharan African origin in various dynasties. This research is necessary and important for several reasons. It provides the ammunition to mount a direct attack on traditional interpretations of ancient Egyptian society as a pseudo-European civilization. The Europeanization of Egypt has facilitated the efforts of historians of Western thought to project the notion of a continuous intellectual history of strictly European lineage. Current research that debunks this interpretation can provide a foundation for reconstructing a continuous intellectual history of African thought that can connect to modern Black/Africana Studies. . . . The examination of value systems in classical African civilizations prior to the emergence of Western political domination can provide exemplars that can clarify the metaphysical and values components of the Black/Africana Studies disciplinary-matrix. In such societies peoples of African descent were rulers rather than subjects. As a consequence, their world views were not shaped by the history of domination that has conditioned much of the thought of peoples of African descent who were kidnapped and transplanted to the West. Studies of classical civilizations have also identified individual figures who can serve as exemplars for contemporary Black/Africana Studies scholar/activists, e.g., Imhotep.[14]

Disciplinary matrices, according to Stewart, comprise four distinct components: (a) metaphysical; (b) values shared by practitioners; (c) symbolic generalizations, observational language, and research methods; and (d) exemplars (concrete examples of the application of the theoretical and empirical framework).[15] Within this matrix, Stewart maintains, "it is critical to understand that the extent to which a system of thought is Afrocentric is only one of many criteria that are relevant for judging the overall usefulness of a conceptual framework."[16] In this regard, Stewart believes, the contemporary emphasis of Afrocentric historiography on

Egypt has not accorded fully with the needs of the African American Studies disciplinary matrix. He contends, "Unfortunately, the vast majority of the scholarship to date is contributionist in orientation, rather than undertaking systematic investigation of the degree of applicability of classical ideas and social formations for the present and future. . . . Little effort has been made to shape these studies in ways that contribute to the generation of the continuous intellectual history advocated previously."[17]

Stewart's references to "applicability of classical ideas and social formations for the present and future" and "generation of [a] continuous intellectual history" derive from his view of the importance of "exemplars" in finding ways to understand and address current conditions, problems, and solutions. Of all the elements of Stewart's conception of the Kuhnian disciplinary matrix, the exemplars component would seem to constitute the most critical link between conception and execution. Quite literally, exemplars, like Du Bois, as Stewart's work through the years has constantly reminded us, "show us how it is done" in terms of the combination of values, subject areas, approaches to knowledge, and standards of presentation that constitute the disciplinary matrix of Black/Africana Studies.

Thus, while no one could validly accuse Stewart of failing to understand the role of ancient historical reconstruction, he suggests nonetheless that "the focus on Kemetic studies needs to be balanced with comparable levels of scrutiny of other classical African civilizations and societies/communities in the Western Hemisphere."[18]

Because Afrocentrists seek a complete break with those who apply more conventional disciplinary approaches to African American Studies, this approach does not lend itself to discourse and reconciliation with other viewpoints within the field. In a manner profoundly consistent with other dimensions in African American discourse, culture, social, and political issues are constructed as bipolar propositions, which then produce polarized results. In African American Studies this tendency is reenacted in microcosm in the tension between "integrationist" extremes at one end, where "black" studies is only the integration of "black content" into conventional studies, and an Afrocentric extreme at the other end, where "Africalogy" is defined as completely independent of any other angle of vision.

Whether this dynamic involves issues of perspective and methodology within African American Studies, or larger political choices in the "real" world, it is usually (that is to say, more often than not) impossible to avoid the polarizing effects of choices presented. Within African

American Studies the difficulty has been the articulation of perspectives that embrace neither pole exclusively, but seek a synthesis better suited to the variations and complexities in the construction of black communities and black experiences. A disciplinary matrix that includes, but is not defined by, the perspective of either pole allows the development of such syntheses, provided that the matrix promotes what Stewart calls "synergistic linkages" among the various approaches in the field.

Transformative Alternatives

Gender, Feminism, and Black Women's Studies

Gender issues suffer in racially polarized discussions, especially the interaction of race and gender. Historically, the struggles against racial oppression on the part of blacks, and against gender oppression on the part of white women, have often interacted to create special problems for black women. The club movement among educated black women at the turn of the century and the modern black feminist movement both reflect the redefinition of reality that occurs when "social truth" is directed to incorporate the unique perspectives of black women. Microcosmically, the emergence of issues related to gender, Black Women's Studies, and black feminism within the Black Studies movement reflect this tendency.

In August 1982 the Institute of the Black World (IBW), a black "cultural think tank" led by scholars like historian Vincent Harding and Howard Dodson (currently director of the Shomburg Collection of the New York City Library), held a conference wrapping up the Black Studies Curriculum Project, which they had undertaken over the course of the previous year. In chapter 1, I refer to that project as an instance when the class-based political economy critique is registered with great authority among those espousing the disciplinary matrix of Black/Africana Studies. The other major consensus from the project was to note the critical absence of Black Women's Studies as a curricular focus in existing courses and programs up to that point. For complete historical accuracy, however, it should be understood that the crucial discussions involving gender issues and black women's perspectives had not been a part of the project's official plan.

The IBW Black Studies curriculum project was ingeniously designed in several stages: collection of existing Black Studies course syllabi from all over the country; review of those syllabi as they reflected basic topical areas in historical, sociopolitical, and aesthetic studies; conferences involving Black Studies scholars from all over the country, where panel and open group discussions considered presentations and reports drawn from reviews of the syllabi; and, finally, a compiled final report that included model syllabi along with the review reports in each topical area. At no stage in the course of this project, up through the printing of the program for the wrap-up conference, were gender issues or black women's perspectives identified as specific areas of concern. As the final conference approached, however, women involved with the project (including the main convenor's wife) launched an uprising—analogous to uprisings occurring among black women scholars across the nation at that time. Thus, these women somewhat forcibly injected gender issues into the discourse of African American Studies, much as African American Studies itself had been injected into the context of broader higher education.

It also seems fair and accurate to say that within the Black Studies movement, black women's perspectives in particular, and gender issues in general, were subject to the same constraints, ambivalences, and ambiguities they have historically faced in the larger movements for black and women's equality. Despite persistent barriers and frequent lack of recognition, black women have been critically involved at all stages, and in all forms, of black political struggle, even as they have always been at the critical core of the cycle of struggle, survival, and continuity of black life and culture in the larger sense. Within the Black Studies movement, the presence of black women as scholars, administrators, leaders, and contributors was phenomenal compared to the presence of white women scholars in many fields in those times. (The first chair of the National Council for Black Studies was a woman; in all, three out of the first five chairs of the discipline's first professional organization were black women.)

However, as a black female graduate assistant remarked to me, it was not "the black women's presence" or "role" or "strength" or "beauty" that was unrecognized by male dominant formations and structures; it was her voice.[19] It not was that she was not seen; it was that she was not heard if her voice was speaking to issues of gender aside from race, of gender extended from race, of gender in combination with race. For example, Deborah King, in a conference on "Afro-American Studies in the Twenty-first Century," noted the manner in which selective presentation of issues (for example, school dropout rates, imprisonment rates, homicide rates, college attendance) suggests that the problems of black communities focus around the issue of the "decimation of the black male." As a result, she argues, "we learn that in the current conceptualization black women are either: (1) invisible, (2) advantaged, or (3) victimizers."[20] Meanwhile, issues especially affecting black women—domestic abuse, sexual assault, impoverished single-parent families, insensitive welfare policies, AIDS as a leading cause of death—are not necessarily seen as "race" problems in a comparable way.

And, conversely, it appears that in the wider feminist discourse about gender, black women are not heard if they speak of race aside from gender, race extended from gender, or race in combination with gender. Thus, black women in academia, like black women aspiring to leadership roles historically and contemporarily, experienced great difficulty accessing channels for voicing their concerns as black women within either the black or the women's studies' movements. As expressed in the creatively constructed title of the pioneering Black Women's Studies anthology *All the Women Are White, All the Blacks Are Men, but Some of Us Are Brave*, black women have periodically and collectively required singular acts of self-assertion to erase their invisibility. Otherwise, common reference would subsume racial identity (blackness) within the collectivity of gender (maleness) and gender identity (femaleness) within the collectivity of race (whiteness). And yet, as King explains, "It is precisely those differences between blacks and women, between black men and black women, between black women and white women that are crucial to understanding the nature of black womanhood," and that also point to the mission of Black Women Studies, both within and alongside of the Black/Africana Studies disciplinary matrix.[21]

The emergence of a distinct Black Women's Studies project, as represented in the confrontation of black women scholars with the previously male-dominated discussion order at the IBW conference, was analogous, in terms of raising new issues of perspective, validity, and authenticity, to the historic confrontation that inaugurated Black Studies as a distinct field of study. As long as existing procedures, customs, habits of thought led predictably, inexorably—as they obviously did in the process of the IBW project—to the exclusion and neglect of issues uniquely affecting black women, a separate initiative called "Black Women's Studies" would seem justified and necessary.

Sorting out how this separate project is to be related to African American Studies, to Women's Studies, and to conventional disciplinary studies involves issues analogous to those that define the relationship of the African American studies to studies of black content in the traditional disciplines. The degree to which Black Women's Studies will remain separate or become integrated into the Black/Africana Studies disciplinary matrix will fundamentally impact the future development of the field. According to Stewart, two tendencies currently exist:

> One school of thought embraces the [African American Studies] field's long standing cultural nationalist ideology. It urges the forging of a new partnership between Africana men and women in pursuit of previously articulated intellectual and political objectives. The second school of thought elevates feminism to a higher ideological status than cultural nationalism. Advocates of the second approach tend to be more directly connected to traditional academic disciplines than are their counterparts and, more specifically, they are clustered in the areas of literary perspectives.[22]

Among the former group the term "womanist" may sometimes be used instead of or in place of "feminist." A high proportion of Black Women's Studies scholars in the second group has tended to emerge within literary studies, according to Stewart. Since literary studies in general is an area which Stewart feels lacks effective synergistic connections within the Black/Africana Studies matrix, he believes that "To the extent that their work is not systematically integrated into the Black/Africana Studies developmental process, the social science-based scholarship of the field will, in all likelihood, continue to be gender-biased."

Regarding the concentration of Black Women's Studies scholars in literary studies, there are exceptions to the trend noted by Stewart. Patricia Hill Collins and Deborah King, for example, are both social scientists who have worked toward developing a theoretical model for the study of gender issues. In addition, bell hooks's work is guided by the postmodern cultural studies paradigm that incorporates both social and literary studies.[23] A body of theory has developed from the work of such black feminist scholars that locates black women's experiences in a hub where race, class, and gender converge, like spokes in a wheel of social constructions, and interact to shape the particulars of black women's lives. Collins's work in defining a "black women's standpoint epistemology," or "angle of vision," has helped to illuminate the inextricable connections among gender, race, and class in approaching issues and problems in social reality to which other black feminists (like King and bell hooks) have also pointed.[24] Thus, King notes, "[t]he triple jeopardy of racism, sexism, and classism is now widely accepted and used as the conceptualization of black women's status."[25]

This body of thought remedies the previous theoretical invisibility of black women, giving black women voices that had been denied in formations based on either race or gender alone. Moreover, these uniquely black feminist voices consistently point to the necessity of addressing all dimensions of human oppressions—termed "non-monism" by King.[26] As such, this body of theory both particularizes a "black women's standpoint epistemology" and universalizes her struggle as the epitome of the human struggle for freedom, dignity, and fulfillment.

Speaking to African American Studies professionals, King asserts that "we have lost a viable means for crafting social issues" by constructing critical social issues as primarily, if not exclusively, male. Since "[t]he ability to discern and comprehend the experiences and circumstances of a variety of African Americans is critical for addressing the complexity of social issues for the community,"[27] this masculinized distortion represents a loss for all. King concludes that, "[a]s scholars, we need to develop conceptual frameworks and conduct historical, literary, and social analyses that are inclusive of the experiences of African American women and men; that are inclusive in their consideration of the dynamics of class, race, gender and other oppressions and that are inclusive in the recognition of the various mechanisms of self-determination, empowerment, and resistance that all African Americans have designed."[28]

In this passage King presents a concern for clarifying special needs and circumstances regarding black women in communion and in connection with a project to enhance "mechanisms of self-determination, empowerment, and resistance" that are of and for "all African Americans." This would suggest an approach compatible (or "synergistic") with the Black Studies disciplinary matrix. Such compatibility is also enhanced in the context of formulations, such as Stewart's Black/Africana Studies disciplinary matrix, that conceptualize the field in terms broader than either an integrationist/inclusionist approach or an Afrocentric approach. Such an "open" discursive framework allows room for other approaches, which could incorporate relevant aspects of each major approach and, as in the case of Black Women's Studies, inject important new elements into the dialogue. Without such an open discourse, the polarized, mutually exclusive character of much of the debate is shown to be inadequate for accommodating issues relating to gender and black feminism. Perhaps more importantly, the interconnections, which black feminist (womanist) scholars have illuminated, of gender and race with class and other oppressions that limit the actualization and expression of humanity is not adequately addressed in the discursive context that polarizes nationalism and integrationism.

When considering the issue of "perspective" one may note that the same facts, words sources and references, and so-called "objective" data—viewed by ostensibly equally qualified scholars—may yield different observations, interpretations, or conclusions. Consider, for example, Asante's assertion, from his reconstruction of cultural and historical reference points from sources such as Diop, that in the course of their work Afrocentrists must reject "any thought, action, behavior and value [that] cannot be found in our culture or in our history."[29]

It can be argued, however, that Asante has turned Diop on his head, based on Diop's own construction of Africa, through Egypt, as "the cradle of civilization." As he points out, "no thought, no ideology is in essence foreign to Africa, which is their birthplace. It is therefore with total liberty that Africans can draw from the common intellectual heritage, letting themselves be guided only by the notions of utility and efficiency."[30]

Rather than seeing African heritage as limiting the framework of analysis or its relevance, Diop's alternative reading of the African legacy constructs it as a window opening to the "common intellectual heritage" of humankind. Thus, while sharing aspects of an Afrocentric historical perspective, such an alternative approach leads to an entirely different conclusion regarding the range and relevance of the subject under consideration. In an earlier article examining alternative approaches to African American Studies I use the terms *transformative* and *transformationist* to refer to the work in African American Studies not circumscribed by either the integrationist or Afrocentrist approaches.[31]

If the inclusionist impulse tends to deny or minimize the distinctiveness of the black/African side of the African American duality, the Afrocentrist impulse tends to deny or minimize the "American" side of that duality. Gates, for example, seems to move in the direction of the former tendency, recalling Stewart's *value-added rationale*, in the following passage: "Making a sharp distinction between the West and the Rest, I suggest, is neither justifiable in theory nor desirable in practice. Indeed, far from being inimical to traditional Western scholarship, humanistic scholarship in Asian and African cultures can be mutually enriching to it . . . it's hard to deny that what you could call the new scholarship has invigorated the traditional disciplines."[32]

In minimizing the "black" aspect of the African American duality, according to Marable, "[t]he inclusionist vision implicitly assumes that African-Americans are basically 'Americans who happen to be black.'" On the other hand, the opposite tendency is reflected in assertions of the "strong claim" of Afrocentrists who feel that every aspect of "Western-ization" must be rejected; seen, for example in the position of the radi-cal Afrocentric psychologists who prescribe the "expansion of an Afri-can definitional system via conscious, collective resistance against external imposition" as a corrective to the "imposition of an alien worldview on a people [that] robs them of their self-efficacy."[33]

The alternative perspective seeks a synthesis that embraces each as-pect of the duality. Indeed, it is perhaps the perspective of "doubleness" or "duality" in affairs involving black social, cultural, and political reality that most clearly distinguishes this alternative approach from the others. According to Marable, "The cultural orientation of the transformative vi-sion is neither 'integrationist' or 'nationalist.' It recognizes the enduring validity of the 'double-consciousness' formulation of W. E. B. Du Bois nearly a century ago."[34]

Stewart, whose contributions range from his complex and subtly nuanced Black/Africana Studies disciplinary matrix to his scholarly in-terpretation of Du Bois's legacy for modern African American Studies, would have to be considered a preeminent example of the "transforma-tive vision." Marable himself, long associated with socialist-influenced historicizing and theorizing within the (cultural nationalist) context of the Black Studies movement, is, of course, another exemplary scholar. Others who could be classified as transformationist include Cornel West, Robin D. G. Kelley, Deborah King, Patricia Hill Collins, bell hooks, Clarence Lusane, and Michael Eric Dyson.[35]

In addition to W. E. B. Du Bois, precepts of this alternate paradigm are drawn from the scholarship and thought of past black intellectuals such as Walter Rodney, Eric Williams, C. L. R. James, and Franz Fanon. In each instance, their work incorporates Afrocentric insights regarding the origi-nal, ancient, or classical history, culture, and peoples of Africa within an analytical framework that also addresses five hundred years of global transformation that created the postmodern world; a world in which Af-rica itself has been unalterably changed, and its peoples dispersed.

The transformationist theoretical perspective has also inherited some of the Marxian focus on economic, social, and structural factors in study-ing black communities. In addition to specifically Marxist-based ap-proaches, non-Marxists within this stream of discourse focus on these structural issues by incorporating a political-economy perspective.[36] My own work has sought to illuminate the role of historical and structural fac-tors in processes of cultural transformation.[37] And, as indicated above, both male and female scholars in this area are making efforts to address issues specific to gender, feminism, and Black Woman's Studies.

Common themes found within this body of thought include the acknowledgment that Africa and its descendants, along with most of the rest of the world, have been transformed in historical conjunction with the expansion of Eurocentric cultural, economic, and political systems to positions of global dominance. Approaches and studies that isolate or hermetically enclose the transforming sensibilities of African descendants from this larger human context introduce their own distortions. There is common acknowledgment that the expropriation of the technologies of destruction, production, and domination, the growth of colonial empires, the role of the slave trade, and the rewriting of history and science in service of the expansion of European imperialism define the legacy and impact of racism in the modern world and the full context of critical issues, conditions, and problems that require comprehension.

Thus, from the transformationist perspective, emphasis on recovering classical African culture and history does not negate the need to study and understand the rest of the world. (This premise is often inferred by those opposing Afrocentrism as part of a discussion about multiculturalism, which has spread into the society at large. Unfortunately, some of the strong claims of Afrocentrists may encourage this perception.) Du Bois left no doubt, surveying the ashes of Europe in 1945, that our task was broader than understanding our own people, culture, and history. That Western culture, and the industrial-capitalist political-economic system that came so close to destroying the world in the process of destroying itself—and which has certainly been able to make the lives of most of us miserable for several centuries—are phenomena we must study and understand with cold, unsentimental clarity.[38]

The transformationist approach connects and contextualizes classical and contemporary African and African American experiences to the wider, global, human experiences. In this connection, it engages contributions from elsewhere in the diaspora, like those of Paul Gilroy, who offers the perspective of a black British subject. In *The Black Atlantic,* Gilroy links the experiences of blacks in the West generally to the "intellectual heritage of the West since Enlightenment," and, more particularly, to the contemporary discourse concerning the intellectual legacy and critique of modernity that has vigorously consumed the attention of European and American critics of postmodernism.[39]

In spite of some controversial and problematic assertions, much of

Gilroy's work appears to be consistent with the transformative vision. In addition to the residual Marxian sensibility reflected in his terms of analyses, Gilroy's work is characterized by a dogged pursuit of the doubleness that constitutes black experiences in all aspects of the what he designates as "black Atlantic." Pointing to racism and anti-Semitism in the works of Kant, Hume, Voltaire, and other Enlightenment figures, Gilroy, like black scholars cited previously, also points out that most of the critical discourse of modernity fails to squarely address the issues and implications of racism.[40]

Unsurprisingly, these are grounds similar to those on which other black scholars have rejected such concepts, schools, or systems of thought. Gilroy's vision of "doubleness," however, infuses an engagement with European philosophers and critics (and a consistently sharp rejection of Afrocentrism) with the unique perspective of a black man from London, England, and seeks to transform the terms of the discourse itself. The debate, Gilroy says, is important for "reasons which have not, so far, been noted from within it."[41]

Gilroy examines the many levels on which race and racism are inextricably tied the social, political, and cultural legacies of Enlightenment rationalism itself. Discussion of the modern and postmodern, then, bears directly on the "shifting relations of domination and subordination between Europeans and the rest of the world." In addition to understanding how the category of race itself was developed and maintained, examination of Enlightenment rationalism also clarifies the historical foundations of notions of politics and nationality that blacks themselves have embraced.[42] Such insights are relevant to arguments I make in the following chapter about the dynamics of black nationalist political formations.

Social Crises: Clarity through Discourse

The emergence of various paradigmatic approaches within the African American Studies discipline is accompanied, appropriately, by continual dialogue and debate among adherents of various points of view about how best to constitute and accomplish the mission of the field. As indicated, such dialogue makes possible greater clarity among all scholars in the area. However, the potential for clarity is greatest when the context of dialogue is most open, when rigid insistence of the validity of only one perspective does not become a barrier to thorough examination of issues and premises, and when there is recognition that "reasonable people can disagree reasonably."

In addition to scholars in history and literary criticism, the recent work of sociologist William Julius Wilson, who joined Gates's Afro-American Studies department at Harvard in 1996, exemplifies a discipline-specific approach to studying conditions in African American communities that has influenced Black Studies.[43] While Wilson did not initially define his work as African American Studies, much of it takes on significance within the Black Studies movement. In part, this is because his work incorporates a historical and interdisciplinary perspective that both sets it off from much conventional sociology and, at the same time, links it to the Black Studies project. Moreover, because his studies focus on conditions in the black community that are of central concern to Black Studies, *The Declining Significance of Race*[44] and *The Truly Disadvantaged*[45] have been much discussed and debated within the field. Indeed, to the chagrin of some, the focus and impact of Wilson's work necessarily make it a part of the discourse of Black Studies. Although subject to controversy and criticism, his work has focused attention on crisis conditions that have evolved among those in the most disadvantaged sectors of the African American community.

It is indeed the urgency of this crisis that further underscores the need and value of coexistence and dialogue among different and varied theoretical perspectives within the African American studies discipline. Acknowledging the prevalence of symptomatic problems like escalating urban violence, drug use, high dropout rates, joblessness, early parenthood, so-called "family dysfunction," and a long list of other conditions symptomatic of the deepening crisis in the African American community, most in the field agree that approaches and solutions are not in great oversupply. Regarding these critical issues and problems, there is certainly much to be gained from promoting discourse within the discipline from several different perspectives.

Afrocentrism's continual return to African historical and cultural themes and references seems to be predicated on an assumption, held by some, that reaffirmations of African classical antiquity will somehow address the current crises and result in institutional and social changes. While not necessarily diminishing the value of African antiquity studies and the cultural reclamation that is at the core of the project, others feel that Black Studies' mission must discover ways to make the subject matter functional in the context of the current crises facing the black community. Diop himself seems to view the reclamation project with caution and qualification, observing, "One sees that what is important for a given people is not the fact of being able to claim a more or less grandiose historical past, but rather be simply pervaded by this sense of *continuity* characteristic of the historical conscience. . . . The knowledge of their own history, no matter what it is, is what is important" (emphasis added).[46] Further, writes Diop, "The African who has understood us is the one who, after the reading of our works, would have felt a birth in himself, of another person, impelled by an historical conscience, a true creator, a Promethean carrier of a new civilization and perfectly aware of what the whole Earth owes to his ancestral genius in all the domains of science, culture, and religion."[47]

The range of issues involved in the current crisis is as deep as it is broad. Issues of culture and identity, development and cooperation, education and aspiration, social transformation and political struggle, history and the future—there are many issues one must confront in generating models for pragmatic change, transformation, or revolution.

The emergence of various approaches, paradigms, and schools of thought indicates how African American Studies, emerging as a discipline out of the sociopolitical transformations of the 1960s, has had to discover new knowledges, affirm new values, create new symbols to express new beliefs, and generate new frameworks to give those symbols meaning. *Yet, we would do well to remain cautiously aware that the moment we free our minds from previous conceptual prisons is precisely the moment when we are most vulnerable to new errors.* These new premises, new paradigms, and new perspectives must be scrutinized from the same center that lead us, in the first instance, to challenge and reject the imposed Eurocentric conceptual constructs. The intellectual practice of principled and critical scrutiny of important issues of our time, through discourse among proponents of various theoretical perspectives or paradigms, represents the final stage of completion in the building of the African American Studies discipline.

In this chapter I have described the conceptual evolution of African American studies in terms of three general paradigms: integrationist, Afrocentric, and transformative. I have indicated that my own approach falls under the rubric of the transformative approach. In chapter 5 I will focus exclusively on a description of my version of this paradigm as I have developed and applied it within the context of my own work. In subsequent chapters I will illustrate the application of the approach in several areas of academic inquiry and policy analysis.

Chapter 5

Systematic and Thematic Principles

As indicated in the introduction, my experience in the historic project I have recounted began as an undergraduate student challenging the academy and has continued through this effort to reflect upon and analyze the field. As my own voice has been raised in this discourse among evolving conceptions in the field, it has found harmony among those in the field who embrace the transformative vision. My efforts have encompassed a dynamic view of culture: while Afrocentric in origin, African American culture is in constant transformation, a dynamic view that seeks to address issues involved with both the Afrocentrist foundations of black communities and the forces of transformation with which they interact. My work has incorporated basic historical and cultural facts and insights and attempted to bring them more clearly and directly to bear on the concrete issues and conditions of black communities in this historical moment.

In this chapter I will present an expanded, updated, and refined version of ideas I first began developing when I entered the field of African American Studies as a professional in the 1970s, and which I first published in a previously cited special issue of the *Journal of Negro Education* in 1984.[1] The ideas I struggled with in 1984 concerned developing an approach, a paradigm, a conceptual framework—an analytical guide for studying, teaching, and researching the "black experience."

Significant contributions have come from different quarters of the Black Studies movement. Afrocentrists deconstruct Eurocentric intellectual bias and endeavor to illuminate a common center for all studies of black life.[2] Womanist analyses, such as that of Patricia Hill Collins,[3] methodically invalidate any framework that ignores or undervalues the perspectives and experiences of black women in contemplating the fact, life, and survival of African American culture and community.[4] Michael Eric Dyson[5] and Henry Louis Gates Jr.[6] are among those who weave cultural and literary criticism into a fabric that links a broad range of cultural impulses associated with black cultural reference frames, spanning from folk culture to "serious" literature to street culture.

However, the problem of developing coherent theoretical approaches for examining the black experience remains prominent. Part of the problem is the "interdisciplinary" nature of the body of knowledge with which *African Americanists* are concerned. Although the subject focus of African American Studies ostensibly spreads across the boundaries of many conventional academic disciplines, it still comprises one discreet, integral, *body* of knowledge. James B. Stewart's disciplinary matrix attempts to construct an integral body of knowledge with "synergistic linkages" between subject areas that would otherwise be divided by disciplinary boundaries of theory, method, and approach.

Currently such linkages are at times still less than optimal. Regarding literary studies, for example, the problem that Stewart sees is that "[w]ithout synergistic linkages between the work of literati and social science-oriented Black/Africana Studies specialists representations of the experiences of peoples of African descent by literati and artists may produce insights that are parallel to, but are unreconcilable with, elements of the Black/Africana Studies disciplinary-matrix."[7]

It is surely not surprising that this trend endures. Before the Black Studies movement, information, knowledge, and scholarship related to the historical and contemporary experiences, conditions, and aspirations of African Americans were produced and housed—usually isolated as secondary or subfield concerns—in the various disciplines referenced above. To this day virtually all scholars in African American Studies programs and departments bring the training and theoretical and methodological approaches of those disciplines to their scholarly practice. The result is that programs and curricula still, more often than not, reflect those disciplinary divisions. More than two decades after Black Studies' inception, Darlene Clark Hine could still write, "In the early years, black studies units justified their intellectual existence on the ground that they shattered the confining and restrictive boundaries of traditional disciplines. Actually, as far as I have been able to discern, most of the individual scholars in these programs and departments have published works that are very much in keeping with the methodological canons of the disciplines in which they were formally trained."[8]

And still, curricular taxonomies typically divide the field into areas like "Black Literature," "African American Politics," and "Black History." While I in no way dispute the importance of these subject areas and approaches, it remains that the task of clarifying, focusing, integrating, and unifying the breadth of insights that constitute the field as a *body* of knowledge is not addressed in these constructions. If, for example, the Harlem Renaissance is presented from an approach that emphasizes the style, form, method, and artistic merit of Renaissance poets and writers, it is, strictly speaking, literature (and part of a "weak multidisciplinary" approach) and not African American Studies. If, however, it is presented as one of several forms of cultural reflection of the urban transformation of the black experience of the early twentieth century—accompanied by insights that detail the historical and social context and the sociodemographic and macroeconomic changes associated with the great urban migration of blacks—then it is African American Studies (and part of an "interdisciplinary" approach) and not strictly literature. (I reiterate that I do not criticize the former approach; indeed, I strongly support its inclusion. That is why my answer to the question debated over the years—whether African American Studies should be integrated across the curriculum or consolidated in free-standing programs or departments—has always been that this is not an "either/or" proposition; and that *both pursuits should be top priorities in American higher education.*)

Stewart further indicates how the Harlem Renaissance experience offers exemplars that distinguish the Black/Africana Studies disciplinary matrix from conventional literary criticism:

> The historical precedent that is most useful for understanding how the primacy of history can be reflected in the work of literati [criterion (2)] is the Harlem Renaissance. It is no historical accident that a major literary/artistic movement bloomed during the 1920s. A variety of factors contributed to the wellspring of black expression including the specific patterns of racial oppression, rural-urban migration, the emergence of a cohort of artist/intellectuals from the relatively favorable conditions for educational attainment that grew out of the first Reconstruction, etc. The work of the literati and professional critics of the Harlem Renaissance was profoundly shaped by the battle for social justice. As an example, Du Bois used his tenure as editor of the NAACP organ, The Crisis, to provide visibility for many Afri-

can American literati. Their works were published alongside analytical analyses and political advocacy.[9]

In several ways, the experiences and products of Renaissance literati fit Stewart's criteria for literary studies that are synergistic to the African American Studies disciplinary matrix. One of Stewart's criteria is the prominence of historical insight in the artistic products of the Renaissance. Historicity is of central importance to formulating conceptions appropriate to the matrix, as previously indicated. Two other criteria exemplified by Renaissance activities involve "synergistic" linkages that minimize, if not actually eliminate, disciplinary lines and separate publication channels that typically divide the insights and products of literary scholars and artists from those of social scientists and political theorists.[10]

The Harlem Renaissance illustration serves further, then, to point to how the problem of "multidisciplinary" boundaries referenced above might be viewed as reducible to a problem of one "meta-disciplinary" boundary—that is, integrating approaches conventionally associated with humanist inquiry (humanities disciplines) with those conventionally associated with social inquiry (social science disciplines). With "Systematic and Thematic Principles," I first tried to address this issue in 1984. This new attempt draws on some of my work since then, and on the work of others, past and present, whose insights have significantly informed my own attempts to gain greater clarity and understanding.

Experience in Search of a Framework

In conceptualizing a framework that addresses transformative dynamics in relation to studies of black communities, I take the view that *all of humanity* is the *progeny* of Africa and seek a reconstruction of perspective that includes and engages, rather than ignores or negates, the presence and impact of other peoples, including whites, in the transforming global reality of all humans. The intellectual, psychological, and political liberation I seek is not just for my blackness but ultimately for my humanity.

I hold that this is *not* reducible to the assimilationism that says, "I am merely an American, or a human, who 'just happens to be black.'" It has always been difficult, however, to maintain a stable, coherent standpoint that holds both African American particularity and global human universalism as reference frames—given the bipolar tendencies long evident in African American political discourse and intellectual discourse—without being perceived by some as anti-black or by others as too particularistic, nationalistic, or narrow minded.

In personal terms this dilemma presented itself to me many times during the early formational period of Black Studies. Especially lucid are memories of periods of activism as an undergraduate student when notions of black power were being tossed around like so many grenades in a revolution some of us thought we were bringing. Sometimes it seemed that militant expressions of blackness were exaggerated in order to avoid being perceived as integrationist or "Uncle Tomish."

Like others in this period, the fear of being shown that others were "blacker-than-thou" sometimes rendered me silent as to addressing distortions, hidden agendas, and other contradictions that were sometimes masked by projections of militancy. Other times, however—I would say about half the time—I would risk being perceived as not black or revolutionary enough, or a "defender of whites" (some of whom I did indeed count among my friends) or "white values," in order to challenge the monolithic overzealousness and questionable logic that sometimes came into play in that dynamic period.

One such episode occurred in a cross-racial "encounter group" in intense 1968.[11] Aside from the pattern of "flagellation" of black anger toward whites that was common in such encounters, the black militant viewpoint that was being established by expressive militants here was that from birth, blacks lived every minute of their lives with the growing consciousness of how white society oppressed them. Consciousness of racism was depicted as the primary determinant of black identity that pushed blacks inexorably toward a separatism that was incompatible with conceiving relations with whites on any terms other than those of anger, rage, and bitterness that were being so freely expressed there, as in other contemporaneous settings.

"Yes," I remember saying as a twenty-year-old, "but there was a time when I didn't know I was black." (That didn't mean I thought I was white. Indeed, in an ironic fashion, it represents the essence of my blackness because it represents the essence of my humanness.)[12] I referred to the first five to seven years of early, mostly primary group, socialization when most children are unaware of the significance of any racial difference they may or may not perceive. It is possible that my experience may have been different if it were not in a virtually all-black urban enclave where there was little opportunity for the social significance of racial difference to manifest itself, while there was great opportunity for norms associated with a coherent, folk/popular tradition to become internalized.

Those who, in my view, take the nationalist impulse to its extreme in their zeal to be free of all externally imposed (white) constraints, tend to conceive of black universes of thought and action as independent of (or "hermetically enclosed" from)[13] outside forces, and they are unconcerned with establishing operational dialogues with other social or cultural collectives. Equability in relations with other groups is not a priority or less of a priority than the rise of the black collective. In political terms this concept of nationalism measures liberation in terms of the degree to which black nationhood is able to function competitively with or, better still, is superior to other nationhoods. As reflected in Afrocentric historical and intellectual formulations, this tendency is provocatively critiqued by Paul Gilroy: "The Africentric movement appears to rely upon a linear idea of time that is enclosed at each end by the grand narrative of African advancement. . . . The anteriority of African civilisation to western civilisation is asserted not in order to escape this linear time, but in order to claim it and thus subordinate its narrative of civilisation to a different set of political interests without even attempting to change the terms themselves."[14]

Like nationalist-oriented scholars, I have sought to identify, enhance, and develop "black perspectives" regarding the key issues of history, culture, and social transformation that shape the concerns of African American Studies. However, in seeking alternative frameworks to establish and legitimate black perspectives I have also always been concerned to locate them in an inclusive human universe, to illuminate a portrait of the black experience in a picture of the human experience. Indeed, it seems to me that the ultimate Afrocentric insight is that Africa is the cradle not only of "civilization as we know it," but also of the human race itself.

Systematic and Thematic Principles: The Interaction

As a Black Studies professional I have tried to address the challenge of capturing the sometimes complex interplay of the particular and the universal, the local and the global, the struggle for both inclusion and self-definition that characterize aspects of black life and culture. As my thinking and practice have developed since that 1984 publication I have refined the approach to one central analytical principle, expressed in the following single, if perhaps somewhat complex, assertion: *It is the inter-*

action of external, objective (systematic) forces (or conditions) on social structure, with internal, subjective (thematic) forces (or conditions) on cultural sensibility, that shapes the lives of black individuals and black communities at any given historical moment.

The external forces or conditions are discernible largely in historically based sociodemographic and macroeconomic terms, and they shape the sociostructural environments in which African American communities evolve. They define varied configurations of socioeconomic hardship, inequality, and oppression associated with a half millennium of globe-shaping Western influence. The changing face of such external forces is seen, for example, in connection with the Great Migration of blacks from the rural South to the urban-industrial North, beginning around the time of World War I (and continuing with a second great spurt following the second outbreak of world war). This period is associated with such macrolevel demographic and economic changes affecting all areas of life for black communities. Thus, this (systematic) level of analysis is central to illuminating sociostructural changes affecting blacks over time.

The internal forces (described in terms of "thematic principles") are in essence cultural. They are comprised from experiences and sensibilities shared among groups of blacks, and they incorporate elements of the adaptation and struggle (physical, emotional, psychological, aesthetic, social, and political) of blacks, individually and collectively, against hardship and inequality. The Harlem Renaissance and the emergence of urban cultural forms and reference frames among ordinary African Americans in this century's early decades are illustrations of the internal, subjective, culturally defined forces that organize reference frames, attitudes, sensibilities, and aspirations, and transform self-perception among black individuals and communities in concert with fundamental historical changes, such as the mass urban migration.

An important corollary to the central principle is that either of these approaches (systematic or thematic) in isolation misses not only the whole experience but also the *essence* of the experience. Consider the work of sociologist William Julius Wilson, whose ideas expressing what he called "the declining significance of race," created much controversy in academic circles as well as in the realm of public discourse. His historical analysis of sociodemographic changes affecting African Americans is guided by what I refer to as *systematic* principles. In those terms it is a formidable piece of work whose impact, whether or not one agrees with its thrust, cannot be denied or ignored. However, his relatively few attempts to incorporate thematic principles—the internal sensibility, the ethos through which African Americans seek to transform themselves and their communities—are weak and glaringly flawed.

His sociostatistical description of this underclass, for example, has been useful, even compelling. However, he has utterly failed to give its people real human faces—to convey their humanness, their spunk, or "attitude." For example, within his perspective there is no accounting for the fact (and implications thereof) that segments of the so-called "underclass" have organized a distinctive cultural voice (presently manifest as "hip-hop") that has significantly influenced "mainstream" culture itself. As a result, the overall impact of his work—aside from inviting confusion of the concept of the significance of race as an abstract statistical category with the concrete reality of race as a sociocultural divider—is to paint an exceedingly negative, and nearly hopeless, portrait of African American communities; especially the so-called "black underclass." (An example of what a human presentation of a social problem represented by that so-called underclass could look like is found in historian Robin D. G. Kelley's collection of essays, *Race Rebels: Culture, Politics, and the Black Working Class.*)

It is important, then, not to assume a one-directional cause-effect relationship between the external-systematic and the internal-thematic. Rather, they should be seen as *wholly interactive and mutually transforming.* In other words, while external forces determining social structure often construct limits and barriers to self-definition, self-determination, and self-actualization, internally generated forces on cultural sensibility often enable individuals and communities to push limits and overcome barriers. Individually, socially, and culturally, blacks shape the cultures of the wider world while being shaped by them.

Duality: A Thematic Principle

This two-way interaction of external and internal forces reflects perhaps the most fundamental, or totalized, form of the basic theme, or *thematic principle,* underlying the form and function of African American identity and culture: *duality.* First called *double-consciousness* by Du Bois, the term *duality* refers to the fundamental opposition of cultural sensibilities that shapes, indeed defines, African Americans as a people. In the broadest terms, the concept of duality describes the opposition of sensibilities of a black culture or reality to those associated with a White reality.

Of all the insights of the most prolific African American man of letters, Du Bois's eloquent and succinct description of this fundamental duality, or double-consciousness—recorded nearly a century ago—is undoubtedly the passage referenced and quoted most often by scholars and intellectuals since then: "One ever fills his twoness,—an American, A Negro; two souls, two thoughts, two unreconciled strivings; two warring ideals in one dark body, whose dogged strength alone keeps it from being torn asunder."[15]

The fact that it is so widely referenced, and the fact that it has probably been applied in almost as many different ways as the number of references, speaks to the responsive chord this idea of doubleness strikes among blacks, as well as to the pervasiveness, the great range of dimensions in which the tensions, contradictions, and paradoxes of this doubleness become manifest in the lives of black individuals and black communities. As Marable noted, "Our identity is always found within the creative and contradictory tension between tradition, ritual and heritage on one hand, and innovation, individuality and assimilation on the other."[16]

However, the nature of the historical encounter between the descendants of Europe, who became "white," and the descendants of Africa, who became "black," is such that doubleness does not usually involve easy compatibility or complementarity. Indeed, it is more accurate to think of African American duality as balancing what in reality cannot be balanced, incorporating sensibilities that are actually mutually exclusive, creating dynamic harmony out of dyadic discord. Incorporating the two warring ideals points to an act of incorporation, a feat of balance, of self-inclusion; the successful possibility of which flows not from reflections of history but from the "dogged strength alone" of those bodies who refuse to be "torn asunder" by the stark existential contradiction of being black and being an American. As discussed later in this chapter, its effect is a constant dyadic tension that becomes manifest in basic as well as complex ways in social structure, political orientation, and cultural sensibility. This tension impels a continual quest for ways to effectively and creatively synthesize the contradictory sensibilities issuing from each aspect of African Americans' dual identity.

Transformation: A Systematic Principle

The fundamental *systematic principle* in this analytical framework is *transformation*. This term refers to the perpetual rearrangement of material and social structures that shape the way people live, think, work, relate, and associate, and points to the dynamic character of cultural and social reality. Within this reference frame black particularities and localities are viewed as interactively connected with global forces and formations. Black identities and cultural sensibilities, rather than being fixed and unchanging, are open and ever evolving. Attending to this dynamic quality in the history of the "black Atlantic," Gilroy notes, "yields a course of lessons as to the instability and mutability of identities which are always unfinished, always being remade."[17] As I have described elsewhere, "The term transformation implies both change and continuity; change which produces new forms continuous with old forms; carrying something of their essence. At the individual level, personalities and perspectives on life are transformed each day through thoughts, feelings, emotions, experiences and perceptions. Each night dreams organize these impressions in the consciousness of individuals. And each morning they are newly transformed. Yet, their selves are continuous. They are essentially the same persons."[18]

Transformation is a term applicable to the history, culture, and experiences of any nation or society, as well as of humanity as one whole: a term that implies both continuity and change. As an analytical principle for examining African American experiences, this framework resolves transformation into important global forces, factors, or conditions that shape the black experience *from the outside* and give rise to the global environments and social structures in which black communities emerge, develop, and transform.

Analyses of these environments and structures are often built around narratives of the construction of race and racism in connection with Western notions of freedom, progress, and enterprise. The Marxian influenced political economy paradigm continues to illuminate the historical record in this regard, connecting Western freedom and prosperity with slavery, racism, and economic domination. In discussing these global aspects of transformation and their manifestations, the terms below represent major interrelated and overlapping themes that frame and direct its impact.

West European Expansion
This term refers to the expansion, over the last five hundred years, of European-based economic, cultural, and political systems to current positions of dominance over most of the world. The proposition that Western Civilization's attainment of world dominion has profoundly affected the development and historical fortunes of the rest of human-

ity is an obvious understatement. In addition to ample signs of this dominance in the material world, it is becoming progressively clear that the very philosophical basis of Western civilization was involved at its core with ideas of racial difference and hierarchy. The conjunction of notions of racial hierarchy at the core of global systems of production of both economics and knowledge is neither coincidental nor surprising, but is far-reaching in its impact and implications.

Technologization

Technologization is a factor in global human transformation when incorporation of technological innovation causes significant change in the basic cultural and social patterns of groups of humans and of humanity as one whole. Ten thousand years ago, for example, the plow revolutionized food production and produced civilization and history as we know it. Three centuries past, the Industrial Revolution, itself connected to the impact of Enlightenment philosophical triumphs of reason and freedom, similarly transformed the global reality of humanity (see *Industrialization,* below). Today, the computer chip, in conjunction with new directions in biomedical and other sciences, is having a similarly profound impact on patterns of living, thinking, working, relating, and associating.

While the common mind generally views technological applications as positive (that is, progress), there are compelling arguments that some innovations are themselves negative (the cross-bow, gunpowder and firearms, dynamite, and nuclear arms), or have unacknowledged or unintended negative consequences (social inequality, depletion of natural resources, loss of jobs to robotic manufacturing techniques, pollution and environmental endangerment, social fragmentation, alienation, and spiritual deterioration). Arguably these consequences do not suggest progress at all—at least, not in a wholly positive sense.

Realization of these negative qualities of progress is one aspect of the cynicism and pessimism often found among participants in the postmodern discourse. Sharing a preoccupation with postwar technological and cognitive changes, these critics have analyzed a perceived "sorrow in the Zeitgeist."[19] Often, however, their ruminations are preoccupied with perceived discontinuities between the recent postmodern and the earlier modern epochs in Western history, rather than framing these recent developments as products of that earlier era—products of historical transformation that involve both change from and continuity with previous eras. With this disposition, Gilroy notes, "there is little attention given to the possibility that much of what is identified as postmodern may have been foreshadowed, or prefigured, in the lineaments of modernity itself."[20]

This oversight poses serious problems for those who believe in "the continuing viability of what Habermas has called the Enlightenment project . . . particularly where they have pronounced upon the idea of progress and the view of civilisation guided steadily towards perfection by secular, rational principles that sustains that idea."[21] Referring to the ongoing philosophical discussion of the relationship between freedom and reason, Gilroy comments subtly that "[t]his [discussion] has gained a special resonance during a period in which technological transformations and political upheavals appear to jeopardise both freedom and reason in equal measure."[22]

It is drearily predictable that the negative effects of technologization focus disproportionately on blacks, people of color, and other disenfranchised groups. Though African Americans make considerable progressive use of technological innovation, transformation related to technological change is conceived as chiefly an "external" factor in shaping the experiences of blacks. This is true because, even when black individuals themselves invent or create technological innovation (and this has happened much more often than most could ever imagine), control over development and application invariably falls to "mainstream" (that is, white-dominated) organizations and institutions.

Colonization

Colonial systems, established as Renaissance Age technological innovations, enabled Europeans to expand the limits of their "known world" and provided the means for organizing the resources of colonies in the non-European world in the name and for the benefit of the European colonizers. "Empire" was the formal conception of these European-dominated transnational formations, and the construction of race is found again among the core dynamics of their ascendance. Du Bois has long identified the slave trade that spanned the historical space between the European Renaissance and the American Civil War, along with visions of the wealth slave labor made possible in the colonial context, as chief causes which "distorted the development of Europe" in this manner.[23]

Moreover, Du Bois argued that in the hands of European intellectuals the role of the slave trade has been "made to occupy a much less important place in the world's history than it deserves."[24] Du Bois's conception is that slave labor occupies a place in history that, while surely significant, is not at all honorable: "The result of the African slave trade and slavery on the European mind and culture was to degrade the position of labor and the respect for humanity as such. . . . There were *new* cruelties, *new* hatreds of human beings, and *new* degradation of human labor. The temptation to degrade human labor was made vaster and deeper by the incredible accumulation of wealth based on slave labor, by the boundless growth of greed" (emphases added).[25]

Du Bois's indictment extends to the "sciences of reason," associated with the so-called "Enlightenment project." According to the tenets of the so-called Enlightenment rationalism, the sciences of reason that guided the development of modern science would also inform a science of humanity that would lead to social harmony. What was produced was the science of racialism and the ideology of racism to cover over the naked brutalization of humanity that went along with building colonial empires. Stripping away those rationalizations, the significant role of race—and its construction and conceptualization—is once again revealed to be critical at "the junction point of capitalism, industrialisation, and political democracy [that] give substance to the discourse of western modernity."[26]

The veneer of rationalism could survive the brutality of the nineteenth-century Age of Imperialism because, through the logic of race, it could be called a period of peace—the so-called "Pax Britannica." On this distortion Du Bois is typically erudite: "The paradox of the peace movement of the nineteenth century is a baffling comment on European civilization. There was not a single year during the nineteenth century when the world was not at war. Chiefly . . . these wars were waged to subjugate colonial peoples."[27]

However, World War I, for nearly the first time since the fall of Napoleon, arrayed the rationalized destructive powers of European nations against each other and exposed a capability and willingness for perpetration of death and destruction that could not be so readily rationalized. The Enlightenment project had somehow not anticipated this deluge of death and destruction among "civilized" nations. The ensuing Second World War, with its geometrically increased capability for destruction and horror, only exacerbated that crisis of modern thought that matured into the seemingly directionless cynicism of postmodernism and has convulsed through the social and human disciplines in recent decades.

Science and the rationalized thought systems that were going to enlighten humanity were critically complicit in endorsing racism as a "science," and led to the postwar cynical world of materialism, consumerism, alienation, pollution, fragmentation, and dislocation; an ethos of insecurity, anxiety, panic, terror, and doom, instead of one of peace, harmony, and prosperity; the "sorrow in the Zeitgeist"[28] that postmodernists have been scrutinizing. Du Bois's early critique establishes both the indictment and the high irony that the same rationalized, based-on-reason, enlightenment-informed sciences that allowed the quantum increase in "man's" knowledge, mobility, productivity, and prosperity (promising the still incomplete Enlightenment project of human perfectibility) also enabled a quantum increase in "man's" capacity, motivation, and willingness to perpetrate cruelty, degradation, exploitation, destruction, alienation, fragmentation, and death.

In the fateful historical moments in which these imperatives took shape, then, it was largely as a result of the drive to seek and exploit resources in colonies around the world that the Atlantic slave trade ensued, giving birth to the African American experience. For peoples of color around the world, the legacies of colonialism include the historical residue of both the material domination to which colonialism subjected them, and the distortion of the historical and cultural record of their experiences and strivings as peoples in the world. Blacks displaced to the Western Hemisphere and other parts of the African diaspora share certain experiences with blacks in Africa and peoples of color in other areas that became domains of European colonial expansion during the last five hundred years of the Enlightenment project. These experiences include racial oppression, cultural negation and destruction, and exploitation of their human and other natural resources. The term *internal colonies*, when used to designate such diasporic populations, links their experiences and the conditions in which they live to those of other colonized peoples through both colonial and postcolonial times.[29]

Industrialization

Wealth reaped through exploitation of slave labor and colonial resources was sufficient to finance new productive technologies that created the Industrial Revolution, leading to the international, industrialized economic system that dominates the globe today. Incorporation of this basic relationship seems necessary for any understanding of how local and global structures of wealth distribution have evolved under Western-dominated industrial capitalism; how racism, through slavery, financed the productive mode, the industrial machine on which the "wealth of nations" described by Adam Smith was built. This historical relationship can be described (in admittedly reductive terms) as an economic transfer of immense historical proportions, a redirection of natural and human resources that must be figured in any attempt to understand current patterns of over- and underdevelopment among nations and collectives in the postmodern world.

It is a relationship hypothesized by Marx, and argued deductively (and portrayed lyrically) by Du Bois.[30] In addition, Eric Williams's *Capitalism and Slavery*[31] stands at the head of a body of scholarship that offers documented analyses supporting the premise of that relationship. The premise is incorporated in the influential work of Walter Rodney and C. L. R. James, among others, and has recently been reiterated by Ronald W. Bailey and William A. Darity Jr.

Unsurprisingly, that premise is accepted by most African American Studies scholars. Mainstream scholars, on the other hand, have ignored or been ignorant of this premise. As Darity notes, the "slave trade remains oddly invisible in the commentaries of historians who have specialized in the sources and cause of British industrialization in the late eighteenth century," except brief mentions in which Williams's thesis is dismissed for lack of foundation.[32]

Sorting out this question, it seems, would provide a very clear and important example of how differences in construction of knowledge figure in defining a unique and valid paradigm for African American Studies. Darity, who has written several articles in economics journals evaluating the thesis and its critiques, provides a most helpful examination of the question of whether or not this "quiet rejection" of Williams's thesis among conventional historians and economists is based on valid intellectual foundation. While perhaps not fully qualified to judge the technical aspects of the argument that Darity engages with apparent facility, this author is certainly indebted to him for making those technical arguments clear, accessible, and persuasive. However, Darity's presentation of how numbers that represent "slave trade profits as a percentage of national income," or "shares of trade in overall economic activity," or "ratios of domestic exports to gross national product," can be reinterpreted as "potentially huge," even after Stanley Engerman has pronounced them "too small to matter in an explanation of British industrialization,"[33] compels Benjamin Disraeli's lamentation that "there are three kinds of lies: lies, damned lies, and statistics."[34]

Reviewing the various technical economic arguments for and against Williams's thesis, Darity concludes that "several theories of growth and trade . . . give a prominent role to the . . . slave trade and slave plantations in British industrialization . . . and none can be dismissed or disproven by [Engerman's] small ratios argument." For the non-economist, Darity's most persuasive qualitative argument points to the views and words of those contemporaneous (eighteenth-century) British voices who spoke unambiguously to this very issue. Darity notes that the invisibility of the slave trade to economic historians "contrasts sharply with the perspective of eighteenth century strategists who, on the eve of the industrial revolution, placed great stock in both the [slave] trade and the colonial plantations as vital instruments for British economic progress." In particular, Darity writes, "Joshua Gee and Malacy Postlethway, once described . . . as Britain's major 'spokesmen' for the eighteenth century, both placed the importation of African slaves into the Americas at the core of their visions of the requirements for national expansion."[35]

Darity's conclusion that "historians of British industrialization have suppressed this story of the industrial revolution, consciously, subconsciously, or unconsciously," recalls Du Bois's indictment of a "system of at first conscious and then unconscious lying about history and distorting it to the disadvantage of the Negroids."[36] In the end Darity quite pointedly indicts the manner in which Williams's key thesis has been absent from modern mainstream discourse: "A blanket of scholarly silence, a cloak of historical invisibility, has been laid by these disputants over the causes of British industrialization and over the significance of the slave trade and the slave plantation. But it is not a golden silence, for it has served only to obscure the richer and brutal story of how the modern world took shape, 'small' import and export ratios and monopoly profits not withstanding."[37]

Removing the blanket of silence is consonant with the task of clearly situating historical transformation associated with experiences of black communities in a global context. Thus, from the moment that historical forces meshed to eventually create the Industrial Revolution, and through contemporary signs of its apparent stagnation and decline, the fate of the black communities and collectives has been linked with the growth and/or decline of industrial manufacturing capacity.

Anticolonial Resistance and Struggle

Resistance of indigenous peoples to the various forms of colonial dominance has always been a factor of historical transformation. In the modern world the impact of such resistance on global transformation has been especially important in the post–World War II period. The twentieth-century "color line" of which Du Bois wrote at its turn became unfurled with the ferocity of a bullwhip in a wave of anticolonial struggles that have "loosened the seams of imperialism," a process Du Bois had also identified in the aftermath of the First World War.[38] The Chinese in 1949 and the Vietnamese in 1954 (Dienbienphu) and again in 1968 (Tet) demonstrated the existence in the so-called "Third World" of forces capable of defeating attempts to maintain or further expand European-based political, cultural, and economic models. African Americans, and others in "internal colonies" (for example, South Africa), were also significant participants in the global pattern of struggle against oppression and exploitation during that period. Such struggles have authored global transformation to a postmodern, "postcolonial" world.

Historical Periodism

For any given historical reference point, external conditions shaping the experiences of blacks may be described in the interplay of these factors of global transformation. In looking at various aspects or dimensions of this body of history, it is often convenient to refer to a historical periodization—a frame of reference in which the historical experience is depicted as a succession of distinct epochs separated by major historical change or transformation. Rather than chronology per se, the focus is on forces, factors, and conditions that characterize social and cultural life in a given period. In the context of the modern African American Studies movement it was Marxists, particularly the Marxist collective known as Peoples College, who initially developed enduring periodization schemes relevant to the aims of the field.[39] In this framework, the *historical periodization* that follows below has been adapted from those early contributions. In addition to adding an African Period that precedes European expansion and links blacks to their historical homeland, the periodization scheme includes added details for framing the relatively complex and fast-moving historical transformations of the twentieth century.

> African Period—before slave trade
> Slave Period—1500 to 1865
> Rural/Agricultural Period—1865 to 1914
> Urban/Industrial Period—1914 to 1973
> Urban Crisis Period—since around 1973

As if on some film screen of history, the factors described in the previous section frame the black experience in the context of global transformation through the centuries. African Americans—parallel to other colonized and oppressed peoples—have contributed their lands and resources, their culture, the value of their labor, and much of their humanity as these transformations have moved history. Financed largely with profits of slave trade, slave labor, and colonial exploitation, the spread of the industrial economy through all parts of the society and the world was a process that stretched through the end of the nineteenth century. The race among European powers (including, eventually, the United States) to stake imperial claims throughout the non-European world was coming to a climax then. The highly competitive situation that developed among the colonial (or "imperialist") powers formed a backdrop for the world wars of the twentieth century.[40]

Black labor was not directly involved in the rapid acceleration of the industrial development in this country that immediately followed the Civil War. Rather, the steady flow of immigrants from eastern and southern Europe provided the labor for the expanding industrial machine, while black masses were held as a virtual captive nation of sharecroppers and tenant farmers in the rural South after the fall of post–Civil War Reconstruction. The First World War in 1914 led to immigration restrictions, creating an increased need for production and an acute labor shortage at the same time that the perfection of assembly-line mass production techniques increased industrial production capability. These conditions comprised a kind of vacuum that sucked virtually entire black communities from the rural/agricultural South to the industrial centers of the urban north.

First in the colonial-slave-rural setting, then—with accelerated industrial expansion and world wars in the twentieth century—as laborers in the industrial centers, blacks constitute the bottom rungs in the socioeconomic system. After a significant period of post–World War II social movements and collective struggle, their fragile positions in this system are threatened in the current period of transition—a result of structural change in the industrial economy that provided a modicum of social and economic mobility through the first two-thirds of this century.

For the Urban/Industrial period of the complex, fast-moving twentieth century, a subperiodization, indicating four separate phases in the period, is additionally useful in looking at these changes.

1. *Urban Transition*—1914 to 1929. In this early phase of transition the rudiments of the complex twentieth-century urban black community emerged dramatically.
2. *Depression Blues*—1929 to 1943. This phase is characterized by adjustments

to changed economic conditions that affected social life, cultural sensibility, and political dynamics.

3. *Postwar Coming of Age*—1943 to 1973. In this era another global crisis loosened economic strictures, and another "victory for democracy" emboldened yet another generation of "New Negroes" to make democracy real for all.

4. *New Waves*—1973 to present. Post-movement generational and class divisions characterize this era when structural economic changes and mainstream attitude shifts have limited progress for some and prevented it entirely for others in black communities.

Duality Revisited

The cultural transformations that characterize the African American experience during this century reflect the increased salience of double-consciousness, or duality, as a cardinal feature of identity among blacks, as more of them experience educational and social mobility, with concomitant exposure to and internalization of mainstream cultural sensibilities, as did Du Bois a century ago. The *theme* of duality reflects the very sense of African American identity in the form of the "double identity," about which Du Bois wrote. The theme is also relevant in framing and examining the dynamics of cultural transformation and reproduction in the context of the experiences of blacks.

I should make clear at this point that my efforts in this area have been guided by certain conceptions regarding the use of the term *culture* and its application to the experiences of African Americans: In simple terms, culture is a shared worldview based on the shared experiences of a group. To speak of culture, however, is not to speak of invariant repetition. Rather, to speak of culture is to speak *also of the process itself* of creating a shared worldview arising out of shared *living* experiences. Previously, I suggested how such processes might operate in various dimensions and terms.

The traits and trends of commonality in life and experience, referred to as culture, arise from minute as well as all-encompassing aspects of the relation and interaction of humans with themselves, their community, environment and society. A feeble listing of some of the components of the process of culture—geography, language, community, socialization, family, mythology, magic, ritual, healing, suffering, symbolism, conflict, contradiction, adaptation, synthesis, transformation—begins to reveal complexity belied in the simpler terms of description.[41]

As a shared worldview, then, black culture can be neither fixed nor monolithic; rather it is multifaceted, complex, and ever changing. The fluid nature of African American cultural sensibilities, reference frames, and orientations has caused some literary and cultural critics to warn against "essentialism" in conceiving, analyzing, and describing black cultural identities. While their apprehension of fixed, limiting categories has validity, my view is that the dynamism and complexity do not make it impossible to speak with some degree of precision about what black cultural sensibilities are, where they come from, and, in some measure, who or what is or is not included in the milieu of black culture.

To say there are "black" or "African American" cultural reference frames and orientations implies that blacks share some unique experiences among themselves, and not with whites, that shape their outlook, their cultural sensibilities, differently than whites. There are two basic sources for such unique sensibilities among African Americans. One source comprises the cultural practices and sensibilities called "Africanisms." They culturally connect African Americans to sensibilities different and distinguishable from the dominant Euro-American cultural heritage of whites. The other set of shared experiences are those based on the social consequences of being "black" (previously "Negro" and other designations) under the social construction of race that has accompanied the modern rise of Western civilization.

While it is true that black individuals and groups of blacks vary widely in terms of the degree to which they share the experiential basis for such sensibilities, it is also true that virtually all African Americans share them to some degree. African Americans also share with each other, and with other Americans, the experiences involved with becoming and being "American." Thus the doubleness, which Du Bois described largely in psychological terms, is also present as cultural duality based on disjunction between or among pools of shared experience from which cultural sensibilities, reference frames, and orientations are derived. In discussing aspects of African culture and its transformation, then, the theme of duality comes up in a number of ways.

Form versus Essence

Duality, resolved as form versus essence, is a way of seeing once again the disparate sources and directions from which emanate factors that shape the experiences of blacks, pointing again to the interaction of the external and the internal. In the context of the African American experience, cultural, social, and political phenomena often involve the infusion of "black," or African-based, sensibilities (essence), in the adaptation of "white," or Euro-American, cultural artifacts (forms). Actual African cultural forms themselves were to a large extent lost, suppressed, or disguised as the cultural forms of the dominant culture, which were imposed on transplanted Africans. Cultural connections to Africa have survived among black Americans largely as "essence," sensibilities based originally on African cultural forms but connected now to new forms.

This is readily demonstrable in the examination of forms of African American music. Virtually all forms of black music developed from the fusion of basic African musical sensibilities with American or Western instruments and musical forms.[42] The African American church and the family, as social institutions, also reflect this pattern. To some degree the pattern of Euro-American form and African American essence follows from or is related to other dimensions of cultural duality, such as those expressed below.

Folk/Popular versus High/Elite (Cultural Traditions)
African American cultural life cannot be understood as one whole without taking into account the "bipolar" character of the experience out of which it emerges. Factors forming the basis for different cultural reference frames among groups of blacks go to the very origins of the African American experience. From the start the persistence of Africanized cultural sensibilities characterized one pole in a spectrum of African American cultural patterns—a "folk/popular" tradition, evolving and maintaining itself in relative autonomy, largely outside mainstream cultural reference frames. At the other pole, the models offered or imposed by nonblacks comprise the basis of a "high" or "elite" cultural reference frame more closely shaped on mainstream forms and sensibilities.

Many observers describe this bifurcation as a legacy of the historical dichotomy between the "field slave" and the "house slave," a metaphor used often by Minister Malcolm X during his heyday in the 1960s. For analyzing basic cultural reference frames, however, this view is misleading. While the "house/field" dichotomy does suggest different orientations among slaves, a more fundamental cultural dichotomy comes from the separate historical legacies of those who were free (and mostly northern and urban) and those who were not (and mostly southern and rural). Specifically, as Richard Thomas noted in 1977, northern free blacks "were developing an urban literary culture at the very same time that their Southern counterparts were developing the more traditional oral nonliterate culture."[43]

The literary culture in which free blacks were participating is part of the culture stream I have labeled the "high/elite" cultural reference frame. According to Thomas this was the "minor strand" of black cultural formation. He notes that "The major strand was obviously born from slavery. . . . This cultural strand, the African/slave Southern folk culture, eventually developed into the predominantly working and lower-class culture. Working and lower classes refer to those blacks who historically have been at the bottom of the black social order. Their assimilation of dominant white culture has always been significantly less than the higher classes of blacks."[44]

Unlike "house slaves," free northern blacks were largely isolated from the masses of blacks, (slaves) whose folk/popular reference frame retained more of the wholly African experience of slave ancestors—including cultural and social ideas, and surviving Africanisms in language, music, and social patterns. Over time these aesthetic elements have transformed in conjunction with the social experiences, shared by most blacks, of poverty and economic deprivation, struggle, and the experience of individual, social, and institutional racism. The high/elite cultural reference frame—relatively isolated from the masses of blacks—has to a greater degree tended toward values and aspirations internalized from the "white," or mainstream, sector of American society.

Ultimately, African American culture as a complex whole generally draws on the mainstream reference frame for its forms while infusing its essence from the black, African, or folk/popular reference frame. Often the importation of mainstream forms into the African American culture at large is a result of high/elite cultural tendencies. Thomas notes that the quasi-assimilationist free black culture's "major characteristic was that it possessed institutions, schools, formal churches (in distinction from the informal folk religion of the slave culture), literary societies, newspapers, conventions and political parties."[45] The conditions of slavery and the ban on literacy that was vigorously enforced in most slave areas meant that the southern slave community depended on the preservation of oral modes of cultural construction, embodying nonmaterial, sometimes nontangible, sensibilities that ultimately identify African American cultural distinctiveness. Thus, states Thomas, "The slave culture could not boast of free African schools, newspapers and political activities and literary societies, but they did have a richer nonliterary culture with a far more ethnically oriented cosmological core. They were destined to outpace the Northern cultural strand and maintain their historical role as the spiritual source of the national black culture."[46]

Although the black experience is historically dichotomized on one level, the prevalence of racism in the cultural life of the dominant society creates a shared experience around which blacks universally identify, making color a more important identifier than class or cultural reference frame in most contexts. For example, even compelling gender issues—brought sharply into focus in a wave of penetrating, black feminist scholarship—are defined by many of these scholars in terms that link them inextricably to a struggle against racism.[47] The shared struggle against racism, then, comprises a basis for cross-class unity as well as cultural diffusion among different groups of blacks. Thus, antebellum northern blacks were fervently involved with abolition—reflecting their recognition of how color tied them to that degraded status—even though most lived in geographic and cultural isolation from slavery. As Thomas notes, "The . . . major and minor strands of cultural formation were based upon the same organic ethos: freedom from slavery in the South and the protracted struggle against racial oppression in the North. As difficult as it was, these two strands continually fueled one another, creating an interaction which in itself constituted an important existential dimension of life in these two nineteenth century Black communities."[48]

Voices of Culture

Nonetheless, the tendency toward bifurcation does manifest itself in the various forms of black expressive culture. Forms of cultural expression associated with the folk/popular tradition are mostly oral. Indeed, for reasons involving indigenous Africanity of spirit, as well as material disadvantage of circumstance, music has provided the definitive voice of the folk/popular cultural milieu. Moreover, it is clear that blues, spirituals, gospels, and other music forms that are authentic reflections of a distinctive black culture in any given period are created from the experience of those folk masses who were captive in the rural economy through the slave period and into the twentieth century. As summarized by Thomas, "If the core cultural products of Black culture have been music, songs, dance and folklore, then the sole responsibility for producing and reproducing must go to the Southern slaves and their social class heirs."[49]

In context with a high/elite cultural reference frame, African Americans express and preserve their experiences for history in literate forms—

letters, biographies, novels, journals, magazines, and newspapers—which, in earlier periods at least, reflected the quasi-assimilationist orientations of the northern literate class that eliminated or minimized cultural distinctiveness. Thomas refers to this dichotomy of expressive media as the "division of cultural labor": "Two distinct Black cultural traditions emerged from this period, and although they would often flow into one another, cross-fertilizing one another, after slavery they still maintained their essential class character. The Northern quasi-assimilationist marginal strand would continue to be dominated by literary cultural products and the Southern former slave folk culture would continue to produce nonliterary oral cultural products."[50]

Such differences in cultural sensibility have historically been the source of tension between the folk/popular masses and the middle-class elites. The division of cultural labor Thomas describes may also lead to bias, or even perhaps unintended oversight, in documenting the histories of black folk that undervalue the experiences of the common folk. In chapter 8 I will point to this aspect of the theme of duality (folk/popular versus elite cultural reference frames) in differentiating alternative interpretations of the history of black cultural transformation. In particular, that history, as interpreted from traditional written sources (the point of view of high/elite culture) reflects middle-class bias and emphasizes the role of certain areas (for example, East Coast cities) as sources and sites of cultural innovation and transformation. However, from the point of view of the folk/popular masses, the movement of blacks up through the industrial heartland of the country is a more valid path along which to trace a description of cultural innovation and transformation.

Inattention to the aspects of African American duality that deal with class and cultural orientation has also led to errors and discontinuities in the way nationalists and Afrocentrists, among others, have interpreted pre–twentieth century black political nationalism. The nationalist lineage of black social thought and cultural practice has a dynamic, paradoxical character that, though hinted at, is seldom presented in a clear fashion. Indeed, such inattention to dyadic complexity has obscured (by oversimplification) the fact that most attempts at nationalist formation in the nineteenth century and before were based on impulses that were, ironically, earnestly and thoroughly assimilationist. Afrocentrism is basically blind to this paradox. Referring to nineteenth-century back-to-Africa movements, Asante glosses right past it when he states, "Those who preached the rhetoric of return [emigrationists advocating a return to Africa] were fundamentally celebrating the survival of an African sensibility in the African American."[51] In fact, however (to the degree to which Asante is referring to a sense of cultural continuity and affinity with Africa), virtually nothing could be further from the truth.

Surviving African sensibilities, though plentiful in the southern oral culture, were virtually absent in the free northern culture, where this movement was enacted. Proto-nationalists like Edward Blyden and Martin Delany were part of the relatively well-educated elite class that was most distant from surviving African sensibilities. By their aspirations they exemplified the inclusionist vision that assumes blacks are "Americans who happen to be black." The historical roots of this vision, Marable says, "are found in the aspirations of the free Negro communities of the North before the Civil War."[52] They were participants in the "quasi-assimilationist" free black northern culture Thomas describes.

Strong assimilationist impulses, in this milieu, were based on the premise that elimination of cultural distinctions between black and white would lead to elimination of distinctions of rights and privileges based solely on color. Their nationalist aspirations always came in the context of the failure of earnest and concerted efforts to assimilate culturally as Americans, which of course were consistently and systematically rejected. Black literary societies, for example, were founded "only after middle-class blacks . . . were thrown out of white literary societies."[53]

This "nationalist" reaction is perhaps more accurately described, as by Thomas, as the manifestation of the "alienation of the quasi-assimilationist marginal strand," when the frustrations of their marginality become manifest.[54] In a similar vein, Gilroy observes that Delany "thought of himself as a man of science . . . his aspirations as a cultivated man of science were intertwined with his political radicalisation in complex ways." Gilroy suggests that Delany's political sensibilities were radicalized after he was denied the right to patent his invention for transporting railroad locomotives.[55] As Delany's experience exemplifies, African Americans' persistent attempts to create a sense of nation that is separate do not arise because blacks have intrinsic separatist proclivities, necessarily. If anything, assimilationist tendencies are more intrinsic among such elites who typically present themselves as cultivated citizens no different than cultivated whites. Seeking to remove themselves from the stigma of color, they want a sense of nation that is their own. This need becomes acutely separatist as they keep receiving the message that *this* nation is not their own.

However, the ideas of nationhood, race, and culture with which black leaders and intellectuals were involved were not based on any ideas or impulses that could be argued to have an indigenous connection to Africa, nor were they substantially concerned with recognizing, reclaiming, or preserving indigenous African culture. The motivation for building such black institutions is their rejection from mainstream social life, in spite of their aspirations for assimilation and inclusion. As both Gilroy and Appiah go to great lengths to stress, nineteenth-century nationalists like Delany, Crummell, and Blyden based their concepts of nation directly on nineteenth-century European ideas regarding state and nation, and *not* to a sense of continuity and cultural affinity to Africa. According to Gilroy, "Delany's primary concern was not with Africa as such but rather with the forms of citizenship and belonging that arose from the (re)generation of modern nationality in the form of an autonomous, black nation state."[56]

Thus, duality, considered in the manner developed in this section, helps resolve some paradoxes. Without considering duality, it is difficult to reconcile the manner in which early nationalism is linked to the impulse to shed rather than retain signs of cultural difference. Efforts to preserve and institutionalize cultural difference occur after acculturative, assimilative efforts have been unsuccessful in the sense that they have not affected or sufficiently ameliorated the stigma of skin color.

Historical nationalism among blacks has thus been based on institutional concepts mirrored by Euro-American mainstream culture and thought—not a sense of cultural continuity with Africa. It was a nationalism that actually required them to culturally reject Africa. Even Marcus Garvey's conception of African culture saw a need for it to be redeemed rather than recognized or reclaimed in some aboriginal indigenous state. Regarding an illumination of this paradoxical dynamic, Asante seems closer to the truth, which remains unnamed, when he summarizes Henry McNeal Turner's turn to emigrationism after a career in the failed Reconstruction politics of Georgia: "Depression, anxiety, frustration, then, were the marks of Turner's conversion; he was a victim of the white man's nationalism, and his response was a black man's nationalism."[57]

Class versus Cultural Reference Frame

While the terms of the transformative framework suggests some overlap among the categories "black/African," "folk/popular," and "lower/working class" on the one hand, and the categories "White/Euro-American," "high/elite," and "middle/upper class" on the other, the overlap may be far from complete. In other words, persons who are middle/upper class in socioeconomic terms may adhere significantly to a folk/popular cultural reference frame. This may be especially likely in the case of upwardly mobile blacks, whose origins or "roots" are within the folk/popular reference frame—and they choose to retain their connections to that cultural ethos. In fact, most African Americans from most classes adhere in some way to elements and combinations involving both reference frames.

Analyzed in these terms black cultural ethos is the product of complex admixtures of "white" or "American" and "black" or "African-based" cultural impulses, attitudes, artifacts, and sensibilities. Important to this analysis is the understanding of where the black (in the sense of African-based) cultural base (the mouth, or source, of the cultural stream) has been—that is, in the historical South and, as blacks migrated north and west away from that "source," in the least culturally assimilated areas of the urban centers in those regions. (The migration created for the first time a significant urban working-class cultural community. This urban working-class community is directly tied to the rural tenant class that was the social and cultural reference frame of the overwhelming majority of blacks only one or two generations earlier.)

Important work in the area of transformation of African American folk/popular culture that incorporates elements of the transformationist perspective has focused on black language or music. (As indicated above, language and music are key elements in the construction of cultural spaces that validate and humanize the lives and experiences of the folk/popular masses.) Geneva Smitherman, a longtime colleague at Wayne State University, conceptualizes black English in terms of its African essence, or "deep structure," and its mainstream (English) forms. The infusion of African linguistic practices (syntax, grammar, pronunciation, and vocabulary) into the practice of English forms transforms it to a distinct language category.

Smitherman's work also specifies systematic or structural factors (migration, urbanization, social class, modernization, or technology) associated with change, development, and transformation regarding the oral culture of African Americans.[58] Her interpretations address the manner in which the rural/folk root of black language has transformed toward an urban/popular root, like other vehicles of cultural construction in a folk/popular continuum. Controversial but practical interest in these ideas regarding the cultural context of African American communication practices has recently been generated in the arena of primary and secondary education policy—after some school systems began to adopt policies based on recognition of the legitimacy of black language, or Ebonics. An examination of issues relevant to these controversies is presented in chapter 8, which discusses the realized and potential impact of ideas connected with African American studies on social and educational policy and practice.

LeRoi Jones (later known as Amiri Baraka) created a major text in African American cultural analysis in *Blues People,* which similarly depicted evolving forms of black music in terms of the interplay of essential African musical sensibilities, Western or American instruments and forms, and forces of social transformation associated with various historical periods. He called the historical black, African-based cultural stream the "blues continuum."[59] Following along this path, my framework uses the term *folk/popular tradition* and relates it dialectically to the black high/elite cultural tradition.

The Quest for Freedom and Literacy: A Principle Theme, a Thematic Principle

As stated earlier, the interaction of external, objective, or systematic forces on social structure, with internal, subjective, or thematic forces on cultural sensibility, shapes the lives of black individuals and black communities at any given historical moment. It was further stated that while external forces determining social structure often construct limits and barriers to self-definition, self-determination, and self-actualization, internally generated forces on cultural sensibility often enable individuals and communities to push limits and overcome barriers. So consistent has been the relationship between the aspirations of African Americans and the limiting conditions of social structure—and so powerful has been the internally generated drive to overcome those conditions—that the idea of struggling for freedom and overcoming barriers has become firmly rooted in the African American cultural reference frame (expressed, for example, in the civil rights anthem "We Shall Overcome").

Indeed, it is axiomatic that the deepest, most widely shared wish of any oppressed people is for freedom. Such strongly held, widely shared ideas have been identified and studied by certain literary critics who examine literature to understand basic motifs of the culture that produced it, using the concept of "pre-generic quest-myths"—prerational, nonmaterial, and extraordinary archetypes held collectively in the consciousness of a people and discernible in their tradition of literary expression. Applying this approach to African American literature, Robert Stepto identifies *freedom and literacy* as the pregeneric quest myth underlying the African American cultural tradition. From the recorded experiences of Frederick Douglass, and through the black community's long struggle for equal educational opportunity, it is not hard to see that African American culture embodies a pregeneric awareness of a basic relationship between the achievement of literacy and the achievement of freedom. Douglass pursued both doggedly, through his life as a slave and beyond; through his career as abolitionist; and as agitator for the rights of African Americans after Emancipation. Educational opportunity has always been at or near the top of the list of practical objectives sought by black movements for freedom and power. Malcolm X's autobiography makes it clear that his self-made prison education was the key to the sense of freedom that allowed him not only to escape his ingrained street-hustler lifestyle, but also to become a leader of international renown—arguably the strongest voice for black self-determination of this century.

Moreover, while "literacy" in the conventional sense is by definition associated with "high," or "elite," culture, the experience of nineteenth-century nationalist elites suggests that literacy conceived in limited, linear terms as Western education was not sufficient for gaining true freedom and equality. In that regard, Norman Harris extends the term *literacy* to refer to substantially more than just the ability to read and write. He suggests that, although the quest for literacy begins with the challenge of decoding the letters, which represent information in this society, it expands to encompass ever-enlarging patterns of meaning. Indeed, ultimately literacy means historical literacy, or cultural literacy— the ability to authentically locate one's self in the context of one's own history and culture.

Novels, autobiographies, and other literary tracts reflecting the assimilationist high/elite tradition are often concerned with protagonists' discovery that literacy, in the sense of knowing what whites know, is insufficient as a basis for sufficiently understanding the protagonist's own experiences. There is often a sense in these cultural records that the tools of literacy do not enable an escape from the condition of blackness (even when, as is often a theme in these works, the protagonist is able to pass for white). In the terms of Harris's analysis, those who struggle successfully with this dilemma eventually turn those tools of literacy to the task of understanding their place in a larger human struggle.

Instead of seeking literacy in order to distance oneself from the stigmatized masses, Harris implies that literacy becomes functional as historical literacy when it recognizes and incorporates the (folk/popular) insight, when it incorporates illumination and transformation of, rather than escape from, the aboriginal experiences of ancestors. Zora Neal Hurston was early among those whose literary work incorporated and transformed the black folk experience to terms of literary discourse.

(Women have dominated black creative writing and literary innovation in the last quarter century. The work of writers like Nobel laureate Toni Morrison suggests that the womanist standpoint may include special insights as to the passing of traditional culture down through generations—the role of the insights of the cultures of their mothers in the contemporary struggle for self, family, and community.)[61]

The theme of freedom and literacy is thus discernible in ways appropriate to both the literate high/elite and the oral folk/popular traditions. The importance of various forms of literacy in the context of folk/popular reference frame culture is discernible in its forms of expressive culture. The one or two slaves on each plantation who managed to become literate in spite of widespread bans against such activity commanded great respect from other blacks. Frederick Douglass evinced sophisticated acuity regarding many dimensions of his social reality, with which he manipulated whites around him into teaching him to read. During Reconstruction ex-slaves who could read almost invariably became community leaders. A folk aphorism conveyed to many blacks by their grandmothers or other elders implores, "get as much education as you can because what ever you get up there [pointing to the head] cannot be taken away from you."

The oral folk culture is also aware of the dangers of "conventional" literacy among those whose sense of identity is not solid. The oral culture warns against becoming an "educated fool," full of "book knowledge" that has no practical use for living. Harris incorporates work from another literary critic, Stephen Henderson, to address relationships between different cultural reference frames using the terms *folk culture* and *formal culture* in ways roughly similar to the use of the terms *folk/popular* and *high/elite* by this author. He indicates that "the 'folk' and the 'formal' were and continue to be competing forces in Afro-American creative life and Afro-American life generally. The 'folk' refers to the African half of double-consciousness and the 'formal' refers to its American half. Henderson describes the relationship between the two as 'perhaps too subtle to be called dialectic.' [Henderson] concludes . . . by noting that the folk has had the most significant influence on the formal during periods of the 'greatest power and originality.'"[62]

Harris adds that achieving historical literacy—the ability to read cultural signs—involves immersing one's self in the insights of folk culture. The quest for freedom, then, is realized with literacy; the ability to conceptualize oneself in an authentic cultural and historical context. The freedom stipulated by Harris is operationalized in terms of individual self-definition and self-determination while confronting systematic barriers to actualization. In practice, he states, "[c]onflict resolution and the ability to move on after certain goals either have not been obtained or have been radically altered depends on the level of literacy achieved by the individual in question."[63] Literacy, in this sense, informs both aspects of the African/folk/popular–American/high/elite duality and at some level attempts to resolve contradictions and tensions between them.

As the quest for literacy and freedom had a particular meaning for blacks in the Slave Period, so does it express a message appropriate for today's black communities, when computerized information superhighways are rendering even more complex the tasks of negotiating paths into an evolving future world dominated by global struggle for limited world resources and a rapidly changing economic structure based on ultramodern scientific, biomedical, and technological applications. In chapter 8, I will argue that the absence of *historical literacy* further handicaps those most adversely affected by the social symptoms of dysfunction—crime, violence, drugs, etc. I will suggest the possibility that social awareness concerning their circumstances as African Americans can actually be transformed into an asset for individuals who struggle against these symptoms of so-called dysfunction.

Literacy and Duality, Transformation and Self-Determination

If the term *transformation* represents the winding highway of history over which African Americans (like all humans) must travel, then *historical periods* represent the places (states, nations, counties) the road has and will put them. And if *duality* represents to the two-barreled carburetor in the engine of black identity and culture, moving across the historical landscape, then the quest for *freedom and literacy* is the fuel that makes that engine go—like a dream, which has to be steadily consumed to become actualized, to become reality, and no longer a "dream deferred."

My current and previous involvement with developing and refining the ideas constituting the framework presented here are based on my belief that such a framework—one that effectively organizes and integrates the full breadth of insight and experience of black life—would be a potentially powerful analytical tool for African American Studies as an academic discipline. The development and application of this framework is reflected in the record of my published and finished pieces of work. Virtually all of these pieces attempt to apply or integrate the fundamental ideas developed here—though these pieces address a broad range of topics, areas, and approaches. It is also a record that reflects consistent attempts to clarify and refine these ideas and make them more accessible to requirements for finding solutions to intellectual problems and practical problems alike. In concluding this chapter, however, I have hazarded that my original closing of more than a dozen years ago might still serve its point, without attempt at improvement or refinement.

> As seen in the lives and works of slaves, intellectuals, artists, musicians, political and community leaders, the quest for freedom and literacy is the story of how blacks continually seek realization in society's terms and ultimately find renewal in their own terms. The quest for literacy begins with the challenge of decoding the letters which represent information in this society and expands to encompass ever-enlarging patterns of meaning. While this literacy brings clarity as to the immediate and extended meaning of one's life, if one is black it does not usually lead to acceptance, in the wider world, of the authenticity of one's experience, vision, or humanity. Yet it is the use of the tools of literacy to authenticate one's own experience, one's own vision, one's own humanity that enables one to, therefore transcend historically structured, socially imposed limitations and experience the true essence of freedom—the freedom of self-determination.[64]

Part 3

In the Vineyard

Chapter 6

Conceptualizing Black Identity

Issues of identity and culture reference frame have always been core concerns, both for Black Studies activists and the larger social/cultural milieu out of which Black Studies emerged. Indeed, radical new approaches to a "psychology of black identity" have been extremely important in the emerging African American Studies disciplinary matrix. In 1972 Wade Nobles published "African Philosophy: Foundations for Black Psychology" as part of a seminal volume on black psychology assembled by Reginald Jones.[1] A year earlier, William Cross Jr. had published "Negro-to-Black Conversion Experience," beginning his career-long examination of changes in psychological and cultural orientation experienced by many blacks during the 1960s and 1970s.[2] Some point to Noble's essay as the beginning of the Afrocentric movement that flowered through the eighties in the works of Karenga and Asante. Meanwhile, Cross and other psychologists have developed *nigrescence,* an approach that studies the dynamics of black identity formation (first conceived as the processes of "becoming psychologically black").

Well received and influential among Black Studies activists, these essays have engendered critical discourses in the field since the early formational stages of the discipline, when I and many others involved in Black Studies were in or newly out of graduate school. This discourse evolved to incorporate related but distinct approaches that have long been recognized and explored for their potential as Black Studies constructs—as frameworks for channeling Black Studies' epistemological approaches into areas traditionally informed by psychology.

In this chapter I will draw on previous work and experience to examine how various approaches within the Black Studies movement, and more conventional approaches, define issues related to identity, cultural reference frame, and relationships between them. The review reveals how different perspectives may each bring both their own contributions and insights, along with their own flaws and limitations in their conception and interpretation of critical issues in the study of black experiences. Similarities and contrasts, scope and limitations, as much as strengths and weaknesses among different frameworks are all important issues to examine while sorting out this subject area's complexities.

The centrality of black identity, and of the cultural reference frames to which black identity relates, is reflected in extensive work by psychologists who are part of, or whose work contributes to, the Black Studies enterprise. As Stewart observed, "African American psychologists have gone well beyond their counterparts in other social and behavioral science disciplines in exploring conceptual approaches that both reject standard approaches and embody values consistent with those of Black/Africana Studies."[3]

Their efforts have been important for overcoming the increasingly more visible inadequacies of conventional approaches to black identity issues. For instance, prior to the new approaches that arose alongside and within the Black Studies movement in the 1960s and 1970s, conventional social psychological approaches to examining aspects of African American racial identity had been based on assumptions that have turned out to be dubious, misleading, and inaccurate. In particular, the premise of widespread black "self-hate" has long been central to studies of identity among blacks. The premise was made famous in the Clark and Clark doll study in which the Clarks reaffirmed findings from earlier works, such as those of Eugene and Ruth Horowitz.[4] These early studies used drawings, photographs, and (as in the Clarks' case) dolls as instruments to assess "racial preference" behavior in young children. A reported tendency of black children to choose drawings, photographs, or dolls supposed to be white, these studies concluded, was an indication of widespread self-hate among blacks.

Cross makes the critical observation that these older studies, and even some recent ones, assumed that measures of individual personality (self-esteem, efficacy, pathology) and racial or group identity (affiliation, cultural reference frame, reference group orientation) are directly related, mutual reflections of one another. Under this logic positive measures of self-esteem and efficacy should directly indicate high levels of racial group identity, and vice versa. This assumption allowed early investigators to draw conclusions about individual personality based on what was really only a test of reference group orientation, or racial preference behavior. Based on such assumptions the premise of racial self-hate had taken root in the oldest psychological studies of blacks.

Hence, at the time various alternative approaches began to emerge in the late 1960s, the general body of research around the question of African American racial identity had left a tangle of paradoxes and contradictions. Since then critical reviews of these findings have convincingly challenged the conceptual and empirical validity of these studies, as well as the concomitant conclusions—namely, that black self-esteem is based on white reference points that promote self-hatred.[5] In particular, William Cross at Cornell University's Africana Research and Studies Institute[6] produced a comprehensive review of conventional psychological formulations on black identity that laid bare presumptions and premises on which these early conclusions were based.[7]

Starting with the first appearance of such research in 1939, Cross's careful reconstruction makes clear that: (1) the assumptions that allowed earlier studies to interpret indices that purportedly assessed aspects of *group identity* (or "reference group orientation") as direct indications of efficacy regarding *personal identity* were unquestioned, though they were never tested, and (2) interpretations leading to the "self-hate" premise were questionable even in those terms. However, even though small sample sizes (as few as five black children were the basis of one of the studies) and ambiguous data splits (often as many as 40 percent or more of the respondents chose "correctly") severely weakened the empirical basis of any such conclusion, the finding of self-hate was the nearly unshakable legacy of this early research. According to Cross, the now commonplace half-truths, distortions, and exaggerations are all embedded in the Horowitzes' early work:

> (1) The subjects in the study are preschool children, yet affirmations are made about the relationship between the study's finding and the probable psychodynamics of Negro adults; (2) although only social attitude is assessed systematically (i.e., racial attitude), the results are discussed "as if" both social attitude and personality had been measured; and (3) *"proof" of depth psychology involvement is equated with anecdotal evidence gleaned from the children's behavior and speech during the collection of social-attitude data.* More important, Ruth Horowitz's study set the stage for the theoretical and methodological orientation to be embraced by researchers of racial identity from 1939 to the present. (Emphasis added.)[8]

The ease with which this conclusion (Negro self-hate), and the virtually untested premises on which it was based (assumption of a direct relationship between measures of personal identity and measures of reference group orientation), passed through the interpretations and findings of succeeding generations of scholarship provides a stunning illustration of the vulnerability of facts and truth regarding black life as conceived (and systematically marginalized) through traditional scholarship. It shows that far from validating empirical facts, the marginalized study of black experiences within conventional disciplinary frameworks frequently produces and reifies distortions and misstatements that have lasting effects. Relief from such distortions is, of course, among the critical needs that African American Studies has emerged to fill.

Thus, even as researchers sifted evidence of "new," positive, or assertive black identities that began to appear in the 1960s and 1970s, the still-untested assumption of a direct relationship between personal and group identity was left largely undisturbed. This may be in part because other inconsistencies in defining and measuring group identity, as well as discontinuities among various methodological approaches, further obscured the problem of this untested assumption. These problems and inconsistencies inhibited integration and reconciliation of various findings regarding this changed sense of black consciousness.

One problem was that definitions and measures of reference group orientation were not consistent. A related problem was that demographic profiles of "black militancy" created from these studies represented at best a snapshot of a particular grouping at a particular point in history, unable to capture the dynamic spread and growth of the new "blackness" among many groups of blacks during the period in question. Another was that, though several studies attempted to associate black group identity with demographic groups and variables, few were built from demographically representative samples.

Barnes, in a 1972 article, presents a clear example of the first set of difficulties mentioned above: how the nearly hidden but highly significant assumption regarding the connection of individual efficacy to measures of reference group orientation has continued to shape discourse. He notes that children who scored favorably on the Ethnic Pictures test, where they are asked to identify pictures that look like them, tended to have parents who favored "collective and militant action" against racism. His conclusion is that the "findings support notion that parental involvement in the black community, and specific beliefs, attitudes, and orientations toward the conditions of one's group, defined as indices of black consciousness, or sense of peoplehood, is *associated positively with more positive self-concepts in children*" (emphasis added).[9]

The conclusion of more positive self-concepts is based only on the subjects' performance on the Ethnic Pictures test, a test only of reference group orientation. The shift from methodology that measures group identity or reference group orientation to an interpretation that focuses on personal identity is so automatic, and so subtle, that it is virtually unnoticed and therefore virtually unchallenged. Cross suggests that the "momentum" of past black identity research drove investigations in that direction, observing that, "After the traditionalists repeated the self-hatred thesis over and over again, the false impression that both PI [personal identity] and RGO [reference group orientation] had been tested adequately was taken for granted."[10]

Cross himself, he admits, was among those who were influenced by this assumed connection: "Initially, observers of Black identity change, myself included, assumed that nigrescence involved comprehensive personality and identity changes . . . . the empirical literature on Black psychological functioning appearing between 1939 and . . . 1968 made it seem that sweeping changes in the Black psyche were in order."[11]

The legacy of previous research has been so formidable that neither the Afrocentric or nigrescence approaches to black identity initially rejected the premises of the studies that defined the subject area they inherited. Afrocentrists assume that indicators of a black sense of group identity or affiliation directly coincide with individual health, efficacy, and optimal functioning. Lack of evidence of such affiliation is a sign of imbalance or disorder. Ironically, this is the same basic conceptual reference frame as earlier studies of black personality pathology. Although later revised, investigators of the nigrescence approach first accepted the premise that the individual who had reached the end stage of nigrescence (that is, change in reference group orientation) was assumed to be more mentally healthy or functional than the individual still in the "pre-encounter" stage. By assuming the connection of personal identity to racial reference frame, they, too, in effect, accepted the "self-hating Negro" theorized in traditional studies.

The second set of conceptual difficulties, related to inconsistent definitions of black identity, is exemplified in studies linking black identity variously with disadvantage or privilege, with adjustment or alienation, or with psychological health or psychopathology. This disparity reflects the inconsistency regarding the conceptualization and measurement that characterized the first analyses of the changes in reference group orientation that emerged among various groupings of blacks in the late sixties. Some conceptualized that levels of militancy, hostility toward whites, or alienation reflected greater racial identification. Conservative writers like Martin Kilson and Thomas Sowell, for example, associated stronger group identity with "black militancy and radicalism [that] follow from experiences of frustration and social alienation and are more prevalent among psychopathic personalities, the chronically unemployed, and the underclass."[12] In contrast, others predicted that high socioeconomic status should correlate with high racial group identity.[13]

Unsurprisingly, these studies have produced a range of results, some of which are at variance with one another. Some, consistent with the conservative thesis, wrote that low-status blacks should show high racial group identification.[14] However, these interpretations were contradicted by a number of empirical studies cited by Cross that found the strongest indicators of black cultural and political militancy among the black middle class youth. Cross himself insisted in 1970 that "Afro-Americans of all types, the rich and poor, the light-skinned or ebony hued, educated or disadvantaged, have been touched by the movement,"[15] suggesting that there was no significant relationship between nigrescence and social class.[16]

One possible factor in these inconsistencies is the focus on static "profiles" that oversimplify and distort the dynamism and complexity of identity formation processes. Nigrescence, defined as "the process of becoming black" begins by addressing these dynamics of identity change. In nigrescence theory the key concept is that a "real-world-encounter" experience will trigger an ultimate reorientation of self that incorporates higher levels of racial awareness and affiliation. By assuming that manifestations of this new "blackness" correlate positively with personal identity or self-esteem, the original conception of Negro self-hate was also incorporated, implicitly.

Recently, however, nigrescence theorists have reconsidered and revised these assumptions in several ways. Revising the implied linear model of "stages of nigrescence" originally proposed, Thomas A. Parham suggested a cyclic process in which the issues of nigrescence, the significance of black identity, or "psychological blackness," may be revisited at several stages in one's life span. A perhaps more significant revision resulted from the collaboration involving Parham, Cross, and Janet E. Helms, in which the "self-hate" thesis was finally revised. Their comprehensive review of studies of personality and reference group orientation found that although a small number of *pre-encounter* blacks fit the self-hate profile, the large majority did not, even though they had not had an encounter that would trigger "higher," and ostensibly healthier, stages of black identity.

In their view, then, the assumed relationship between reference group orientation and personal identity did *not* hold up. As Cross notes, this is a significant finding: "The lack of a relationship between PI [personal identity] and RGO [reference group orientation] in Black identity means not only that a white preference does not predict pathology but that a Black preference or being Afrocentric does not predict mental health."[17]

On the one hand, changes in reference group orientation widely manifest since the late 1960s do not automatically imply concurrent or proportional changes in levels of personal efficacy and esteem. On the other hand, most blacks were not "self-hating Negroes" before these group identity changes occurred. Regarding this significant reconceptualization, Cross notes, "in the excitement of explicating the process of change, I overlooked another important dimension embedded in my notes: continuity."[18]

National Survey of Black Americans

Meanwhile, as these issues have been refined and debated among Afrocentric psychologists and nigrescence theorists, social scientists utilizing more conventional modalities have made it possible to consider the third set of difficulties noted above. As indicated, although several studies attempt to associate black group identity with demographic groups and variables, few were built from demographically representative samples. Prior to 1981 all studies in this area were based either on local samples or upon nonrepresentative national samples: that is, samples of the national population that did not have a nationally representative subsample of blacks.[19] In spite of the great influence of some of these studies, then, there is valid reason to question their reliability and generalizability regarding association with social class, age, region, or other demographic variables.

The first studies based on a valid representative sample came from data collected for the important National Survey of Black Americans (NSBA), conducted during 1979–80. In designing the first nationally representative sample of black Americans, the original researchers countered what had been a significant problem in looking at demographic variables—such as age, region, and education—in relation to issues like racial group identity. The NSBA data provided the first opportunity to explore the involvement of sociodemographic factors like age, region, and social class with measures of racial group identity using an accurately representative sample of black respondents. While the survey of this sample population covered a wide range of other topics, a number of studies have been published from this data that looked specifically at aspects of racial group identity.[20]

I examined the data from this survey while a member of a sociology department. Reviewing studies published by the original research group, and reviewing and manipulating the data itself when it was released to the public domain in 1989, I felt that basic issues were being raised once again about how to constitute valid knowledge on the subject of black peoples and communities. In essence, these were epistemological issues to be addressed in assessing these studies and the data on which they were based. There was no basis for direct quantitative comparison of black identity, as measured in these studies; but with the conceptions postulated and measured by Afrocentrists and nigrescence theorists, it seemed nevertheless that the question of analyzing trends and qualitative differences in approach, concept, and results could at least be addressed.

The clear contribution of those using conventional social-science statistical approaches is the fact that they can, as did the NSBA, provide so-called "objective data" for empirically testing and validating information relevant to studying black individuals, collectives, and communities. It is true that many in African American Studies challenge the validity of so-called "quantitative" approaches and methods, and are especially opposed to their overuse and misapplication. Complete rejection of such approaches, as some advocate, however, may be too extreme.

When limitations and qualifications are observed in the use of quantitative methods they have been useful in documenting and predicting social behavior and attitudes. Moreover, as long as these methods are continually used to characterize and analyze the lives and experiences of African Americans, based often on poor techniques and distorted interpretations, the existence of a valid set of data is critical for those who wish to investigate how these methods might document alternative interpretations of these African American realities.

Studies of the NSBA data have been undoubtedly useful in identifying sociodemographic factors that affect or correlate with measures of racial group identity. Some findings challenge, contradict, or force clarification of the new the conceptions of black group identity being developed by Afrocentrists and nigrescence theorists. However, generally lacking theoretical frameworks that tie together relevant but disparate-seeming aspects of black life, these studies are unable to clarify or illuminate the significance of these items. In other words, these findings are presented in ways that suggest precisely the kind of cross-disciplinary problems affecting studies of African Americans that often arise (sometimes unnoticed) in the work of scholars focusing on a conventional disciplinary and methodological approach. Thus, while data from this conventional approach can be used to challenge and force clarification, limitations in the conventional interpretive framework are still problematic.

While conducting my study of the NSBA data I encountered a number of issues of conceptualization, categorization, measurement, and interpretation in which I found bases for questioning or differing from the original group's approaches, based on the framework developed from my involvement in the Black Studies movement. Included among these concerns were: (1) basic definitional issues about racial group identity: how and when it is assumed to develop, its relationship to black identity and other issues of identity and culture (such as militancy, Africanity, Afrocentricity); (2) the relationship between racial group identity as defined and the actual variable constructed to "measure" it; (3) the effect of how important variables, specifically age and region, are categorized and defined on the validity of results produced; and (4) how to categorize and interpret qualitative historical changes and their effects on the lives and attitudes of black individuals.

All these factors (assumptions about the development of group identity, the age at which to look for period effects, and the basis on which to categorize historical periods) were involved in the eventual definition of the age category used to look at the measure of racial group identity in relation to possible historical period effects. In my view, all were contestable in terms that could justify alternative categorizations of relevant variables.

These issues all bear on the central questions of epistemology I have been exploring relative to the emergence, and the salience, of African American Studies as a field of study: what processes of thought, reason, conceptualization, categorization, and analysis lead to valid knowledge regarding the experiences, conditions, and aspirations of black individuals and black communities (and, in reverse, which processes do not)? When I analyzed this data I employed the paradigm developed from my previous work to address this problem. In particular, I found ways to employ some of these constructions, and make a case for their validity, in making statistical inferences from this data.

Data Analysis

The total number of respondents in the National Survey of Black Americans, collected in 1979–80, selected by multistage sampling procedures designed at the Survey Research Center at the University of Michigan, was 2,107. These data represent the first nationally representative, randomly selected cross section of the adult black population in the continental United States. Information about this data set is detailed by Jackson et al.[21]

The instrument used in the NSBA survey was derived from Gurin's definition of group identity, further described below.[22] The original studies found that racial group identity, as measured with this particular instrument, was stronger among older blacks, southern blacks, less-educated blacks, and among non–Western educated urban blacks, suggesting, in effect, that group identity is eroding, particularly among younger blacks. This is counterintuitive to expectations flowing from either Afrocentrism or nigrescence. In the theoretical terms of either approach, increases in racial group identification are associated with the emergence of "black consciousness" during the social movement period, involving precisely the younger blacks whose group identity, as measured in the NSBA, is apparently eroding. Conversely, several studies by nigrescence theorists see no relationship between social class and the reference group orientation changes that define the process of nigrescence, while studies from the NSBA data find that at least one social class indicator (level of education) did affect its measure of group identity.

No adequate explanation of these findings or their significance is evident in the NSBA studies, given the degree to which these observations defy the expectations of many black identity theorists. One possible response to this paradox is to examine the instrument employed in the NSBA. It consisted of a series of eight questions that asked the respondent "how close do you feel in your ideas and feelings about things to blacks who are": (1) poor, (2) religious, (3) young, (4) middle class, (5) working class, (6) older, (7) elected officials, and (8) professionals. The available responses ("very close," "fairly close," "not too close," and "not at all close") are given the respective scores of 4,3,2, and 1. The index is derived from the mean of each respondent's score on all items.

Here Helms's speculation seems helpful. Discussing issues of complexity, she notes that "racial identity development is multidimensional. Accordingly an individual's racial identity might differ depending on what aspect of his or her life one is considering. Thus, a person's racial identity concerning the world of work might be governed by one stage of racial identity, whereas his or her racial identity concerning social relationships might reflect another."[23]

The concept of racial group identity defined by this survey instrument is not synonymous with *black identity* or *black consciousness* as those terms would be conceived by Afrocentrists or nigrescence theorists. For these approaches additional and more complex sensibilities are anticipated as reflections or measures of black group identity.[24] In addition, my analysis of the data produced by this instrument (further below) points to the fact that the original conventional studies did not satisfactorily link explanations of findings with important historical factors that frame social and cultural phenomenon in black communities.

Taking such factors into account, my study does not conclude that later born blacks necessarily have weaker racial identity than earlier born blacks. Rather it suggests that for younger, nonsouthern, educated blacks the cultural foundations of individual and group identity are different and more complex than they were in earlier periods, when blacks as a whole were more separated from the cultural mainstream. This effect, identified below as "class interference," may reflect increasing social diversity among blacks resulting from urbanization and other modern sociodemographic changes, rather than a "weaker" sense of black identity.

However, to the degree one recognizes that the instrument detects only one of many possible aspects of a multidimensional black racial group identity, it may still be seen as a valid measure of some aspect of self-group orientation. In addition to its geographic and socioeconomic representativeness, the age range of the sample was so great (18–101) that it reflects history in some important ways. Several crucial transformations have occurred during the span of history represented in this sample. It is, therefore, highly conceivable that one's orientation toward group identity would be affected according to how one's individual life span was positioned among these periods of transformation. At least two studies from the original research group attempted to address this possibility by categorizing age groups in terms of historical landmarks.[25]

Like these studies of this data, part of my analysis created age and regional categories by grouping respondents according to historical period of birth and region of residence. My categorization of those variables sought to operationalize terms and principles of the transformative theoretical framework outlined and developed in previous chapters. The result was an alteration of how age groups were aggregated, and of how states were grouped into regions, that produced small but significant differences consistent with the theses proposed below.

In presenting my alternative construction of the age variable, two issues embedded in the previous studies require excavation. One is the nature and timing of the processes by which racial group identity is assumed to develop. Studies of the NSBA data undertaken by the original research group incorporate James Jackson's assumption that group identity is largely *preceded by* personal identity development in early life and is reflective of experiences and relationships encountered outside of the immediate, primary socialization environment. Specifically, according to Jackson, "group identification and consciousness develop out of the relationships of blacks to a broader set of influences and referents, specifically blacks' relationships and experiences in white-dominated environments."[26] Based on their acceptance of the premise that external, secondary socialization factors determine racial group identity, Jackson and the original researchers chose the age of sixteen as a point at which to look for connections between measures of racial group identity and qualitative historical changes.

The concept that racial group identity comes from later contact with white environments in secondary socialization contexts seems based on sociocognitive developmental theories of racial group identity formation. Rather than looking directly at racial group identity, some theorists in this area have looked at how and when children understand and internalize race as a biological and social concept. Apparently the inference has been made that a child's racial group identity itself cannot begin to form until such understanding is in place. (Findings suggest that such understanding is constructed around age eight or ten.)

This conception addresses only externally generated factors that define blacks as a group (with whom to identify) from the outside and give no importance to internally generated sensibilities that shape identity formation and cultural orientation from the earliest periods of socialization in family and close community contexts. There is no intrinsic reason to assume that factors shaping racial group identity are not in place prior to a child's cognitive understanding and internalization of race as a social concept. Personality and identity development is a complex process, made more so when issues of cultural and racial difference are involved. The assumption of discreet, sequentially separated personal and racial group aspects of the identity formation process is an arguable one. Support for an alternative view—that primary socialization experiences are significantly involved with group identity development; that personal

identity and group identity are coincident rather than sequential developments—comes also from reports of sociocognitive theorists indicating that
the elements of racial group identity are in place by the age of seven or
eight, and often by age five.[27]

My assumption that historical period effects would be seen at earlier
ages than those indicated by Jackson is one basis for altering the contours
of the age category in relation to historical periods. The second basis for
my alteration of the age category is the way in which fundamental factors
of historical change or difference are conceived. The original research
group chose to define historical periods in terms of public policy events
(the New Deal and the *Brown vs. Board of Education* decision). However, my
argument is that the public policy events which Jackson, Broman, and associates chose to mark the periodization were themselves the result of
more fundamental economic, sociopolitical, and demographic changes.
Arguably, these more fundamental changes constitute a more valid basis
for demarcating historical periods (and hence the age groupings that
define the age category) for purposes of examining period effects.

Broman et al. defined birth year groups as including individuals
who were at *least sixteen years of age* during four historical periods the
authors believed to be significant for Black Americans. The four periods
were the following: "pre-Roosevelt," from 1878 (the birth year of the
oldest respondent) through 1931; before *Brown vs. the Board of Education*,
from 1932 through 1953; "protest," from 1954 through 1968; and "post
protest," from 1969 to 1979 (the year the data were collected). Therefore,
respondents who were at least sixteen during these periods were born
between 1878–1915, 1916–37, 1938–52, and after 1953, respectively (the
youngest respondent was born in 1963).

My analysis assumes that the impact of historical and macroeconomic changes influence primary socialization experiences. In defining
historical periods I argue that the most important experiences occur before the age of sixteen and are important factors influencing group identity. Although historical events in later life also have impact, such impact will not fundamentally alter personality structures already formed
in primary socialization experiences. In addition, my periodization also
assumes that fundamental historical and macroeconomic changes and
events are a better basis for demarcating the Black American historical
experience than the public policy events used as historical signposts in
the previous study.

Based on the historical framework of transformation presented in
the previous chapter, then, I look at a periodization in which data are

regrouped by birth year in the following intervals: 1878–97, 1898–1912, 1913–27, 1928–42, 1943–57, and 1958–63. The names of these birth year groups reflect the inclusion of individuals born shortly before or during certain important historical periods: the nineteenth-century group, the turn-of-the-century group, the World War I group, the Depression/World War II group, the postwar movement group,[28] and the post-movement group. Since the size of the oldest (nineteenth-century) group is small (*n*=23) those cases are combined with those in the next (turn-of-the-century) group to create a subsample of adequate size for statistical comparison. This group is the "pre-migration group."

Results

Table 1 is based on the age categorization of the original (Broman et al.) study, along with a similar one based on the alternative age categorization discussed above. The table is broken down by age-group category and indicate the size (*n*), mean score as measured by the group identity instrument, and the standard deviation of each. In addition, the means of each pair of adjacent age groups were compared using *t*-tests to determine if observed differences between group means were large enough to be considered statistically significant. The *z* value in the last column of each row is generated from the *t*-test comparing that group's mean with the mean of the group in the line below. A *z* value greater than 1.96 indicates significance at the 0.05 level (meaning that chances are at least 95 percent that observed differences were not merely random fluctuation); a value greater than 2.58 indicates significance at the 0.01 level (implying a 99 percent chance that differences are not random).

The alternative periodization produces a somewhat sharper differentiation between the group with highest group identity measures (1913–1927; mean=3.57) and the next (younger) group (1928–1942; mean=3.42) than the differentiation between similar groups in Broman's study, where the means were 3.57 and 3.49. *T*-testing those groups in the Broman study generates a *z* value of 2.25, indicating 0.05 level significance, while the *z* value yielded from comparison of similar groups in my alternative periodization is 4.45, indicating significance at the 0.01 level.

My interpretation is that, although each categorization produced significant differences between age groups, the alternative periodization more clearly reveals the beginning, or increase, in factors influencing this particular measure of group identity from one generation to the next. The alternative categorization would support an argument that the conditions related to the relatively high means of older groups contin-

Table 1. Group Identity by Birth Year Groups

Original Periodization

		n	mean	std dev	z
Pre-Roosevelt	(1878–1915)	258	3.57	0.44	2.25
New Deal	(1916–37)	511	3.49	0.45	7.89
Protest	(1938–52)	585	3.27	0.50	3.34
Post-protest	(1953–63)	379	3.15	0.53	
	Total	1733	3.35		

Alternate Periodization

		n	mean	std dev	z
Premigration	(1878–1912)	205	3.54	0.44	0.76
World War I	(1913–27)	316	3.57	0.43	4.45
Depr/WWII	(1928–42)	395	3.42	0.47	7.13
Movement	(1943–57)	673	3.20	0.51	1.25
Post-movement	(1958–63)	144	3.14	0.53	
	Total	1733	3.35		

ued to affect those born up to 1927, while the previous categorization brackets the age groups in a way to suggest that changes occurred earlier, with those born after 1916.

Both sets of birth year groupings confirm a significant difference in means between the first postwar group and the previous (older) group. Broman et al.'s New Deal and protest groups have respective means of 3.49 and 3.27 (z value, 7.89), while my study's depression and movement groups have respective means of 3.42 and 3.20 (z value, 7.13). However, the different conceptions of factors that shape or bracket historical change employed in the earlier studies created birth year cohorts that overlapped with those proposed here in ways significant in assessing these alternative perspectives. Here, it seems, the lack of a qualitative historical framework worked to handicap or limit the usefulness of the original categorizations.

For example, the earlier studies included in the same (1938–52) group individuals born before *and* after 1943, when accelerated war production began to drastically alter economic and social conditions for urban and migrating blacks, leading to the relative affluence under which the postwar "baby-boom" generation was socialized. My

periodization assumes that those born between 1938 and 1942 are better placed with the group born and socialized during the era of the depression. As indicated, however, in the previous study the first postwar
group included birth years 1938–54 (protest), while this study groups
birth years 1943–57 (movement).

Based on this conception I anticipated that a comparison of the mean
of the 1938–42 subgroup with that of the adjacent younger 1943–47 subgroup would have special significance for assessing each model. The age
categorization employed in the earlier studies included both these subgroups as part of the same birth year cohort. If, as my alternative categorization assumed, they were actually from qualitatively different historical
milieu, then (a) their means would likely be significantly different from one
another; (b) the mean of the older (1938–42) subgroup would not be significantly different from the overall mean of the cohort (1928–42) with
which my categorization grouped them; and (c) the mean of the adjacent
younger subgroup (1943–47) would not be significantly different from the
overall mean of the cohort (1943–57) with which my categorization
grouped them. The results of this analysis are presented in the table 2.
(Note that the z values represent the t-test comparing the mean of the row
containing the z value with that of the row below.)

As I had anticipated above, the mean of the 1938–42 subgroup (3.38)
is significantly different than the mean of the adjacent younger (1943–
47) subgroup, with which Broman et al. had grouped them (mean equals
3.21; z=3.14). In fact, the mean of the 1938–42 group is much closer to
the depression group mean of 3.42. Indeed, the t-test comparing the
means of those groups indicates no significant difference (z=0.91).
Unsurprisingly, the final t-test comparing the 1943–47 subgroup (mean
equals 3.21) with the overall postwar movement (1943–57) group (mean
equals 3.20) reveals no significant statistical difference (z=0.23). I interpret this as support for the alternative age categorization, since, accord-

Table 2. Comparison of Birth Year Sub-groups

Birth Period	n	mean	std dev	z
(1943–47)	195	3.21	0.54	3.14
(1938–42)	153	3.38	0.47	0.91
(1928–42)	395	3.42	0.43	4.81
(1943–57)	673	3.20	0.51	0.23
(1943–47)	195	3.21	0.54	

ing to the terms of my analysis, it shows that the sharp change in the measure of group identity is essentially a postwar phenomenon.

In my study, the two youngest groups (respective birth year intervals, 1943–57 and 1958–63) are somewhat more similar to each other than the two youngest groups in the Broman and Jackson studies (birth years 1938–52 and 1953–63). The z value yielded from comparing the movement and post-movement groups of my study (respective means, 3.20 and 3.14) is 1.25; not enough to assert statistical significance. On the other hand there is a significant statistical difference between the means of the previous studies protest and post-protest groups. The t-test of their respective means (3.27 and 3.15) yields a z value of 3.34. The fact that the younger groups are not significantly different when grouped according to my periodization coincides with my view that these two postwar groups are indeed similar in terms of their reflection of class interference.

Regional Data

Analyzed by region the data reflect highest measured group identity in the South, followed by the North Central, Northeast, and West regions. The previous study categorized regional data in accordance with standard census bureau designations. This writer attempted to alter the regional designation to more closely reflect the historical pattern of dispersion of blacks up the Mississippi and Ohio valleys and into the industrial Midwest and Northeast. In terms of data groupings, the only result of this alteration was that the data from the state of Pennsylvania—a part of the heavily industrial economy that has historically drawn large numbers of blacks from the South—were included with the other North Central states[29] The new alignment was labeled the "Industrial" region.

Again, while the effect of this alteration is small, it does serve to further differentiate the Midwest from the Northeast region. The difference between the means of the alternate "industrial" and Northeast regions (respectively 3.25 and 3.21) is greater than that between the census North Central and Northeast regions (respectively 3.24 and 3.23). A closer look at the Northeast shows that the large number of respondents from New York City and near New Jersey (130 out of 336) account for the difference between the two northern regions. When those New York City area cases are separated, the rest of the industrial Northeast is quite similar to the industrial Midwest (mean = 3.25), while the New York area is more similar to the West (mean = 3.17).[30] This possible "bicoastal" effect is suggested in the third set of columns in table 3.

Table 3. Regional Comparisons

Census Regions			Alternate Regions			Bicoastal		
reg	n	mean	reg	n	mean	reg	n	mean
NE	336	3.23	NE	246	3.21	NYC	130	3.17
NC	404	3.24	Ind	494	3.25	NE	116	3.26
So	965	3.46	So	965	3.46	Ind	494	3.25
We	109	3.17	We	109	3.17	So	965	3.46
						We	109	3.17

Obviously the South region is significantly different from all the others. When my regional categorizations are applied, especially when the New York City area is treated separately, the differences between the extreme East Coast and the remaining Northeast region is made larger (but not significantly so), while the Northeast region outside of New York City area is made more similar to the Midwest industrial region (mean equals 3.25). The differences are not large, but they are consistent. Moreover, while the difference between the New York City area and the rest of the industrial Northeast is not statistically significant, in my categorization, it does arguably *approach* significance ($z = 1.51$).

Effects of Education Level

Analyzed by level of education, the data in table 4 suggests that higher education levels correlate with lower group identity measures. However, in the Midwest and South the measure is higher among those with the highest level of education. This study uses two different categorizations of education level to indicate this relationship. Like the previous study, the first categorization groups those with grammar school education or less, those with high school and no diploma, high school graduates, and college attendees. The category of college attendees includes both college graduates and those with some college but no degree. The second categorization of education level separates college graduates from those with some college.

The first categorization shows the overall negative correlation between education level and group identity measure. However, the second categorization reveals that college graduates have significantly higher measures of group identity than college attendees with no diploma.

A look at education levels broken down by region shows that this effect is entirely accounted for in the South and Midwest regions (table 5). In the Northeast and West, college graduates have lower scores than

Table 4. Group Identity by Education Levels

level	n	mean	std dev	z
0–8 Yrs	370	3.59	0.44	4.98
9–11 Yrs	392	3.42	0.50	3.95
H.S. Grads	587	3.29	0.51	3.56
College*	465	3.18	0.49	
Some College	300	3.15	0.50	2.14
College Grads	165	3.25	0.47	

*All college attendees.

college attendees, though the size of these subsamples (fewer than thirty) is inadequate for valid statistical comparison. In the South and North Central/Midwest regions there is a consistent and statistically significant rise in the measure among college graduates over attendees with no degree. In the Northeast, this trend emerges when the cases from New York are taken out. Once again, treating the New York City area separately causes the appearance of greater similarity between the remaining Northeast and the industrial Midwest, and points to possible similarities between the extreme East and West coasts. Although the subsample is small, the New York profile of group identity measures by education level is similar to that of the West, where the index continues to decline with college graduates.

In summary, age, among all sociodemographic variables, has the strongest effect on measures of group identity. (In studies using both historical period groupings, older groups tend to have higher measures of group identity than younger ones.) In addition, region and education are found to correlate in various ways with group identity measures. (The appendix contains detailed tables and discussions of (1) age groups within regions, (2) age groups across regions, (3) education levels within age categories, (4) age groups while controlling for education level, and (5) education levels across regions.)

Overall, those in the South have highest group identity, followed by the Midwest (or North Central), Northeast, and West. Education was negatively correlated with group identity, except among college graduates outside the West and the extreme East Coast. It was found that lower education levels correlated with higher group identity within all age groups; that older groups had higher group identity scores than younger groups with the same education; and that southerners and

Table 5. Education Level within Regions

	Northeast (Census)		Northeast (without Pa.)	
	n	mean	n	mean
0–8 Yrs	42	3.42	31	3.37
9–11 Yrs	66	3.35	51	3.28
H.S. Grads	126	3.23	85	3.23
College*	81	3.10	63	3.01
Some Coll	55	3.13	42	3.13
Coll Grads	26	3.06	21	3.02

	North Central (census)		Industrial (includes Pa.)	
	n	mean	n	mean
0–8 Yrs	52	3.40	63	3.43
9–11 Yrs	97	3.38	112	3.40
H.S. Grads	125	3.18	166	3.19
College*	113	3.11	131	3.12
Some Coll	88	3.05	101	3.06
Coll Grads	25	3.32	30	3.31

	South		West	
	n	mean	n	mean
0–8 Yrs	249	3.65	8	3.69
9–11 Yrs	195	3.48	17	3.43
H.S. Grads	270	3.38	42	3.18
College	220	3.29	30	2.98
Some Coll	124	3.28	22	3.03
Coll Grads	96	3.30	8	2.81

	New York City		Northeast (without New York)	
	n	mean	n	mean
0–8 Yrs	14	3.35	17	3.38
9–11 Yrs	29	3.32	22	3.23
H.S. Grads	40	3.14	45	3.31
College*	36	3.08	27	3.11
Some Coll	27	3.16	15	3.09
Coll Grads	9	2.86	12	3.14

Includes attendees and graduates.

midwesterners had higher means than those in other regions in the same educational category.

Putting It All Together

Many of the differences noted between previous study results and my study of the NSBA data are small. However, the support demonstrated for the validity of the alternative categorization of the age and region variables points to more significant theoretical issues. Clearly Broman and others who have analyzed the NSBA's racial group identity data do not account for the apparent dramatic changes in cultural, psychological, and political orientation that seemed widespread among black youth and others during the tumultuous period of social movements. These changes were highly visible among younger blacks, who registered a drop in levels of racial identification from their elders, according to the NSBA instrument. And while education was negatively correlated with group identity as measured by the survey instrument, the nigrescence phenomenon, as described by Cross and others, was highly visible among educated blacks, particularly younger blacks in institutions of higher education. On the other hand, nigrescence theory, at least at the outset, was not prepared to find, or explain, the evidence of strong black affiliation and group identity among older blacks, the majority of whom were assumed to be in the pre-encounter, or least advanced state, of black identity.

The NSBA instrument clearly taps into the issue of reference group orientation, which, according to nigrescence theory, underwent significant change among those whose new sense of black identity was emerging. Why then does the cohort most associated with the "new black identity" show less evidence of racial affiliation in the NSBA survey than their grandparents? And conversely (and separately), why do their grandparents show evidence of such strong affiliation when their pre-encounter sense of black identity was supposed to have been so weak?

Beginning with their revision of the "Negro self-hate" premise, discourse and collaboration over the years among Cross and other nigrescence theorists has allowed at least a partial reconciliation of this paradox. They assumed initially that changes in reference group orientation observed in the 1960s reflected the transformation of negative attitudes to positive ones. However, they concluded that empirical findings did not support that assumption.[31] By picturing the "Negro-to-Black" conversions of the 1960s as a nearly total break from the past, critics, analysts, and many original participants themselves, all obscured the strong sense of connection to the past that was also involved. Nigrescence theorists finally surmised that the dramatic ascendance of black identity in that particular (movement) period may have been based directly on psychological strengths passed from previous generations. Describing the student subjects of one study, Cross realized that "some of the strengths the students identified in themselves, and that helped them account for their success at college, could be traced not to identity change but to their socialization by their (Negro) parents and extended families. The students' vision of their past was far from a tangle of pathology, though they could readily associate the traditional, or Negro, identity with many, if not most, of the significant others from that past."[32]

Regarding the strong association with age, the original NSBA studies made no attempt to interpret whether the association was based on biological age or historical period. The paradigm from which the alternative periodization is derived, however, offers not only a different set of years with which to define periods, but also an analytical structure for explaining possible period effects on measures of group identity. Viewed in terms consistent (or "synergistic") with an African American Studies disciplinary matrix, the fact that 90 percent of all blacks born before World War I were born and socialized in the South is of key relevance. In the South at that time a rigidly segregated social structure made the issue of class fairly irrelevant to the issue of black identity. That is, blacks identified with each other as a group regardless of class. For one thing most blacks were part of the same rural tenant class. And to the degree that there was stratification among blacks in the South, those in the upper strata were, in social and usually economic terms, inextricably tied to the black community.

Taking these factors into account, however, my study does not conclude that later born blacks necessarily have weaker racial identity than earlier born blacks. (The fact that a single measure of a single aspect of racial group identity appears to change does not invalidate the perception that widespread and dramatic identity transformations did, and do, indeed occur.) Rather my analysis of the NSBA data quickly focuses on how the NSBA measure clusters in a close alignment with the historic, geographic, and socioeconomic patterns of diffusion and transformation of folk/popular cultural sensibilities in various historical periods.

With respect to the data and results of the NSBA survey, the groups which scored high in measures of group identity in the NSBA are those identified in the paradigm as closest to the folk/popular tradition, or the blues continuum, which have been the historical bases for the distinctiveness and cohesion of black cultural life. Older blacks (those in the older, higher-scoring groups who grew up basically before the Great Migration) almost unanimously have strong southern roots. The proportion of blacks growing up in the North before the time of the migration was quite small. Even as late as the 1960s more than half the black population still lived in the South.

Thus, my analysis does suggest that NSBA index and survey items are a valid measure of some aspect of self-group orientation; and the measured phenomenon is something that is altered by migration from the South, urbanization, and educational and social mobility. Along this conceptual path is the suggestion that younger, nonsouthern, educated blacks are historically, geographically, and culturally more removed from the original, primary, and fundamentally separable cultural ethos that developed among older blacks before the Great Migration, when blacks as a whole were more separated from the cultural mainstream; and that for younger, nonsouthern blacks, the cultural foundations of individual and group identity are more complex. In my analysis this sharp change coincides with the acceleration of stratification and the class interference referred to above.

In the South and Midwest (or Industrial) regions, college graduates report higher measures of the identity variable than college attendees who did not graduate. This is an interesting finding, considering the overall negative relationship between level of education and score on the identity measure. An explanation may be suggested in terms of the Cross theory of nigrescence, which postulates that encounters with people or situations in which the stigma of race is keenly felt stimulates black consciousness. Attending college long enough to get a degree, it may be hypothesized, increases the likelihood of such an encounter.

Moreover, with the period of migration, the rural folk cultural tradition was transformed to become the urban folk/popular tradition, based in the working-class, relatively unassimilated black communities in urban industrial centers. This is consistent with the data reporting that urbanized, less-educated blacks who make up these communities show higher levels of group identity, as it is defined and measured by Broman et al. When the western data is taken out of the national sample, a tendency toward stronger group identification emerges among urban, educated blacks. Many of this group actually have roots (that is, early primary socialization) in those working-class urban communities and got their education in the age of opportunity that allowed so many of us to pass through the hallowed halls of higher education. Not all of us lost or severed our connections or sense of closeness to our folk/popular roots. Depending on what items are measured, however, it appears some have.

The basic analytical principle shaping the development of the paradigm used in this analysis is that the interaction of external, objective (systematic) forces on the one hand, with internal, subjective (thematic) forces on the other hand, shapes the conditions and sensibilities of individual blacks and black communities. This interaction creates the fundamental duality underlying sociocultural domains in the black experience while shaping both social and individual reference frames.

In the case of sorting out data and theoretical formulations concerning black group identity, the analysis derived from this paradigm points to issues involving the distinction between cultural (internally generated) and social (externally shaped) aspects of group identity, which are tapped and measured by the items in the NSBA survey. The cultural dimension refers to a range of sensibilities that are internally generated within black communities. The more a black community is culturally isolated from the mainstream, the greater is the degree to which these sensibilities make up a worldview, or way of life discrete and separable from that of the mainstream. The second dimension, which I call social/ structural, refers to blacks' orientation and accommodation to social structures imposed from outside the black community. The impact of such structures on black racial identification processes can be seen to vary in concert with historical and demographic changes that blacks have undergone.

This study, then, suggests the term "group identity" may be misleading or incomplete as a description of the phenomenon that actually emerges with this interpretation of the data. My interpretation is that internally derived *cultural aspects* of black racial group identity, characteristic of the South before integration, form the basis for similar responses among those groups showing higher group identity in the NSBA. In this view it seems unlikely that racial group identity—at least that aspect measured by the survey instrument—would be determined by secondary socialization experiences like those stipulated by Jackson. He suggests that racial group identity develops as a result of interactions with and interpretations of the world outside the immediate community. According to the approach developed here, shared cultural sensibilities developed in arenas of primary socialization will have already anchored a person's self-group orientation by the time secondary socialization experiences begin to have significant influence.

At that point, the social foundations of group identity may be altered in interaction with larger group, social, and institutional forces. What develops from that point are what I have referred to as the social structural components group identity, the causes and manifestations of which may be numerous. The addition of these components to black identity structure lead to the sense of double consciousness, or duality, which Du Bois described so eloquently and succinctly, nearly a century ago, as "two warring souls in one dark body . . . whose dogged strength alone keeps it from being torn asunder." The cultural transformations characterizing the African American experience during this century reflect the increased salience of double-consciousness as a primary factor in self-group orientation among blacks as, like Du Bois a century ago, more of them experience educational and social mobility concomitant with exposure to and internalization of mainstream cultural sensibilities.

In this study the increased salience of duality is inferentially evident in increased class interference, which my analysis concludes is measured by the variation, according to age, region, and educational attainment, documented in the NSBA data. While these findings differ from other studies, and from many expectations, regarding which groupings of blacks should show stronger indices of group identity, they can fit into, and be elucidated from, the perspective of transformationism. These findings suggest the need for further investigation of this data to clarify and disentangle the effects of duality and class interference on racial group identity among various subgroups of blacks.

Chapter 7

The Songs of Black Folks

Among all areas of African American expressive culture, music has arguably been the most distinctive and important contribution of folk/popular sensibility.[1] At the same time, African American music is the aspect of black culture that is most clearly and thoroughly American. (It has been the basis for almost any identifiably "American" music.) The very distinctiveness of African American musical sensibility makes its influence on the music of American culture readily apparent.

This is a paradox that seems to reproduce itself perpetually. In its myriad forms, black music functions to validate black humanity in cultural spaces separate and distinct from the dominant culture, in the folk/popular reference frame of unassimilated segments of black communities. It is also arguably the strongest form of black influence on the wider culture. Ironically, this influence shapes mainstream sensibilities in such as way as to reduce the effectiveness of given forms as markers of cultural differentiation—again, especially for those most distant from the cultural mainstream. In certain instances, this leads to the emergence of new markers of differentiation. To assess the significance of African American musical culture in connection with the overall experiences of black individuals and communities, it is necessary to examine the various aspects of this paradox. This chapter, then, will examine the role of folk/popular cultural sensibility as a record, or reflection, of black life in general, and as the principal source of distinctiveness in African American musical sensibility in particular. I will also look at how African American musical sensibilities interact with and significantly influence mainstream culture.

As argued in chapter 6, cultural sensibilities most directly connected with the African heritage of black Americans—by one definition the "purest" forms of African American culture—tend to be retained, cultivated, and transformed within an African American folk/popular reference frame. This is due to the effects of structural isolation. Contexts where dominant culture norms are absent or relatively inoperative—such as New Orleans's famous Congo Square (where enslaved Africans gathered by the hundreds outside the purview of any masters), the slave quarter, or a basement "rent party"—often function as repositories for African American cultural sensibilities in their most distinguishable form, differentiated from and independent of the dominant framework.

As black culture has transformed through the decades, the least culturally assimilated sectors of the black cultural landscape, where African orality and rhythmicity are strongest, have generally tended to coincide with the lower socioeconomic strata among African Americans. That is to say, the "mouth" or "source" of the historical stream of sensibilities connecting black Americans with an African cultural heritage has always been located among the least assimilated sectors of the black community. Historically this was the South. Today it also includes the least assimilated, structurally isolated urban areas.

Recalling an assertion from the previous chapter, there are two basic sources for unique sensibilities shared among African Americans that shape their outlook—their cultural framework—differently than whites: surviving Africanisms and the shared social consequences of being black in a racist society. These terms, in a sense, define the parameters of a cultural reference frame predicated from the unique experiences of blacks. Moreover, these two principal sources of culturally distinctive experiences are both clustered closely along this folk/popular cultural stream.

As the source of unassimilated sensibilities in contemporary black culture, the folk/popular reference frame often provides elements of innovation that keep black culture distinct as it is transformed. As I have already suggested in chapter 6, each of several transformations in black musical culture preserved aspects of pure African sensibility while joining them to Western musical forms and instruments. African sensibilities may be identified in such qualities as the emphasis on rhythmic syncopation, melodic improvisation, and audience performance participation ("call-response"), which characterize most African American musical forms.[2]

It turns out, then, that sociostructural isolation not only leads to survival of these root sensibilities but also to cultural environments highly supportive of significant innovation that engages those sensibilities. In this context forms of black music function to validate a distinctive sense of black humanity in cultural spaces separated and differentiated from the dominant culture; spaces in which the scorn, devaluation, and rejection of the dominant culture are replaced by affirmative expressions of self. This is an especially salient function of music, especially, among other expressive forms, in the folk/popular reference frame of relatively unassimilated segments of black communities.

Here it is important to distinguish between maintenance of alternative *cultural* frameworks in the folk/popular milieu and the construction of alternative *institutional* frameworks in the milieu of the high/elite black experience. There is, in other words, a distinction between a "cultural cohesion" based on indigenous folk/popular sensibilities, and an institutional nationalism historically associated with the high culture aspirations of an educated elite.

Both traditions eventually embrace the idea of constructing alternative frameworks for culturally validating black humanity. As suggested in chapter 6, however, institutional nationalism emerged historically from failed quasi-assimilationist aspirations to remove the stigma associated with cultural difference. Creation of institutions that embraced cultural separateness occurred when those attempts to assimilate were rejected. Within the framework of sensibilities that shape attitudes in the folk/popular context, however, preservation of an alternative system of cultural affirmation is not based on a frustrated aspiration to remove cultural difference but on a sense of always knowing the difference; of always knowing that affirmation would not come from the dominant culture but would be generated from within. Rather than being initially concerned with removing cultural difference, folk popular sensibilities highlight and celebrate cultural difference and the possibility of self-affirmation it offers. Rather than being a sign of stigma, cultural difference is embraced as something valuable that black people "own," which validates their own distinctive sense of their humanity, independent of the oppressive mainstream.

The Medium Is the Music

At the core of this indigenous cultural framework are African-influenced religious and spiritual sensibilities. But music, easily transversing boundaries between sacred and secular dominions, is that core's principal medium of transmission. Music is the ethereal medium through which African influenced sensibilities flow, the framework that supports the structure, the mortar that holds it tight, the palpable substance that makes it real, the extra-corporeal soul that gives it life.

In a previous chapter I proposed that forms of music have been the definitive voice in the documentation of experience and history within the folk/popular cultural milieu. Therefore, music has been essential in interpreting the experiences of blacks. In addition to manifesting the aspect of duality that involves adaptation of Western forms to contain, house, and express an essence comprised of sensibilities derived from an African heritage, musical transformations incorporate social sentiments peculiar to historical moments in which they emerge—reflecting unique conditions shaping African American social reality and cultural expression in given periods and contexts. Implicitly, these observations point to the importance of popular music in the construction of historical impressions that accurately and comprehensively reflect the experiences of black folks at any given point.

As an example of a social theme, it has been established that the blues developed in the southern rural black culture of the late nineteenth century.[3] Blues represents on one level an amalgamation of Western form (the 12-bar, standard 1-4-5 chord structure of Western folk music) and African essence (especially melodic improvisation, including use of melisma ("smeared tones") and blue notes (tones that do not appear in the standard Western diatonic scale). On another level, the blues is informed socially by sentiments peculiar to the African American experience at that historical moment in which it emerged. In particular, the betrayal of Reconstruction after 1877 taught the newly emancipated blacks that, in the words of a contemporary white blues-influenced songwriter, "freedom is just another word for nothin' left to lose."[4]

In this regard, perhaps the most brilliant and enduring assertion in LeRoi Jones's landmark analysis of the social context of black music is his association of blues—evolved in the rural world of late-nineteenth-century sharecroppers—with this ultimate betrayal of black freedom that the faith of slave-era spirituals had prophesied. Only as ostensibly "free" persons whose freedom was cynically betrayed, Jones stated, did blacks have the experience to create the blues.[5] At least as much as any of the poignant renderings of educated leaders, protesters, poets, or other voices of the elite leadership class, the blues expresses the tragicomic irony and pathos arising from the circumstances of black Emancipation and betrayal that led to the Jim Crow era. Representations of this critical junction in black history (post-Reconstruction nineteenth century) seem incomplete if they do not prominently privilege the information and sentiment incorporated in this body of cultural expression. Indeed, it is generally true that any aspect of the African American experience must be augmented with the perspective found in the folk/popular tradition in order to be accurate and comprehensive. Typically, however, traditional literate historical and interpretive approaches to presenting black history and culture tend to undervalue the experiences of those folk.

The transformative paradigm developed here incorporates this aspect of duality—reflected in the "division of cultural labor" that Richard Thomas noted (see chapter 5)—as the basis for discerning what might be seen as two different, distinguishable but related perspectives on African American cultural history. One perspective would be derived from the legacies of those who were free or otherwise removed from the experiences of the masses of enslaved African Americans. This view emphasizes the antebellum northern urban community of free blacks, dating from colonial times, which was based in the northeastern cities of Boston, New York, and Philadelphia and contained many of the historically visible black leaders of the nineteenth century.

They were continually involved with progressive ideas and political struggle. However, culturally this community was divorced from the rural folk sensibilities of the vast majority of blacks of that time, and tended to embrace the forms of the American mainstream. For example, the nineteenth-century northern black church, while providing a vocal and effective antislavery leadership vanguard, employed a worship style more like the white denominations from which they emerged than like the heavily Africanized worship style of the enslaved brothers and sisters on whose behalf they campaigned. Specifically, the musical repertoire of southern black folk church was wholly different from that of the northern independent black churches, which evolved directly from northern white Protestant denominations. According to Portia Maultsby, the church services of this elite middle class "strictly followed the established liturgy and sang from the official hymnal."[6]

Of course the separation between the religious worship experiences of northern and southern blacks is not complete. There are continuities that flow from the involvement of northern churches with abolition, their role in helping escaped slaves, and the consequent presence of southern-bred blacks in their congregations. However, in a trend that has been consistent when southern black culture is transplanted in the North, southern black folkways are scorned and discouraged by northern blacks, who see them as a mark of difference that, in the context of

American racism, is a badge of inferiority. Thus, officials of black independent churches noted harshly that some in the congregation were "clapping and stamping the feet in a ridiculous and heathenish way." Such behaviors constituted "undesirable practices," and northern clergy "seemed to associate demonstrative forms of religious expression with the 'unenlightened.'"[7]

Again, Afrocentrism, either in the approach represented by Molefi Asante, or Maulana Karenga's more pragmatically oriented one, is not able to make these significant distinctions in its conception of how African Americans are, in fact, culturally and historically related to Africa. Asante, commenting on expressions of nineteenth-century black abolitionist oratory (much of it housed in the northern black churches), notes that *nommo*, the African invocation of the power of the spoken word, is "not clearly sensed in . . . the political and social rhetoric of Afro-Americans [in this period]. Probably only within the religious experience, when worshippers and leaders . . . interact does this concept blossom into its full communicative significance."[8]

This observation seems to obscure critical factors that distinguish the northern independent institutional church from the southern folk church. Many of the northern leaders were in fact involved with the northern independent black church movement. However, by imposing his Afrocentric paradigm on northern leaders like Delany and Garnet, and by not differentiating between cultural practices of the northern and southern black churches, Asante's analysis does not acknowledge how the various actors in this passage have different connections along a high/elite-folk/popular continuum that differentiates a spectrum of cultural orientations among blacks. The sensibilities that circumscribe and define the unique characteristics of African American worship styles are not operative in the context of the nineteenth-century northern black church. Those religious practices Asante associates with nommo (call-response, emotional worship, possessions rituals) are, in the nineteenth century, associated with southern black religious practice that is culturally closer to Africa and therefore more Afrocentric in this regard.

Karenga, in his treatment of the historical role of the church, points to the distinction at the same time that he determines to erase it. He notes that although previous research "divides the church into the 'invisible church' in slavery and the institutional church which began with the founding [in the North] of the African Methodist Episcopal Church in 1778 and the first African Baptist church in 1788, for the purpose of this section and to stress historical continuity, the division will not be made."[9] Apparently the "purpose of this section" is to stress a "historical continuity" that is, in fact, not present, given the cultural discontinuities that differentiate the two religious traditions. Again, however, the imposition of the Afrocentrist concept in this case obscures this fact.

From the standpoint of the high/elite perspective cultural transformation in the modern, urban context is seen to occur in New York (as reflected by the Harlem Renaissance) and the East, nurtured by influxes of blacks from all sectors.[10] However, blues, spirituals, gospels, and other music forms along the blues continuum, which Jones felt was an authentic, grassroots reflection of the black experience of any given period, are clearly created from the experience of those folk masses, who were captive in the southern rural economy through the slave period and into the twentieth century urban migration period. From the standpoint of this folk/popular experience the transformation to urban forms might be seen as an impulse that went first up the Mississippi Valley from New Orleans to Memphis, Kansas City, St. Louis, Chicago, Detroit, or other places to be transformed before going east, or later west, to be recognized.[11]

As told in the folk/popular voice the model for the flowering of African American culture in an urban setting—visible as the Harlem Renaissance among "literati"—was in place at the turn of the century, actually before the bulk of the northern migration occurred. New Orleans, with one of the largest urban concentrations of African Americans in the late nineteenth century, is specifically important in this regard. The city provided many of the elements that would make up modern urban black culture from the aesthetic and social elements that merged with the ancestral spirits of that city's Congo Square, from the 1890s through the early twentieth century. The Crescent City was a crucible in which these sensibilities were forged, and out of which boiled the major musical innovation in North American history, the musical form which sprang into the wider culture as "jazz."

This original "New Orleans synthesis" involved Euro-American forms, instruments, and influences but was grounded wholly within a black, folk/popular reference frame. The city's large black population—especially large after hardening post-Reconstruction laws defined the numerous light-skinned Creoles as black for segregation purposes—provided aesthetic elements, social context, and economic support for this musical transformation. The Creole tradition, forced by Jim Crow to socially redirect itself, brought band instruments and European training and performance styles. Creole bands (said to be adapted from French tradition of military marching bands), string orchestras, and other musical ensemble forms contributed these new instruments and instrumental arrangements that—like ragtime in relation to the piano—could be used to re-express African-derived rhythmic, tonal, and improvisational sensibilities provided mostly by uptown blacks.

The New Orleans tradition of brothels (as in its much-remembered Storyville red-light district), sporting establishments, and the like made it a significant center of ragtime piano music, since such establishments were prime employers of ragtime players.[12] Through jazz's developmental years, Mardi Gras, funeral and other parades, picnics, dances, private parties, and other mostly but not entirely black affairs also provided an economy sufficiently organized to support jazz's innovators at the turn of the century.[13]

Blues, as a musical force and as a philosophy of life, came with the increasing numbers of residents from the Delta areas in Mississippi and other rural enclaves. In New Orleans and other black urban environments, the equivalent of the field holler—described as the roots from which rural blues grew in the late 1800s[14]—was heard in the cries and chants of street hawkers selling vegetables and other goods, each with their unique cry, who sometimes accompanied themselves on harmonica or homemade flute.[15]

Western Form, African Essence

Evolving from this dynamic context, jazz (like ragtime, which developed from similar contexts) illustrates how the emergence of new forms involves the ascendance or reemphasis of African-derived musical sensibilities that are retained in the folk, popular, or traditional African American cultural reference frame and contribute critically to the periodic reformation of distinctive musical forms. Piano ragtime was achieved from the imposition of African rhythmic patterns on piano playing styles—a syncopated attack on Western musicological sensibility that subordinated and extended Western harmonic concepts with the drive of African polyrhythms, and in the process transformed the piano into a rhythm instrument.

With jazz's emergence, instruments designed in the European literate tradition of "reading" music fixed on paper were adapted to the African oral tradition of finding it "by ear." Led or directed by fluid, syncopated rhythmic patterns, this "aural" proficiency enables melodic variation, or improvisation. Ensembles comprised of those instruments—which in the

European tradition play fixed arrangements together—were redefined to accommodate fluid flights of polyphony in which the various instruments collectively improvised melodic variation on a polyrhythmic foundation.

Ragtime songs provided materials and concepts for adapting these instruments and arrangements to polyrhythmic and improvisational techniques in band performance. The multi-instrumental format, featuring several musicians instead of just one piano player—allowed a geometrical increase of layers of rhythmic complexity and degrees of improvisational freedom.[16] Blues contributed an approach, a performance style, a body of melodies, a "vocal tonality" (techniques that shape the sound of instruments—especially in jazz horns—to imitate the human voice, recalling the rural cries, moans, and field hollers), and a pattern of improvisational interplay.

This saturation of Western form with African music sensibility imbues the emotional directness—a unity between composition and performance—characteristic of black performance styles. From this synthesis emerged a unique musical form that still reemphasized black aesthetic and cultural sensibilities in the form of African-derived orality and rhythmicity.

During jazz's early formative period—from the mid-1890s until around 1905—the new sound was largely invisible to whites, indistinguishable from the honky-tonk and ragtime music associated with fast, sinful living.[17] Charles "Buddy" Bolden—a musical ancestor claimed by virtually every one of the early New Orleans innovators—was trying his new sound as early as 1895. And though their eventual contribution to jazz was considerable, the light-skinned Creoles initially scorned Bolden's new sound as honky-tonk music.[18] Meanwhile "Papa" Jack Laine, considered a "white father" of New Orleans Jazz, claims he had never heard of him at this point, although he apparently was familiar with some of the Creole players.[19]

Resisted by the established Creole musical community, and unnoticed by the adjacent white culture, jazz clearly emerged as a phenomenon of the folk/popular masses, the least structurally and culturally assimilated sector of the community.[20] By 1905, however, black New Orleans was thoroughly in tune with the new music. Creole musicians had been won over, or had adapted to it by necessity, and over the next ten years the rest of the city followed suit.[21] From these rich beginnings jazz innovators eventually moved up the Mississippi Valley to Chicago (also Kansas City and St. Louis), where jazz's potency spread into the consciousness of a broader world and became a social phenomenon.[22]

As innovations like ragtime and jazz emerge from such relatively unassimilated cultural spaces they become visible to some whites, who view them initially from the safety of their own side of the cultural boundary. Assessment of the role of white attitudes toward expressions of African cultural sensibility in this process is confounded by several factors. White America has often become exposed to emerging forms of black popular music, for example, as part of some more general confrontation of social mores and cultural sensibilities in which the source of these innovations is invariably dehumanized and devalued. Thus, whites' consistent interest in black rhythmic/musical sensibilities is often obscured or distorted by racist habits of thought and association that provoke suppression and denial, even while conjuring powerful attractions. Aesthetic attraction produces dissonance that must be resolved by interpreting the attraction in ways consistent with the social construction of racial hierarchy.

Plantation diaries and antebellum travel reports consistently refer to whites' awareness of and interest in blacks' rhythmic sense, along with other cultural traits they found peculiar yet fascinating, whether in the context of religious worship, work practices, or other observed activities. Typical is the observation of George W. Moore regarding the mistress of the Baring plantation: "I have often seen Mrs. Baring, when the Negroes were singing, catch the motion of their bodies and do just as they did."[23]

Likewise, New Orleans's Congo Square attracted not only congregations of blacks who came to re-create aspects of the various African cultures from which they came, but also interested white observers, whose recorded fascination now forms part of our contemporary window to that time and place where African rhythms reverberated, possibly in their most potent form in North America, through much of the antebellum period and into the 1880s.[24]

From their side of the racial boundary, then, whites often describe their fascination, sometimes disguised as disgust or horror, in terms consistent with their own perceived cultural superiority. This framework of superiority is incompatible with recognition of innovation as genuine artistic or aesthetic achievement. Thus, as stated above, initial reaction to new forms of musical expression is consistently negative and resistant, at least on the surface. Ragtime, for instance, came to general awareness initially as part of the "sporting life"—a euphemism usually associated with brothels, bars, gambling establishments and other sites where sins of the spirit and flesh are partaken—and therefore rejected by "polite" society. Commenting in

1918 on what eventually turned out to be ragtime's redefinition of the American piano tradition, the New Orleans *Times-Picayune* instructed its readers that "[r]hythm, though often associated with melody and harmony, is not necessarily music." Indeed, it was an "atrocity in polite society, and . . . we should make it a point of civic honor to suppress it. Its musical value is nil, and its possibilities of harm are great."[25] Eventually, however, ragtime revolutionized American popular music, in addition to influencing European and American "serious" composers like Claude Debussy, Igor Stravinsky, and Charles Ives.[26]

Jazz was similarly associated with guilt in connection with the social environment of its formative period, which overlapped and paralleled that of ragtime in the late nineteenth century. Perhaps because its associated social activities were indeed probably quite familiar to most residents, the established press' first mention of jazz that was not derogatory did not occur until 1933, according to one source.[27]

As this summary suggests, the high/elite bias of some views of the black historical experiences likely parallels the contemporaneous rejection of folk/popular sensibilities that literate or more assimilated classes among blacks have always expressed to some degree. For example, during the Great Migration newly arrived southerners were encouraged to abandon their "country" ways on arrival, often through ridicule. In the view of the more assimilated northerners, distinct cultural traits evident in folk/popular language, music, or religious practice were too closely linked with stereotypes that they had struggled fervently to oppose, negate, and overcome. Such distinctive cultural traits contradicted the assimilationist strategy of maintaining there was no difference, other than skin color, between blacks and whites.

In resisting the raw sensibilities of the folk masses, many blacks who considered themselves sophisticated were following a sense of culture associated with the mainstream society. Even when positive images of an identifiable black culture were expressed in the Harlem Renaissance, the premise was that the development of "high" cultural forms based on black life would finally prove that blacks (the "New Negroes") deserved a place in the American mainstream. Significantly, the music that developed in black urban areas during this period was not recognized by many artists of the Renaissance as the musical analogue of what they themselves were expressing literarily about the so-called New Negro. (Langston Hughes deserves mention as the most prominent exception to this tendency.) The closer the music was to the traditional folk roots of rural black culture, the more "gutbucket" and disdainful it was considered.[28]

On the other hand, the overall working-class, southern-folk character of the new urban black culture was more predominant in northern cities like Detroit and Chicago, cities whose great industrial capacities attracted a large proportion of the migration. In such areas, the folk/popular sensibilities imported from the South found root in spite of initial rejection by northerners. Chicago, for example, was not only the blues center of the North in the early part of the century, but was also the place where Louis Armstrong and his contemporaries were transformed from traditional New Orleans band musicians to pace-setting jazz innovators. Then he went to New York to facilitate the spread of jazz into the consciousness of the mainstream culture.

Thus, despite initial resistance and ridicule from more assimilated blacks, from middle or upper-class blacks, and from the mainstream culture, innovations in language, music, and other forms of expressive culture manage to survive and diffuse into the wider culture in a very consistent manner. Repeatedly over time, new forms emerge from the folk/popular traditions, survive initial criticism and rejection, and become definitive cultural reference points for African Americans as well as pervasive influences in the wider culture. The fact that jazz, ragtime, R&B, and other forms have become firmly entrenched in American musical culture in spite of typical resistance and rejection by both whites and mainstream-oriented blacks suggests a kind of authenticity—as a voice for the masses of blacks as well as in terms of maintaining African-derived, distinctly black cultural sensibilities—that mainstream culture fails to negate. Indeed, such innovation is eventually recognized to have authenticity, vitality, or other relevant expressive qualities by those—among blacks and in the wider culture—who initially resist or reject it.

From Folk to Popular

As modernity has progressed in the twentieth century, the degree and level of isolation characterizing the social and cultural distances among groups of African Americans, as well as between blacks and the mainstream, has been altered. Concurrently, the dynamics that keep black culture distinct, even as it is transformed in conjunction with mainstream cultural interaction, have become more complicated and salient. Several issues of modernization affect this process.

To begin with, the march of modernity has caused the folk/popular reference frame to move along the continuum, becoming less "folk" and more "popular." Beginning with the phonograph, and continuing through today's computerized, synthesized music and recording devices, technology has profoundly influenced both the nature of the sound, as well as the way in which the sound comes to the audience, or consumer. The minute the blues was recorded, and could therefore be heard outside of the actual context in which the sounds were made, and even by people who—because they were not black—had little emotional or psychological connection to the experience that created the blues, the music lost some of its character of traditional folk culture and took on a little of the modern character of popular culture.

Moreover, as part of engaging the evolution of popular culture from premodern folk cultural roots, modern technology, media, and various other factors have appeared to blur the distinction between what music or culture is or is not black. The blurring begins with the involvement of those who control entertainment and recording businesses in determining who and what is heard. As the business side of popular culture has developed, control over the music entertainment industry by others has affected the ability of black performers to determine the output of their own creative impulses. When record companies discovered in the 1920s that a market existed in the newly migrated, folk-urban community for their so-called "race records," their business interest started to become a determinant of the kind of music those communities heard. Recorded blues were, therefore, less directly a reflection of folk cultural sensibility than were forms of blues performed live as part of an indigenous, folk context.

Recorded music coexisted with, but did not preempt, live performance as the primary context in which music was heard by most black people until perhaps the late 1950s and early 1960s. Since then, with the introduction of sophisticated recording and music synthesizing technology, it seems safe to say that what happens in recording studios is a more important determinant of how popular music develops than any indigenous performance context (except possibly the church). That is, it *seemed* safe to say, until hip-hop boiled up from the street cultures of an emerging "underclass" of "maroons" during the current period.

Popular culture, then, involves the packaging and commercial redistribution of elements of folk cultural expression, a process which itself influences the direction of erstwhile indigenous cultural impulses. While this discussion has been mostly focused on music as a form of cultural expression, changes in its development as a cultural medium are related to more general changes in culture and society, black and white, as the highly industrialized, highly urbanized, supposedly highly civilized society we live in has ensnared more and more of humanity in its web of profit and deceit. The fact that the purely folk character of the culture is changed is therefore consistent with the fact that the purely folk character of the experience has changed. Popular culture remains an authentic expression of distinctive sensibility as well as community sentiment, as long as one recognizes that the "folk" themselves are products of these transforming experiences. The folk-popular continuum has become less folk and more popular. Many other agents, institutions, and forces now stand between the act of creation and the act of celebration of musical culture. This correlates with the fact that culture, social and individual identity, and community life in general are similarly more complex relative to the past.

Another aspect of modern complexity and blurring of distinctions, in conjunction with cultural and technological modernity, is manifest when black artists change and tailor their styles to appeal to nonblack audiences. Especially since the 1960s the strategy of appealing purposely to white audiences, perhaps as a kind of economic protection against white appropriation, has been successful for a number of black artists who have tailored their music for the so-called "cross-over" market. Many artists, from Motown to Prince to Ice Cube, have appealed to this extremely lucrative audience while maintaining their black following. Today, some see more confusion regarding these distinctions in the "reverse cross-over" phenomenon, when white artists so successfully incorporate musical styles associated with rhythm and blues that even blacks listen to them. These tendencies, in addition to the existence of groups comprising mixed nationalities, have made it less accurate to speak of black popular music than of the "black influence on popular music."

Nonetheless, the complexity of blurring and changing cultural lines increases rather than diminishes the salience of the fundamental theme of duality in the black experience and further complicates the dynamics of culture and identity for African Americans in the context of postmodern society. One side of an individual or collective African American psyche might accept such blurring of boundaries as an aspect of progress with respect to recognition and valuation of black culture and humanity in the wider culture. However, another side of an individual or collective psyche might interpret the loss of cultural distinctiveness as a negative event—indeed, as a loss of self.

Thus, it appears the attraction of whites to black musical forms contradicts or interferes with the function of those forms as markers of a distinctly black cultural reference frame—especially the folk/popular reference frame of blacks who are the least mainstream oriented. Put another way, as new forms emerge to influence and even dominate mainstream musical culture, so also do events that lead to appropriation, on various levels, of such aesthetic innovation by the white-dominated wider culture. One aspect of this process is the tendency of the forms to become dissociated from the African American experiential context that created them in the discourse and perceptual framework of the white-dominated mainstream. Actually, it seems more accurate to say that for the white-dominated mainstream the separation of the musical phenomenon from the people, and hence from previous negative associations with black people and black culture, is a necessary accommodation to the accomplished fact that such penetration has occurred, in spite of previous criticism and rejection.

At the point at which ragtime's influence was expressed in the work of classical composers, the "influence" seemed to be far separated from the folk and the experience that created it. As part of a "classical" composition, or a popular show tune, the rhythmic influence of ragtime (the name came from the fact that the syncopated rhythmic approach sounded like "ragged time" to Western ears attuned to conventional rhythm) had become diluted and was no longer connected to blackness, or to the stigmatized association with "low" life and culture.

In addition to separation of the aesthetic and experiential dimensions, it also seems that the perception of economic value, and the subsequent impact of market forces, contribute to this dissociative tendency. In the case of jazz both aspects are evident. The process of obscuring the association between black culture and jazz was evident even before most New Orleans jazz players had been heard by outsiders. Although riverboats and vaudeville tours had been spreading the new jazz sound over many regions in the early 1900s, what became widely accepted as jazz were derivations of the original "New Orleans synthesis" that came into wide popularity following the first release of a jazz record made by the white—and inappropriately named—"Original Dixieland Jazz Band" in 1917.[29] In other words, by the early 1920s—when New Orleans originals like King Oliver and his cornetist, Louis Armstrong, pianist Jelly Roll Morton, and reed-player Sidney Bechet had settled in Chicago to further develop and expose the new art form—jazz was already, in the minds of many, associated with white musicians. Armstrong and Ferdinand "Jelly Roll" Morton, pivotal figures linking New Orleans jazz with future forms, were in their most fertile, creative, and innovative periods during the twenties.[30] Under the precepts of the recording industry's segmented marketing systems, however, recordings of their music were distributed on "race record" labels geared specifically to blacks, and remained invisible to most whites.[31] By that time music recorded by white dance bands, led by Paul Whiteman, was being introduced to mainstream whites as "jazz" through record labels and performance venues specifically marketed to them.

Twenties "symphonic jazz" was not particularly or closely associated with blackness or with the "low culture" contexts in which these forms arose. Whiteman ostensibly performed "symphonic" jazz by "taming" its "primitive rhythms" and making it more acceptable to white audiences.[32] The ironic result of this appropriation is that the music eventually lost much of the emotional directness and rhythmic vitality that made it distinctive and provoked attraction in the first place.

In cultivating and exploiting this audience Whiteman exemplifies an especially odious result of this pattern of appropriation: reaping value and economic profit from aesthetic innovations emerging from the tradition of cultural sensibility among the masses, the common, the ordinary blacks, who remain mostly as disadvantaged, and disfranchised as ever. Whiteman became "King of Jazz" in this market, grossing one million dollars in a single year during the 1920s.[33]

Among Armstrong's white fans during his early days in Chicago was a group of high school age youths, several of whom later became important jazz figures. This group included Bix Beiderbecke, described in most sources as the best white jazzman of the latter 1920s.[34] From his apprenticeship in Chicago, Beiderbecke went on to facilitate the spread of jazz with the Wolverines, a young white band that played colleges, amusement parks, and resorts throughout the Midwest during the early 1920s.[35] Among the white dance bands he enlivened later in his career was the Whiteman band, where his presence no doubt constituted the closest that band came to having an authentic jazzman.

Meanwhile, Jelly Roll and several other original innovators were ending their lives in ignominious obscurity by the time band jazz became "swing" in the thirties. Regarding Jelly Roll, who died in 1941, one writer observed, "In Morton's fifty-six years . . . are to be found the whole course of ragtime and jazz, their acceptance, their rejection, their triumphs, and their subtle spurious "improvement" by the music business, the swift alternations of the true masters between comparative riches and fame, and complete oblivion."[36] Armstrong was more fortunate, although his earnings were less than one-tenth of Whiteman's.[37] Though many came to associate his popularity with "Uncle Tomism," his career and fame survived through the thirties, in part because he *did* successfully appeal to whites as well as blacks.

Some (for example, Whiteman) might be guilty of crass commercial exploitation of aesthetic innovation; but it would be inaccurate to say that, once a form is accepted into the broader cultural milieu, *individuals* orchestrate the struggle over what the valued phenomenon is and who "owns" it. This process of appropriation often has indifferent or tragic results for black innovators. Attitudes and orientations among whites who are owners, producers, agents, and performers may range from cynically exploitive to wholly or at least relatively sympathetic, like Bix Beiderbecke, Benny Goodman, or Johnny Otis (a white "rhythm-and-blues" pioneer). Regarding the results, in which white participants are disproportionately recognized, rewarded, and compensated, it may be that the exploitive individuals are more numerous or more powerful. Or such results may simply illustrate that this struggle for "cultural ownership" is perhaps not especially a struggle of individuals—that systemic forces are prominent in this process. The effects of racism, prejudice, and stereotypes, along with custom and "habits of thought," on white-dominated mainstream social, institutional, economic structures seem to lead inexorably to reproduction of patterns of inequality of recognition and compensation based on race without needing a self-conscious conspiracy of individuals.

Indeed, the outcomes seem oblivious to the individual wills of the Bix Beiderbeckes, Benny Goodmans, Elvis Presleys, and John Lennons of the music world. Beiderbecke is often considered a sympathetic character in the story of jazz, and some even portray him as another victim of the process of appropriation.[38] Still, market segregation practices of that time meant that the millions he may have played for had never heard of Armstrong, much less appreciated and appropriately rewarded his contributions to America's most original art form. Beiderbecke's presence in various white bands in the segregated music world of the 1920s helped spread the idea of jazz as a music not connected with the black experience, no matter Beiderbecke's will or intention.

As forms of jazz developed into the 1930s, the emergence of white swing bands and the depression helped further legitimize the idea that jazz was not connected to black culture. The precise arranged style of "swinging" that became the national phenomenon emerged among a group of black bands (Fletcher Henderson, Don Redman, Duke Ellington, Jimmie Lunceford, among others) who played regularly for predominantly white audiences.[39] In adapting the "hot" style of playing to appeal to these audiences those black "pre-swing" bands may have been guided by an optimistic sense that their merit as musicians and entertainers would be recognized, accepted, and fairly rewarded. Likely, however, the very popularity among white audiences of the arranged "riffing" style that emerged between 1929 and 1935 contributed to its eventual appropriation and domination by whites. The combination of the effects of the depression on recording, broadcast, and performance, and the appropriation of the swing style in the appearance of white bands (led by Goodman's but including Artie Shaw, Glenn Miller, the Dorsey brothers, and a host of others) severely limited black exposure in this mainstream market and led to disproportionate distribution of the rewards and recognition of swing.

In the recording industry session, opportunities for black band musicians became severely limited during the thirties. Similarly, the lucrative big-band dance/concert circuit of the thirties and early forties featured fewer than a handful of blacks among the names associated with that storied era of swing. Moreover, so-called "jazz polls . . . began in the middle thirties wherein no Negro players won top positions, few Negroes even made the listings, and Harry James [Benny Goodman's trumpeter] invariably won top trumpet over Louis Armstrong."[40]

Fletcher Henderson's position as Goodman's chief arranger represented the proscribed pinnacle of mainstream recognition and compensation available to black musicians. Economics and recognition were not necessarily the most important terms in which losses were to be measured. Not only did the industry built from jazz—sprung from the very bosom of black life—not support black musicians economically, in the public mind the music itself was not even particularly associated with blackness. Jazz could no longer function as a living definition and affirmation of what it meant to be black in that time.

Appropriation and Cultural Meaning

As I discussed elsewhere, co-optation and expropriation of this kind tends to render innovations in areas such as music or language ineffective in a key culture function—that of marking and affirming black ethnicity and identity.[41] Moreover, such episodes or tendencies are consistently accompanied or followed by innovations that refocus and reemphasize black sensibilities, allowing reformation of indigenous African American identities once again set off from whites. In the area of music this usually involves reemphasis of rhythmic and polyrhythmic techniques and other aspects of the orality of Africa's heritage.

Like Congo Square—which allowed a maximum degree of coalescence and coherence among African slaves from many different cultures, in an environment outside of the immediate purview of their dominators—each innovative period or context features increased cohesion among blacks (including erstwhile disparate elements) as a community as a result of both external and internal factors. The New Orleans jazz synthesis occurred during a period in which cohesion had been largely imposed by Jim Crow definitions of social orientation after the failure of Reconstruction. The sense of hopeful inclusion evident in the Jazz Age 1920s was betrayed during the thirties, when economic depression forced many musicians out of the mainstream music economy in the thirties.

Thus, in some ways this thrust toward new cohesion was imposed from without. As Jim Crow laws had forced uptown blacks and downtown Creoles together in New Orleans, so did depression economics force many who had thought in terms of an integrated musical universe to reconsider their options. Socially alienated and economically displaced, black musical practitioners looked inward—in terms of community, and perhaps also in the psychological sense—to find their aesthetic and economic constituency. And while the white icons of swing raked in the big bucks, black bands played to and were revitalized by all-black audiences on this "chitlin circuit."

In some ways this turning inward was an aesthetic choice. With swing, the rhythmic sense of jazz became watered down and improvisation became limited and restrained. Before the stock market crash black musicians played venues in which they "used more and more Western song forms, incorporated Western harmony, and played for increasingly integrated audiences."[42] All-black bands on the "chitlin circuit," however, especially the Southwest circuit that included Kansas City, St. Louis, and Oklahoma, according to Jones, "had developed very much differently than the big Northeastern bands . . . They had always remained much closer to the older, blues tradition, even after they began to master some of the instrumental techniques of the Eastern bands, they still . . . relied heavily on the blues."[43]

Popular on that circuit was the band led by Bennie Moten and later by Count Basie, where many future innovators, including Lester Young and Charlie Parker, served apprenticeships.[44] In addition to theaters and other venues that catered to blacks, this "chitlin circuit" included small clubs in city neighborhoods, southern rural roadhouses, and private house or rent parties—especially in the South, Southwest, and Midwest regions, where African American folk masses have historically been concentrated. These were settings for a revitalization, a reconnection to indigenous roots, to primordially African rhythms, residing as they always have in the cultural world of the folk masses.

Relieved of the necessity, and stripped of the motivation, to alter their expressive mode to appeal to white sensibilities, black musicians found the space and the means to refresh their musical art by emphasizing those elements that made performance spaces distinctly African American, remaking black identity in cultural terms, re-forming the framework of ethnicity that defined blackness and distinguished it from whiteness. Largely invisible to the swing mainstream, this flourishing black "underground" moved the contemporary black expressive forms away from assimilationist pretensions and back toward the folk/popular/African roots of core African American culture.

Thus, the folk/popular tradition continues to function as the primary source of cultural continuity—and of "authenticity" regarding living connections to an African heritage—in the modern context, in spite of the complicating factors cited above. So that while band jazz was appropriated to the national phenomenon of "swing"—centered at the communication distribution points on the East and West coasts—groups of black musicians based in the South and Southwest—the Memphis–Kansas City connection—delivered unappropriated, blues-based forms of band jazz to black folk in communities throughout the urban diaspora. Harbored in this musical community were the innovators of two forms of music that would revitalize black music in the post–World War II period—forms that became known as "rhythm and blues" and "bebop."

The boppers launched a revolution based on the merging of sophisticated harmonic theory and technical virtuosity with a retrieval and restatement of basic African sensibilities of rhythm and melodic improvisation. "Jump blues," the black popular music that emerged after the war to become known as "rhythm and blues," is my main concern here in documenting the evolving folk/popular tradition or reference frame. R&B took its rhythmic pulse from the boogie-woogie sounds emerging from thirties' underground culture—a "fast shuffle" that anchored a pulsating dance rhythm at rent parties and juke joints. It came with an attitude that projected much more of what was considered unpretentious, down to earth— even "raunchy" and "gutbucket"—about black life and much less of what was considered sophisticated and highfalutin; as if deliberately making cultural space between itself and perceived mainstream sensibilities; as if their wish was to make sure they were not mistaken for someone trying to appeal to "white" or otherwise pretentious tastes.

As was the case with early jazz in New Orleans, some blacks—middle-class, assimilation minded, or ostensibly sophisticated—resisted the "ethnicity" evident in the new R&B, characterizing it as gutbucket and unrefined. And, as with the New Orleans synthesis, this "underground" was largely invisible to mainstream whites. Major record companies showed no initial interest in this "lower-class" black music. The result was that a bevy of smaller, independent record companies, some which were black owned and most of which more closely reflected folk/popular tastes and sensibilities, became important institutions in the "rhythm-and-blues world."[45]

Conceivably, early R&B's perceived raw, raunchy attitude made it unattractive to major companies, as it was for some middle-class blacks. It is also conceivable that this very attitude, along with the pulsating rhythm, *did* help make it attractive to some young whites. With radio playing an important role (records had been important in the 1920s and 1930s) the sound of R&B drifted in and apparently was music to the ears of a generation of young whites with or without reasons to rebel.[46] Eventually the R&B term "rock and roll" (which meant to have sex) became a label for music that included elements of R&B (for example, Bo Diddley, Chuck Berry, and Little Richard) and a lot of younger, mostly white, groups and musicians, like Elvis Presley and Bill Haley, trying to move with the pulsating rhythmic sense that drove R&B.

The initial rock 'n' roll explosion seemed to energize a new generation of white youth with its electrifying dance rhythms. As the dynamics of appropriation proceeded, however, the initial energy seemed to become diluted as even middle-of-the-road white entertainers attempted to rock and roll. As white imitations grew paler, with the "plastic posturings of the Fabians and . . . Avalons,"[47] it proved problematic for maintaining a sense of the distinctiveness and value of African American expressive culture. Nearly to the extreme of Whiteman's "symphonic jazz" in the twenties, this "rock 'n' roll" (later classic rock and disco) came to represent a redefinition of black music forms for nonblack uses. R&B\rock 'n' roll pioneer Little Richard clearly understood this, reminiscing on a Home Box Office television special how a version his rock anthem, "Tutti Frutti," reached the number-one spot on the pop charts: "By Pat Boone," he said, grimacing to the camera.

Soul music, which flowered in the sixties, seemed in part a reaction to the rock 'n' roll appropriation of earlier forms. Aesthetically, the evolution of R&B into soul music emerged from fifties innovators like Ray Charles and Sam Cooke, who obliterated tenuous barriers between sacred and secular worlds, bringing gospel-inflected harmonies and gospel-style fervor (and call-response rhythmicity) to their decidedly secular performances.[48] It functioned to reestablish a distinctive black musical sound, an instrument of cultural cohesion, in context with the shared consciousness and heightened cohesion accruing within the social movements of that period.

Soul music's effectiveness as an instrument of cultural cohesion, as well as of musical innovation, was in part related to the mainstream music industry's inability to control it. Although many of the early companies specializing in R&B were no longer in business, independents still controlled the market as soul music bloomed through the sixties. The most important were New York–based Atlantic Records, Motown in Detroit, and Stax-Volt out of Memphis, Tennessee.[49] With these legendary "indies" continuously pumping out soulful sounds, the pale imitations offered by major companies during the late fifties and early sixties were of small effect.

By the middle 1970s, the apparent success of the previous decades' movements may have led some to believe that the cohesion of the sixties was less necessary and less relevant. In the early 1970s, when the "heart of soul" had moved from the Detroit-Memphis-Chicago triangle to Philadelphia (specifically, to the studios of Philadelphia International Records), many who began as lower-class adherents of soul experienced upward mobility in the wake of the 1960s' movements for equality.

The "sound of Philadelphia" moved toward smoothness and commercialism on the one hand and slid down into funk on the other. By the end of the 1970s, commercial funk amalgamated into disco, and the end of a trail defined by both generation and class was reached.[50] Disco emerged after the dominant black or black-oriented independent record companies came under influence or control of major record companies and other large corporations.[51] Once again, music forms from African American innovation and creativity became redefined, aesthetically and culturally, as a result of white participation.

In the 1970s, however, after furious evolution of media and communications techniques, popular dance music could not be as easily or completely divorced from black culture as it was in the 1920s or 1930s. In the earlier period market channels were so separate that blacks who were "lined up for Bessie [Smith] or Ma [Rainey], never heard of Paul Whiteman," and vice versa.[52] In the later period, the channels of cultural separation were, by comparison, considerably more porous. Eventually, however, the notion that "raceless disco" meant "white" in the dominant reference frame became as clear as the image of actor John Travolta, whose "white-dancin'-fool" character in the movie *Saturday Night Fever* became for the mainstream the disco star of the 1970s. Moreover, the brazen attempt of Music Television (MTV) to take to the air with virtually no videos by black musicians (rationalized again in terms of its projected "mainstream" or "classic rock" market) showed a still-enduring tendency to redefine blackness out of mainstream conceptions of popular music, in spite of its thunderously obvious presence.

Class separations and ideological inconsistencies evident in other areas of black life in that period were manifest in music as well at this time. While images of disco–pseudo sophistication dominated the 1970s, the countercurrents of regeneration—a "funk underground" or counterculture can also be found in that same period. More visible than the depression-era underground, this strain of popular-culture innovation was still significantly removed from the mainstream venues where disco reigned among sophisticates of all colors.

Like other innovations in black music history, the emergence of funk in the 1970s involved a new synthesis of mainstream form with essential black rhythmicity. Electrified instruments, instrumental techniques, along with the form of self-contained bands were adapted from the rock world of that era. As is usual in such instances, cultural absorption involved subordinating this technology and instrumentation to the primacy of an African-derived rhythmic sense. The resulting sound rejected the pretentious sophistication of disco in favor of the melodically stripped-down, rhythmically souped-up riffs of James Brown's "JBs," George Clinton's "P-Funk," and other stars of seventies funk. The sound was especially audible in the South and Midwest, where black community concentrations abounded, while it was heard less distinctly around the East and West coasts, where disco chic was all the rage.[53]

During the thirties the cultural underground provided a context for reenergizing black musical sensibilities, for incubation of bebop and R&B, new forms that emerged during the following decade. During the late seventies, while the sophisticated, the elegant, and the beautiful queued up outside the popular discos downtown, a scruffier, more streetwise constituency held forth in the uptown "joints," where elements of the dominant sound of the next decade met and mixed; elements that erupted in the eighties as rap and hip-hop, newly "radicalized" forms that began once again the pattern of diffusing into and transforming mainstream culture itself.

The Folk/Popular and the Folks

Thus, the added complexity of modernity has not changed the basic dynamics of innovation, interaction, and diffusion with respect to African American musical sensibility. Despite blurred or changing cultural boundaries, a discernible folk/popular strain of African American culture remains the chief source of distinctiveness, as well as the main source of innovation, regarding black musical sensibility. In spite of modern complexity, the black culture of celebration and renewal continues to revitalize itself by refocusing basic sensibilities retained within a folk/popular cultural tradition. The recent eruption of black urban youth culture as hip-hop and rap illustrates the continuation of these dynamics.

The elements and techniques that produce rap involve both retrieval and restatement of African indigenous cultural traits and sensibilities, and redirection of technology, instrumentation, and musical forms available in the wider culture. Oral rapping is, in fact, as old as African culture itself. In African American culture rap has been present in many forms. The streets of my own childhood in the 1950s still reverberated with the oral raps of a previous generation called the "Toasts." Like today's rap they were considered vulgar and existed as a part of an underground culture. Today's urban culture combines traditional orality with an intense emphasis on rhythm in the delivery of the rap.

Originally, raps were delivered by disc jockeys playing records in dance clubs and private parties. They would talk over the records, often attempting to enliven the dance floor by imploring dancers with call-response exhortations, like "Everybody say yeah!" and "Par-teee!" In form and substance they were also drawing on a tradition of earlier black radio personality DJs, who used rhyme and clever language to enliven their broadcasts.

The disco-era practice of blending the bass lines and rhythm of the record ending on one turntable with the one beginning on another—allowing the dance crowd to "boogie on" nonstop—required the DJ to manually stop or move one of the turntables ahead or backward to synchronize the rhythm. One technique that came from these early practices was "scratching"—that is, creating rhythmic patterns using the scratching sound caused by the phonograph needle when records were moved manually.

Sometimes the DJ would switch back and forth between turntables, moving the needle back and forth, playing the same snatches of music over and over while rapping over the music. This led to "sampling"—another technique that became a regular part of rap production. "Sampling" now involves new and sophisticated audio technologies that capture (usually in digitized form) segments of rhythmic and instrumental background from existing songs. These segments are then used to build musical backgrounds for new rap songs. (As suggested above, musical material from the "funk underground" rather than the mainstream disco culture provided these samples. In particular, James Brown was sampled more than any other single act, leading him to launch a lawsuit against several rap groups.)

These techniques illustrate again how black musical innovation consistently involves redirection, or use of existing technology and instrumentation in ways and for purposes other than those for which they were designed. It is comparable, for example, to the way ragtime and boogie-woogie piano players essentially turned the piano into a rhythm instrument; or the way that horn players have developed techniques that allow them to project qualities of the human voice in their instruments' sounds, or that extend the range of their instruments. (According to one saxophone player, "false fingerings" have extended the tenor sax's pitch through most of the alto range, making the alto sax itself unnecessary and accounting for the dearth of alto players on the jazz scene.)[54]

As early rhythm and blues expressed a rejection of attempted middle-class sophistication, today rap music also rejects pretentious sophistication in favor of knowing in the starkest terms "what time it is."[55] Like early rhythm and blues in the late 1940s, rap has survived and grown largely on independent record labels, despite lack of interest, rejection, and even attempted suppression on the part of the mainstream record companies and radio stations.[56] Rejection, criticism, and attempted censorship by mainstream whites and blacks has not prevented young blacks from identifying strongly with rap music and hip-hop cultural symbols like language, dress, and "attitude." Moreover, the significant and growing attraction of rap for some white middle-class youth affirms the historical pattern of diffusion of indigenous cultural sensibilities into the wider culture.

Regardless of its objectionable features, today's urban "street" culture has followed the historically consistent pattern of folk/popular innovation, reaching out and embedding itself—making its mark—in the wider culture at large, despite the objections, resistance, and rejection of more respectable, refined folk. In redirecting and subordinating Western form, technology, and instrumentation to the imperatives of African rhythmicity and orality, hip-hop continues the folk/popular tradition of interaction, innovation, and transformation in which elements that redefine the distinctiveness of black culture emerge from the least-assimilated sectors of black communities.

Moreover, like the blues a century ago, rap/hip-hop is linked to social themes connected with the historical moments in which it emerged. In particular, there is a direct connection between the contemporary bursts of youth culture and the marooned "underclass" described by Wilson and other social scientists. Black youth culture in isolated urban areas directly reflects postwar structural changes, significantly exacerbated during the eighties, that marooned them outside the legitimate socioeconomic structure even while wealth was accruing and concentrating progressively at the top of the structure.[57] While it may be inaccurate, or overstated, to say that rap/hip-hop is *the* voice *of* this so-called black "underclass," it is pretty clearly *a* voice *from* that sector. It is an authentic voice, dense with social messages.

While widespread misogyny and vulgar sexuality are legitimately criticized, they are not the only, nor necessarily the essential, sentiments being expressed. More essential are messages about being "dissed" by a society that has seemingly tried to evolve without them, creating structural barriers that circumscribe the marooned "underclass" whence this radical voice comes. Like the stable boy in the *Emperor's New Clothes*, this group is most outside of the structure of legitimacy. Unlike the members of the court in the emperor's fable, they have no motivation to shape their perceptions to accord with mainstream expectations.

While the voice comes from that marooned sector, the frightful images and realities associated with the so-called "underclass" have a message for all of us. It is that we created them. We created the marooned socioeconomic island where they spawned. They are as much a core description of 1990s America as any of the rest of us, as much as President Bill Clinton or Bill Gates.

In the world these artists describe, police are viewed as violent enemies of the community, and may even be involved with drugs themselves; violence, vulgar sexual exploitation, and corruption are normative. This description is not as foreign, off the mark, or inaccurate as citizens of polite society might want to believe. Police brutality and corruption are significant issues affecting police-community relations in many communities. Sexual exploitation and other forms of corruption of human intimacy are significantly widespread behind veneers of respectability and propriety. Ruthlessness, driven by pursuit of profit, spans from the criminal underworld well into the arena of supposedly respectable enterprise. Drug abuse and other addictions are and always have been virtually equally widespread across race and class in a structure that better conceals, better protects, and better supports the activities of privileged groups.

The difference between the raw world reflected in youth culture and the supposedly polite world becomes frighteningly transparent when one looks twice at how some remarkably well-organized and efficient drug-dealing enterprises emerged in "maroon" areas; enterprises run by urban youth using standard business practices to build corporatelike enterprises. They are different from mainstream business organizations mainly in that their commodity of trade happens to be a harmful illegal substance (not that different from some perspectives) and that they are young, black, poor, and violent (use of violence may also be considered only a marginal difference of degree).[58]

If ever there was need for a good illustration of the anomie of pursuing "socially approved" goals through "socially disapproved means" (adding the caveat of socially disapproved people), such instances would appear to suffice. In addressing the crises gripping African American communities today, such themes should not be missed.

It is a message that may be hard put to get through. Rap and hip-hop image, energy, and culture have been gladly expropriated all through Hollywood and Madison Avenue. Yet the underclass, or marooned class, of young black males and females are currently under vilification, objects of ranges of fears; at risk and seemingly ready to be sacrificed.

In this chapter I have looked at how African American music has functioned, aesthetically and socially, to express and affirm black humanity in a variety of sociohistorical contexts. Chapter 8 will look at how initiatives connected with African American Studies (like Afrocentric curricula and Ebonics) have influenced public discourses in primary and secondary education. In addition, part of chapter 8's discussion will be an examination of how the frustration in the messages expressed in contemporary popular culture—palpably linked with the lack of access to approved means of mobility—might conceivably be channeled toward positive or productive outcomes.

Chapter 8

Crisis, Culture, and Literacy in the Community

With its origins in the social movements of the 1960s, Black Studies has always embraced an *instrumental* mission to change oppressive conditions in African American communities. This chapter explores potential roles for Black Studies in addressing contemporary problems that have endured through the 1990s, especially in those African American communities caught up in the urban crises of calcified poverty, blight, and decay. Framed in terms of the pursuit and practice of "freedom and literacy" the discussion starts with a look at how African American Studies is affecting public discourses, particularly in primary and secondary education. Then I explore further how concepts, policies, and interventions aimed at impacting the acute symptoms of social crises—approaches that link the African American Studies project with the special needs in these communities—might be developed.

This discussion is aimed at those connected to the policy development processes of institutions, such as education, public health, social welfare, and criminal justice, who must deal with constituencies of poor, black, or minority people and communities. These are individuals whose institutional role offers them opportunities to influence the definition of objectives and strategies of implementation in critical areas of public policy. The discussion is also aimed those, such as academics, intellectuals, and other professionals, who may be in a position to influence policy makers.

An important part of the historical mandate embraced by activists in the Black Studies movement was the instrumental mission to link processes of knowledge construction to processes of social change. In pursuing its *instrumental* mission, Black Studies activists have been like progressive intelligentsia in postcolonial settings throughout the world who have sought to transform educational processes to instruments of empowerment and liberation. Originating within the larger struggle for racial equality (and that within the larger domain of postwar anticolonial struggles) the Black Studies movement represented a quest not just for new knowledge but also for a blueprint to change the world.

As I had learned in graduate school, amidst the rich mixture of peoples of color who were my compatriots, the common history of oppression in connection with Western colonial dominance gave us much to share in the way of methods of struggle. The reflections of Paulo Freire, the Brazilian educator renown for his contributions to Third World literacy, ring true also as a prescription for Black Studies activists. "In reality, when you work toward convincing the students, your effort is in relation to a political victory that takes place outside of the university. Your act of convincing seeks to obtain support for your greater dream, not simply to be a good professor. If you accept that your teachings do not go beyond the wall, in my opinion you are making a mistake, that of elitism."[1]

Rejecting ivory tower elitism, Black Studies activists looked outside the walls of academia with the visions of change that were, in the period of Black Studies' emergence, quite radical. Indeed, helping bring on "The Revolution," variously defined, was the ultimate goal of Marxists, Pan-Africanists, and others in this dynamic period. As maturity, disillusionment, pragmatism, and realism have all worked to modify those visions the goals have become perhaps less broad, but no less urgent, given the period of crises now evident. In that connection, the need to maintain concrete linkages between a program and "the community" has been continually reiterated among those in the field who have carried this activist tradition.

A significant area where African American Studies–related ideas and initiatives have been recently visible is in public policy discourses connected to primary and secondary education. The emergence of Afrocentric materials, curricula, and so-called "African-Centered" schools in urban areas serving black youth, and the recent controversial initiatives of some school systems to adopt policies based on recognition of indigenous black language patterns, or Ebonics, are both examples of such of linkage and potential influence. Later I consider these trends and attempt to draw from them the elements of a pedagogical paradigm. I incorporate aspects of Paulo Freire's model that conceivably could be applied in or outside of formal classrooms across a wide array of institutional fronts in the struggles of black communities against symptoms of dysfunction.

The insistent emergence of initiatives such as those involving Afrocentric curricula and Ebonics, despite contested interpretations of their success, points to the atmosphere of urgency that engulfs many communities today where these initiatives have appeared. These communities face a perplexing array of conditions symptomatic of the deepening crisis among the so-called "underclass" in the African American community. Many of the symptoms are rooted in the impact of structural changes in the U.S. economy on sectors of the black community. Emerging since the 1970s, these structural changes have lead to a general stagnation in major manufacturing industries, and it is clear that the communities that grew on their previous strength will suffer the effects for some time.

As manufacturing industries retooled they trimmed their workforces, both to streamline and accommodate increased automation. As a result, the number of jobs this sector provides has been greatly restricted. Entry-level, "unskilled" jobs have practically disappeared.[2] Unlike the industrial workforce of the recent past, young, uneducated, unskilled workers have no viable role in the economy. Hence, another scholar, social philosopher Tommie Lee Lott, refers to this young, "underclass" group as twentieth-century "maroons"; they are isolated, in pockets, from mainstream society.[3]

The cumulative weight of ancillary effects from economic restructure has fallen heavily on this group. The impact of deteriorated municipal services, public safety, and public education systems, the increases in school dropouts, functional illiteracy, early parenthood, out-of-wedlock births, and long-term joblessness has accumulated heavily on the shoulders, and on the aspirations, of the young maroons of our communities. For this group the economic restructuring of the last quarter century has created barriers, making paths of educational and economic mobility extremely difficult to access—making their marooned status an institutionalized fact. Joblessness among young black men particularly—age twenty to twenty-four—increased sharply during the mid-seventies and has remained high.[4] In many communities, unemployment, or lack of adequate employment, is an everyday reality.

In 1990 the Sentencing Alternative Project, based in Washington, D.C., released the first startling report that one in four black men in their twenties was in prison, on parole, or on probation.[5] Even more startlingly, the incarceration rate of black males in this country was more than four times the rate of black males in South Africa at the height of the antiapartheid struggle.[6] In 1995 a follow-up report from the same organization showed a worsening of this symptom; the proportion of young African American men under the jurisdiction criminal justice authorities rose to one in three. These figures point to a large portion of an emerging generation being lost, in one way or another. For the maroons of the underclass, these frustrating conditions severely limit their opportunities to self-actualize; to engage in activities that affirm them as productive human beings in this society. It is no wonder that frustration and anger lead to high rates of youth violence, among other symptoms of "dysfunction" in these communities.

Putting people in jail for drug offenses and violent crimes may be considered necessary, but hardly completes the job. The punishment of perpetrators does nothing to prevent new victims or new perpetrators. Regarding the spread of violence in poor African American communities, there is, in fact, a double tragedy being enacted here. One aspect is the increasing number of victims of fatal and injurious violence in the heavily black urban centers; the other aspect is the increasing number of youth from these same communities who are in some form of incarceration when they should be in school, training, or in some way developing productive pursuits for their lives.

Violence, substance abuse, and other problems are symptoms; they are reflections of structural barriers issuing from institutionalized racial inequality and socioeconomic disadvantage that keep large numbers of our community in poverty and social isolation. In focusing on symptoms, officials who may be either black and/or well meaning have focused on objectives that are incorrect and/or incomplete. This is especially true when officials are acting in a crisis atmosphere. For example, the "war on drugs," born during the Bush administration in the late 1980s, was fought almost entirely on a law enforcement front, with little new support for prevention and rehabilitation.[7] In terms of funds allocated and spent and programs pursued and developed, law enforcement personnel and apparatus have been favored conspicuously over programs aimed at social and educational assistance and health promotion.[8]

I will not suggest that treating symptoms is unimportant. Some educational and other intervention programs, in fact, have been impressive. However, effective programs must at some level address, indeed, become part of, processes of larger social change. A question that points to a strategy is this: How can we help "at-risk" persons—who are so much symptoms of the problem—to become part of the solution?

Communities often come to see a critical connection between severe inadequacies in public education and other symptoms of crisis. Loss of tax revenues from fleeing industries and affluent residents has exacerbated problems in central cities. Municipal services, public safety, and especially public schools have been affected. Dropout rates have increased in some cities. Many who finish high school do so without grade level reading and math skills. Meanwhile, essentially all growth in entry-level, low-education requisite jobs has taken place in suburbs and nonmetropolitan areas far removed from growing concentrations of poorly educated urban minorities. In this troubled atmosphere education is often seen as an important focus for intervention, and some communities have been motivated to look for alternative educational approaches and strategies. Thus, primary and secondary education are areas outside the university that have become open to direct and indirect impact from African American studies, especially in major urban areas with large black constituencies and where blacks occupy positions of responsibility.

Afrocentric Curricula and Schools

Schools have been incorporating black history, literature, and other "black content" into their curricula since nearly the start of the Black Studies movement. As urban crisis symptoms have worsened in recent years communities have been motivated to deviate even further from traditional practices perceived as inadequate or ineffective. The trend of adopting "Afrocentric" curricula and creating "African-centered" schools, for example, has gained considerable force in such areas.[9] Despite criticism and controversy, major districts are even adopting *systemwide* mandates to develop what is termed Afrocentric curricula.

Here it should be remembered, as noted in chapter 3, that conceptions, articulations, and implementations of "Afrocentrism," particularly outside the academy, are far from uniform or consistent. Of course such inconsistency, among many other factors, helps confuse public discourse on these efforts, leading to confusion and discord as well as to assessment of the effectiveness or impact. The range of ideas, methods, perspectives, and sensibilities embraced as Afrocentric in these settings is broader than the body of thought defined by Afrocentrists in the academy. The prominence of African cultures and civilizations is usually present in these programs, possibly reflecting the direct involvement of prominent Afrocentric university scholars as consultants in several of these projects. This aside, however, there appears to be greater emphasis on *African American* history and culture in programs that call themselves Afrocentric in the wider educational arena.

It is not my purpose here to attempt a comprehensive or systematic assessment of the success of these efforts as a class, or of any particular one. The variation in the kind and quality of materials, diversity of approaches, and character of political climates would make such an assessment dauntingly complex. I do intend to suggest, however, that in this era of black community crisis this is one area of institutional policy being influenced by discourses generated within or associated with the Black/Africana Studies movement. It may be argued that the involvement of schools, teachers, administrators, school boards, communities, and media in often vigorous public discourse on these areas of curricular change is itself a highly suggestive indicator of the salience of this influence.

Ebonics

Vigorous discourse among educators and the public was recently generated when several school systems moved to adopt policies based on recognition of indigenous black language patterns, referred to as "Black English," or "Ebonics." This issue has been visible in educational policy discussion since at least 1979. At that time a decision in the lawsuit that became known as the "Black English case" was rendered on behalf of a group of black elementary school students in Ann Arbor, Michigan, who had been assigned to "special education" classes because of presumed scholastic inaptitude. Using the published work and testimony of Geneva Smitherman, then director of the Center for Black Studies at Wayne State University, the plaintiffs successfully argued that their clients' language patterns were indicative of a legitimate, though different, language tradition, and not low scholastic aptitude or intelligence meriting their assignment in "special" classes.[10]

In ruling for the plaintiffs Federal Judge Charles Joiner did not, as some assumed, order that Black English be taught to children in the classroom. Rather the court stipulated that the school had an obligation to teach standard English reading and writing skills using approaches that would "take into account" students' indigenous language patterns. The linguistic principles underlying this argument are that differences in language patterns exhibited by many African American students are the result of the same factors that produce other variations in language patterns among different groups. In the case of African Americans, these factors include the historical amalgamation of African vocabulary, pronunciation, and grammatical practices reinforced and cultivated by many decades of isolation from mainstream cultural venues.

The same kinds of factors have caused variations of English in the United States or in Australia to evolve into dialects distinctly different from the variation of English considered "standard" in the United Kingdom. Fostering teacher awareness or "appreciation" of the nature of these language differences would, ostensibly, lessen the tendency to stigmatize students merely for the way they speak. The speech of these children could, therefore, be seen in terms of skills and knowledge that children can build on to develop proficiency in the "standard" English of mainstream commerce and culture, rather than being viewed as evidence of lack of capacity or competence. In the interim years several schools have adopted approaches that embraced Ebonics on an experimental basis. However, the controversy surrounding the issues in the Black English case was largely forgotten until the Oakland, California, school board took steps to create the first districtwide policy based on this idea in late 1996.

The Ann Arbor and Oakland cases, though quite different in some respect, both stemmed from the perceived failure of current school practices. Plaintiffs in the Ann Arbor case argued that the nine poor black boys at the mostly white (and ironically named) Martin Luther King elementary school had been virtually abandoned, shunted into special education classes designated for "slow learners," based on the way their language was misperceived by their teachers. In the case of the Oakland school district, the board emphasized that they were motivated to develop alternative instructional strategies aimed at improving the overall 1.8 grade point average of the systems' African American students. The policy they adopted called on schools to increase African American students' proficiency in standard English (what Smitherman terms the "language of wider communication"), through strategies that recognized the legitimacy of Ebonics, their primary language.

The public dialogue around this issue has been significantly muddled by the fact that basic terms and concepts in this discussion have been used in different ways, and have meant different things to various participants in the dialogue. Noting that "[o]ne uncontroversial principle underlying the Oakland Unified School District's December 18th 'Ebonics' resolution is the truism that people can't learn from each other if they don't speak the same language," Charles J. Fillmore, linguist at the University of California, Berkeley, summarized this confusion quite succinctly in an analysis appearing as part of a report by the Center for Applied Linguists during the controversy: "You might think that all these people speak the same language, but the evidence contradicts the appearance. All of the key words that keep coming up in these discussions clearly mean different things to different parties in the debate, and that blocks successful communication and makes it too easy for each participant to believe that the others are mad, scheming, or stupid."[11]

It is quite striking that in both the Ann Arbor and Oakland cases the most vocal aspect of the attendant public discussion was opposition to the perception that Black English would be taught to students in the classroom. This idea persisted despite numerous attempts in both cases to specify that standard English proficiency was the intended objective. The nature of the "news-gathering" enterprise and the media's misunderstanding and misreporting are a major cause of the confusion. In journalism it is said that when a dog bites a man (Oakland Schools moving to improve African American students' standard English skills), that's not news. However, when a man bites a dog (a school district recognizing the legitimacy of Black English, or Ebonics), that's news.

For example, on December 21, 1996, three days after the Oakland board's action, *San Francisco Chronicle* reporters Elliot Diringer and Lori Olzewski reported: "Amid all the furor over the Oakland school board's decision to recognize Ebonics as a distinct language, one key point seems to have been lost: The goal is to help black students master standard English."[12] Yet Olzewski had also reported the *Chronicle*'s original report of the action two days earlier. Under a front-page headline of "OAKLAND SCHOOLS OK BLACK ENGLISH: EBONICS CONSIDERED DIFFERENT, NOT WRONG," the article's lead sentence read: "The Oakland school board approved a landmark policy last night that recognizes Ebonics, or Black English, as a primary language of its African American students, making it the first school district in the United States with such a system-wide approach."[13] The rest of the sixteen-paragraph story never really specified that standard English proficiency was the objective of the initiative. However, even when it is made clear that the reason for "recognizing" Ebonics is to implement strategies for elevating standard English skills, those who reject the initiative typically do not change their positions.

It seems that whites, unless they have particular knowledge of the linguistic principles underlying the debate, generally find the idea of something called Ebonics or Black English quite strange, if not downright ridiculous. Even more striking, however, has been the depth, breadth, and strength of the negative reaction to Ebonics from African Americans, of all classes and regions. The core of their opposition seems to be a fundamental notion that nothing other than standard, "proper" English should ever be considered legitimate. Thus, they reject Black English as mere slang or street language that should never be given legitimacy by being recognized.

Regardless of the supposed goal of such programs, many have vehemently opposed recognizing Ebonics or elevating it to the status of legitimate language on grounds that doing so "is just admitting our kids can't learn to speak correctly like others" (or, in another variation of this argument, that it represents giving up on schools' responsibility to teach "correct" English). Usually the notion of expectation becomes part of this argument; for example, "If we have high expectations students will achieve accordingly," or, "If our expectations are that students learn proper English, they will."

This aspect of the debate seems especially ironic because the concept of expectations lies at the very core of the pedagogical principles on which the Ebonics initiative is based. Three decades ago it was established that teacher expectations are a major determinant of student academic performance. Teachers who expect their students to succeed tend to produce more students who succeed.[14] Supporters of the Ebonics initiative argue that some teachers wrongly associate the language patterns of some black students with low competence and, therefore, approach such students with low expectations rather than as people who just talk differently. This may result in Black English speakers being inappropriately placed in "slow learner" tracks, as were the nine Ann Arbor boys, or in other ways abandoned educationally.

Familiarity, acceptance, or recognition of the legitimacy of Ebonics may work to change the expectations of teachers by changing their association of difference with inferiority or inability, and the low expectations that go along with such perceptions. Thus, according to linguist Fillmore, "An important step toward introducing this new practice is to *help teachers understand the characteristics of their students' speech* so they can lead the children to an awareness of the difference" (emphasis added).[15]

For opponents, the issue of expectations breaks down quite differently. "If we recognize the legitimacy of Ebonics," they argue, "we're saying that the way they speak is 'OK,' and that we don't expect them to be able to learn proper English." In order to communicate the expectation that African American students should learn to speak properly we must make it unambiguously clear to them that the way they speak—variously characterized as slang, street language, or just wrong—is not acceptable and must be corrected. Recognizing or legitimizing these students' current language practices may provide excuses for them not to learn acceptable language skills.

Cultural Literacy and Liberation Pedagogy

This sense of expectation involves exactly the kind of stigmatizing of current language practices that proponents of the Ebonics initiative had hoped to avoid. Thus, although the same word is used, the concept of expectation is enjoined in nearly opposite ways by opposing sides in this debate. From this writer's standpoint, a core issue involves the need to recognize and validate African American cultural experience as it is lived by all segments within the black community. It is, therefore, critical to look for ways of educating blacks in poor urban communities that also validate, rather than negate, their experience and their culture. It may well be that methodological approaches to literacy made famous in Freire's well-known work *Pedagogy of the Oppressed*, which first appeared in 1970, can be adapted to needs and objectives in poor African American communities.

To begin with, the conflict of outlooks expressed in debates around the Ebonics initiative calls to mind the critique of conventional approaches to literacy made prominent by Freire. The insistent rejection by opponents of the Ebonics initiatives of the legitimacy of the language skills and habits that children bring to school is reminiscent of the "banking concept of education." Conventional educational pedagogy assumes that recipients of education and service are like empty vessels, or accounts, into which deposits can be made.[16] Freire has been consistently critical of this tendency: "I am always astonished by the disdain with which schools, with a few happy exceptions, treat the perceptual, existential, 'lived' experience acquired by the child outside the school confines. It's as though they want to erase this other form of language, which constitutes the child's way of being, sensibility and initial vision of the world, from his or her mental and physical memory."[17]

Freire's reference to "lived experience" suggests that more than just the words of students are devalued in this process. The language patterns students bring to the educational process are critical carriers of their still-evolving senses of identity and of their cultural reference frame. In a 1980 conference publication exploring the ramifications of the Ann Arbor Black English case I referenced Freire's seminal work[18] to apply this concept to the Black English issue: "Blacks, whose history of social and political oppression and economic deprivation binds them to oppressed peoples the world over, have for too long been subjected to a 'banking concept of education.' . . . As victims of the presumptions of this pedagogy, the Black student's world is negated—not only the language, but also the very experience out of which the student's language is forged."[19]

When the primary language and culture frameworks of students are suppressed and denied legitimacy, the students role in their own educational process becomes passive, an object, rather than proactive, a subject. Accepting or empowering the language practices students bring to the educational setting is consistent with Freire's conception of the alternative model that, according to Freire, is "dialogical" and "problem-posing," based on an immersion in and authentic understanding of the cultural world of the students. To recognize the authenticity of these language patterns is, therefore, to begin to recognize the cultural and social realities of the worlds they inhabit. The similarity between Freire's approach and the rationale for recognition of Ebonics is striking in Freire's own comments:

> It must never be forgotten that, long before they begin to form letters, the very young have learned to speak, to manipulate oral language. Through their family experience, they "read" the reality of the world around them long before they can write about it . . . .
>
> Literacy work must take this reality as its point of departure and refer to it constantly so as to make possible, thanks to the greater depth of knowledge that reading and writing confer, a more profound decipherment, a "re-reading" of the world once it has been discovered.[20]

This conception, which sees literacy as a point of departure to more profound personal transformation, or "re-reading" of the world, is consistent with notions of literacy, referenced in chapter 5, that have been advanced within the Black Studies movement and have served to organize the various discussions in this book. In that context, cultural, or historical, literacy signifies knowledge relevant not only to decoding letters but also to negotiating the social arenas and institutions of the world those letters represent.

The social symptoms of dysfunction, crime, violence, and drugs manifest the confrontations of a large sector among the black "underclass" with the legacy, the momentum of their history; they are a large segment, especially among young people, who sorely lack these special tools of literacy. These "maroons" could surely benefit from greater levels of literacy, in both the conventional sense and in the extended sense of cultural, or historical, literacy. Relevant is Harris's observation that "[c]onflict resolution and the ability to move on after certain goals either have not been obtained or have been radically altered depends on the level of literacy achieved by the individual in question."[21]

With this sense of cultural literacy as a goal, I propose that approaches, similar to those that have already been adapted to the needs of struggling people in many countries,[22] can also be adapted to fight against symptoms of community crisis among African Americans. The relevance of literacy work is obvious in relation to actual education programs; but the modalities of this approach might also be adapted to settings in and outside of formal classrooms, across an array of institutional fronts, as a liberation pedagogy that mobilizes cultural literacy as a tool to address other aspects of community dysfunction. For example, programs that attempt to address symptomatic problems like violence, drug use, high dropout rates, early parenthood, and so-called "family dysfunction."

Praxis versus the "Banking Concept" of Education

Those opposed to the "banking concept" conceptualize approaches that validate the lived culture of students as part of the educational process. While the banking concept assumes that desired knowledge can be imparted based on predetermined concepts of the "correct" information and skills, the goal in liberation pedagogy is to elicit, through dialogue, "critical thinking by posing problems in such a way as to have participants uncover root causes of their place in society—the socioeconomic, political, cultural and historical context of personal lives."[23] For blacks, in essence, this approach to literacy seeks to create culturally relevant knowledge concerning participants' circumstances as African Americans—knowledge which may actually be transformed into an asset in their individual struggles against substance abuse, violence, and other symptoms of "dysfunction."

Codifications

In the liberation approach, dialogue is structured around actual, concrete images that represent critical themes in the lives of the participants. This is called "problem posing." The images that serve as objects of dialogue are called "codifications" or "codes." Codifications are representations, usually visual—as in a drawing, painting, or photograph—that contain deeply felt themes and critical issues. The critical themes, and the codifications that express them, are developed from dialogue between educators and representatives of a program's ultimate constituency. The goal is to present themes and representations that authentically express the lived reality of the participants themselves. In practice, a codification can be a range of many other kinds of concrete representations of an identified critical theme or issue in any form, including role-plays, stories, slides, photographs, and songs.[24] Thus, video technology has been used in a youth violence prevention curriculum developed for Roxbury tenth graders by Dr. Deborah Prothrow-Stith—who is associated with both the Boston University and Harvard Medical Schools. The curriculum uses a problem-posing approach.

This curriculum was adopted by several other schools in Boston and elsewhere. The program blended technological innovation to facilitate the conditions for reflective, problem-posing dialogue through a unique aspect of the curriculum in which a role-play of a fight situation is videotaped, including its precursor events and its aftermath. Through this technique, students are able to consider many elements of the issues involved in such confrontations.[25]

While literacy programs in the conventional restricted sense are associated with formal educational institutions, the problem-posing approach to cultural literacy as conceptualized here can be appropriate in other arenas. A program in health education aimed at youth alcohol abuse prevention describes its use of codifications in this manner:

> Each code re-presents the community reality back to discussion participants and enables them to project their emotional and social responses into the object for focused discussion. An effective code shows a problematic situation that is many-sided, familiar to participants, and open-ended without [immediate] solution . . . People are asked to (1) describe what they see and feel, (2) as a group, define the many levels of the problem (3) share similar experiences from their lives (4) question why this problem exists and (5) develop action plans to address the problem.[26]

Similarly, in the Prothrow-Stith model, by reflecting on video images of themselves, the participants engage in dialogue that clarifies perceptions, meanings, and alternatives regarding situations leading to violence.

Applications of this principle in acutely stressed black communities would have to be conceived and carried out with great care to recognize, account for, and speak authentically to an appropriate set of cultural sensibilities. Indeed, the banking concept of education is a bankrupt concept of education for these young blacks. They are largely uneducated, and many cannot read, but they are not dumb. In the current economic climate, the message of middle-class assimilation, which the "banking concept" carries, is a sham; they see this clearly, and in dress, linguistic behavior, rap music, and other modes they demonstrate an established cultural reference frame that expresses their rejection. The method of dialogue in the liberation approach—and a key to its effective application in our crisis—is of nonhierarchical dialogue; that is, unlike the conventional banking concept, there is no "talking down" to the maroons of the "underclass." Thus, according to Freire, "teaching should always take into account the differing levels of knowledge that children bring with them when they come to school. This intellectual baggage is an expression of what might be called their cultural identity and this, of course, is linked to the sociological concept of class. The teacher must take into account this initial 'reading of the world' that children bring with, or, rather, within them."[27]

The issue of cultural reference frame is fundamental in the engagement of reflective dialogue within any given application. The banking concept assumption that participants come to the situation with no cultural insight, and that deposits of "correct" information can be made into that empty vessel, is fundamentally incorrect. Maroons in our society have a cultural reference frame made distinct by their structural isolation from the economic and social mainstreams and labeled "pathological" by those in the mainstream. Rather than dismiss it as pathological, liberation pedagogy incorporates Lott's suggestion to address destructive behaviors without rejecting the culture itself.

In constructing codifications that express meaningful themes in the lives of student constituents, Freire suggests that educators become familiar with the popular culture of their students by "studying books and newspapers, listening to television and radio, listening to people talking in the streets."[28] Rap music, for example, which Lott describes as a kind of "black man's television," the vehicle in which the cultural voice of poor blacks is best represented, has "declared war against the dominant ideological apparatus."[29] Although legitimately criticized as misogynist and overly vulgar, the wide variety material produced in this genre of popular culture includes a significant portion that is analytical in concept, has its own critical terms and dimensions, and shows political astuteness. The use of such rap images to code or codify critical themes that emerge in reflective dialogue may have great potential and certainly should not be overlooked. There are many products of hip-hop culture that conceivably could serve the role of codification for purposes of problem posing or centralizing and channeling dialogue. To illustrate, the late Tupak Shakur's rap song "Dear Mamma" could potentially become a potent vehicle for posing issues for critical dialogue. In addition, the actual production of raps by program participants could be focused on creating reflective dialogue and giving analytical voice to critical themes in their lives.

Reflective Action

The goal of group reflection through nonhierarchical dialogue in liberation pedagogy is both to tap the strongly felt critical themes of a constituency and to forge new plans of action based in a new understanding of underlying issues. Often, and not surprisingly, participants realize that some aspects of the problems they uncover have no immediate solution. Arguably, that constitutes further reason their understanding of self has to be linked to the history, local and global, individual and social, of struggle against systematic aspects of oppression, which African American Studies represents. Conceivably, action designed in the context of deeper understanding has a new character, a new salience, and a new relevance. As Harris noted, the ability to move on when goals are not met, or are radically altered, depends on the degree of literacy—cultural and historical—achieved.

The process of active reflection and reflective action deepens. New actions from participants can encompass individual or social realms. In the alcohol-abuse prevention program the students initiated a communitywide effort based on peer influence and aimed at reducing alcohol-related problems. In the Prothrow-Stith curriculum, students focus on concrete anticipation of issues involved in confrontations that typically lead to fights. They consider ways of dealing with issues that avoid violence and injury. In a school-based violence-reduction program in Atlanta, Georgia, that employs cultural symbols—from African philosophy to rap music—to engage reflective dialogue among young men, participants have formed an operating team that uses cultural codes of their own device to communicate to their schoolmates and among themselves, and monitor potentially violent behavior in the school environment.

Action, whether individual, collective, or social, that is based in critical consciousness informed by dialogical reflection will have greater measures of authenticity than action not so informed. For example, reflective dialogue might engender a renewed focus on self-improvement, educational pursuits, spiritual clarity, or other personal objectives that sound, and indeed are, individual and mainstream. If engaged within a dialogically informed perspective such pursuits will tend to be less alienated and more relevant; efforts will be sustained by a greater sense of drive; the activities involved will have palpable meaning; and in the final analysis there will be a greater likelihood of their success. Moreover, there is reason to believe that successes at this level will contribute to social action and to cultural action at the larger social levels; the same drive, salience, relevance, palpability, or authenticity that informs individual efforts at personal transformation will also inform collective or social efforts involving broader levels of social and political transformation.

Social Action

"To undertake a challenge to . . . systemic problem[s] [like] violence, we must take a systematic approach."[30] Analyses of symptoms of community crisis tell us that many problem areas must be addressed in programs that would effectively address any one symptom of socioeconomic and health inequity. Liberation pedagogy informs us that the converse statement can also be true. A program approach that authentically addresses one symptom can also be adapted to address many problem areas. Models developed from the basic concepts set out here—cultural competence, or literacy; nonhierarchical dialogue; codification of critical, culturally relevant themes; and reflective action—can be effective in programs in a number of areas.

As my examples have shown, public health and health education programs have usefully employed many of the concepts, as have conventionally defined educational programs and curricula. I see no reason why similar concepts could not be adapted to substance-abuse prevention and treatment programs, juvenile diversion and alternative sentencing programs, prison-based literacy programs, education programs, parenting programs, and a whole host of other applications.

A dialogical approach like that associated with Freire ensures that the objects of learning arise out of, and have concrete meaning within, the cultural reference frame of the constituency; it is not a framework imposed from without by a white middle class or even by black educators and professionals who presume to have relevance for others in our community. Knowledge or insight, if it has authenticity for participants—that is, if it has concretely useful value, or is relevant, as we used to say—emerges from the participants' existing reference frame. Activities and forms of communication that engage the elements of that reference frame in tasks of reflective dialogue initiate its mobilization. In this way people authenticate their own experiences, their own insights, their own lives.

A people's own culture is the context in which proactive behaviors are shaped, defined, and have meaning. It is, therefore, important to recognize that a people's own culture constitutes the medium in which communication takes authentic meaning, whether that communication is in the context of teaching, rehabilitating, intervening, or even punishing. Thus, the alternative approach, the liberation pedagogy, is based on dialogue leading to praxis, the process of reflection and action, through which oppressed people transform themselves from Objects to become Subjects, from spectators to actors in the processes shaping their lives.

The Problem and the Solution

In the case of youth violence and other destructive behavior, it is useless, even counterproductive, to attempt to persuade youth not to be angry and frustrated, as the banking concept would dictate. Anger is, as the Prothrow-Stith violence-prevention curriculum presents it, a normal, potentially constructive emotion. It should, in fact, be channeled toward, and linked with, an elevated or enlightened sense of social consciousness. This may be accomplished through avenues of dialogue in which participants come to see their private troubles as public issues and act accordingly; to engage themselves at the level of social action and expend the energy generated from anger and frustration there, rather than at the level of destruction of their own, or someone else's, person; to stop being part of the problem and start being part of the solution.

To achieve this awareness is to achieve "literacy" as conceptualized in the paradigm developed in this and previous chapters, in the sense of being able to authentically locate one's self in the context of one's own history and culture. As discussed in chapter 6, literacy becomes functional as historical literacy when it recognizes and incorporates the "authentic" (folk/popular) insight of ancestors and forbears. Incorporating the current perspective of that folk/popular tradition, historical literacy represents a state of knowledge in which the tools of conventional literacy are focused on the need to address concrete conditions of oppression.

Nonhierarchical dialogue comprising active reflection and reflective action, or praxis, begins this process. It is incumbent on us, as professionals and community leaders, to develop programs that cultivate reflective dialogue in the cultural context of our communities and our youth; we must seek, within that context, the terms for constructive social action. It is incumbent on us, in our institutional stations, in our social and institutional networks, and within our community relationships and associations, to find effective ways to be part of the solution. By allowing the perpetuation of the bankrupt banking concept of education, we risk becoming part of the problem.

I have looked at three dimensions in which African American studies–related insights have been tied to public policy and programmatic community change: (1) incorporation of black content and Afrocentric curricula; (2) recognizing Ebonics, indigenous black language, as part of language skills development programs; and (3) application of dialogical pedagogical principles in and outside of formal educational settings to address crisis conditions in the community. From somewhat disparate origins, these three discourses converge around key issues that African American studies can and should engage: discovering and valuing who black children, students, participants, and constituents are and what the experiences are that make them who they are; and drawing out and developing from those personal identities, tools, resources, and capabilities for engaging and negotiating communities, institutions, and systems in the wider social world. These tasks define current and future missions for African American Studies—a future I look toward in the epilogue.

Epilogue

Working in African American Studies

Despite initial doubts regarding its practical value, African American Studies is increasingly acknowledged as a critical component of educational programs on all levels for blacks and nonblacks alike. The schools of thought, controlling ideas, and paradigms that issued from earlier recounted struggles continue to advance and define the field today as, despite all previous predictions and tendencies, programs, departments, and institutes have endured to institutionalize them. Remaining controversial, and continuing to struggle against marginalization, African American Studies has nonetheless demonstrated both its legitimacy and its tenacity in the three decades of its tenure in academia. Furthermore, signs of renewed activism, reminiscent of the movement out of which the discipline originally emerged, have further energized African American Studies scholars to continue to interpret and develop the original mission of discovering and developing knowledge relevant to purposes of social change.

Institutions and Schools of Thought

From the original schools of thought, the integrationist/inclusionist approach is exemplified most prominently by the department at Harvard, headed by Henry Louis Gates Jr. and now also including philosophy and religious scholar Cornel West from Princeton and sociologist William Julius Wilson from University of Chicago (not to mention African philosopher Kwame Anthony Appiah from Cambridge University). Within the academic establishment and in larger public discourse this array of intellectual stars obviously carries great weight. Opposition from Black Studies movement activists, therefore, has not prevented this approach from evolving into an important if not dominant position among the tendencies and schools of thought that make up our field today.

Afrocentrism, which emerged to become a leading voice among those who opposed this approach, found its flagship program at Temple University, under the intellectual and administrative leadership of Molefi Asante. As the first bona fide Ph.D. program in this field, the achievements of this program are historic. Moreover, when one considers the large number of Ph.D. candidates the program has attracted in relation to the small number of black doctorates awarded annually these days, one realizes that the potential influence on and responsibility for the future of black intellectual thought is quite immense.

I am of course aware that, at this writing, the department at Temple is undergoing multilayered crises, the details of which remain quite controversial, and, in any case, fall outside the parameters of this discourse. Whatever the specific outcome, it seems that one likely result will be a less hegemonic place for Afrocentrism, in both the national discourse and within the local department at Temple. However, the "Afrocentric Idea" is still a potent source of inspiration for many in the field and will, in all likelihood, continue to resonate for some time.

A capstone program or department that institutionalizes an alternative, "transformationist" approach, as Temple and Harvard do for the others, may possibly emerge at Columbia University. Since becoming director of Columbia's Institute for Research in African American Studies, Manning Marable has brought in scholars such as literary scholar Gina Dent, cultural critic Michael Eric Dyson, and historian Robin D. G. Kelly, who all represent such alternate perspectives. Similarly, while well-known feminist scholars (Patricia Hill Collins, for example) are associated with Black Studies programs in several institutions, Duke University houses a program that gives prominence to gender issues, black women's experiences, and black feminism. There, Karla Holloway has recently taken over the African American Studies program and made historian Paula Giddings one of her first hires. Furthermore, in public statements and other venues, like the conference on black women that this program hosted in 1996, Professor Holloway has indicated that she will seek to make black women's studies a priority.

Another recent trend involves applying the cultural studies approach, associated with the British Birmingham School, to looking at black people. Here, I am including some who claim a new disciplinary status for what they call "black cultural studies," and whose presence raises issues about the relationships among cultural studies, black studies, and black cultural studies.[1] In a certain way these relationships parallel the "British Invasion" led by the Beatles and Rolling Stones that transformed the musical popular culture in 1964, a year before my class entered college. These British rockers were essentially reflecting back what they had learned about music from black people.

Paul Gilroy, prominent in this more recent British invasion, tied the history of the postmodern critique of modernity to the articulations of blacks like Douglass and Du Bois, who identified flaws in the Western heritage of perfectibility long before it became the discourse of postmodernism that cultural studies now engages. Perhaps Gilroy should have also included us, the Black Studies movement, as part of this black intellectual tradition of critiquing Western modernity. I hope I have shown that our Black Studies movement, as much as any of the other postmodern critiques, involves challenging, deconstructing, and reconstructing the basic epistemological foundation on which knowledge is built and truth determined. As surely as any, we challenged the "master narratives" of Western progress; we raised basic questions of epistemology, of how knowledge is generated, how truth is shaped, and for whom. All of these issues continue to consume ongoing postmodern, poststructuralist, postcolonial discussions.

The point is that the Black Studies movement is the parent in relationship to these discussions of cultural studies and black cultural studies. I should point out here that my colleague in North Carolina, Mae G. Henderson, is making this argument from within that discourse, pointing out that the interdisciplinary breadth and the challenge to conventional epistemologies and political structures characterizing cultural studies movement were presaged in the Black Studies movement.[2] Indeed, the appreciation of cultural diversity in America and in the world that is now encouraged in many educational curricula is a product of dynamics first brought to academia by the Black Studies movement. The emergence of multiculturalism in educational and social arenas in the 1900s owes its genesis to the seed planted in the form of the challenge, posed by activists in the 1960s, to the tendency of European particularisms to be "translated into absolute standards for human achievement, norms, and aspirations."[3] In ways that are different but complementary, then, blacks and whites alike benefit from the connection to a vital part of the American social, cultural, political, and historical landscape, which African American Studies illuminates.

Activists and Academics Revisited

Along with continuing discourse among these Black Studies academics, the field is also being shaped by trends and events in the larger political arena. This is reminiscent of the movement's original constituency, when a larger social movement shaped campus activism. Recently, a growing restlessness has been evident among activists and the black community at large about the traditional civil rights leadership's perceived ineffectiveness in dealing with the problems of the late twentieth century and the approaching millennium. This concern was profoundly apparent in the thunderous response to the call for the Million Man March in October 1995. That black men (with the support of most women) were willing to mobilize, fully one million strong, for that event clearly showed a broad-based, deeply rooted mandate for bold, aggressive activism from the community. That they were willing to follow the call of Minister Louis Farrakhan and the Nation of Islam showed clear defiance of the wishes of the power structure and of the mainstream black leadership. Such attitudes typically go along with separatist sentiments, movements, and organizations, and are most evident during times of greatest disaffection with mainstream society.

Veterans and others in the Black Studies movement were active and involved in the march mobilization; including Maulana Karenga, who wrote the march's mission statement, and Leonard Jeffries, the controversial City College professor who was one of the platform speakers. Described in one review as a penultimate "nationalist moment," the mobilization created a forum through which Minister Farrakhan was arguably poised to become the most important and influential black leader in the country.[4] Aside from the general and even profound sense of inspiration and commitment to community involvement experienced by many march participants, however, evidence of sustained organized actions has been much less visible and dramatic than the march itself.

Along with other events, however, the march movement has focused the attention of community on the need for dramatic collective action to address seemingly intractable problems characterizing black communities. One year after the march a conference on the state of African American

Studies was hosted at Columbia University's Center for African American Research.[5] The lineup of scholars and activists and the themes they addressed seem to suggest the coalescence of a new activist-oriented intellectual and ideological center for the field, distinct from both the Gates-led Harvard model and the Asante-led Afrocentric approach. Issues of class and gender, the need for African American Studies to maintain an activist relationship in the wider community, and the impact of economic globalization were prominent themes of discussion at that event.

Several from that meeting also participated prominently in another recent gathering, much smaller numerically than the Million Man March, that may nonetheless be significant as a bellwether of renewed black activism: the Black Radical Congress. This gathering was constructed from a process, mounted through the Internet and other technologically enhanced communication modes, that linked a far-flung network of old and new activists in a vigorous discourse around defining new perspectives, objectives, and imperatives for advancing the cause of progress for African Americans. The organizers took pains to characterize the event as "nonacademic," notwithstanding the significant presence of African American Studies scholar-activists—particularly from the left-leaning "transformationist" school—among the fifteen hundred labor and welfare rights activists, low-income housing advocates, educators, artists, and writers who participated. Recalling the 1968–74 period, when the Black Studies movement was connected to broader social movements for equality and social justice, this constituency converged on Chicago from June 19 to 21, 1998, with the objective of creating a radical new agenda for the twenty-first century.

This process was generally led by Marxists, feminists, and other leftist radicals, generating complaints that some important nationalists from the Black Studies arena (like Maulana Karenga) and from the larger political community (like Ron Walters) were "left out" of the process in which this event was constructed.[6] In response, one participant pointed out that, with the advent of "cyber-democracy," any of those supposedly "left-out" spokespersons could participate. Indeed a variety of nationalists did participate in the initiative.[7] In addition, Gerald Horne wrote that not being invited by the organizers despite his leftist credentials did not make him conclude he should not participate, nor did it prevent him from doing so.[8] Finally, it was noted, the fact that it was to be a *Black* Radical Congress suggested a nationalistic formation in itself.[9]

Complaints aside, the discourse generated in the process of organizing and conducting the congress clearly rejoined the vibrant Marxist/

Nationalist interchange that had been central in the context of that earlier movement period. There were (only) a few instances of repeating missteps of the earlier debate. More frequent were indications that some lessons were learned and taught by each side in the previous rounds of discourse; operational unity, rather than ideological dominance, should be the goal among them.

Though undoubtedly premature, one may also be tempted to situate the initiative alongside other historically important events, such as the Niagara Movement in 1905, when a small band of "radicals" met to construct a new agenda after expressing growing dissatisfaction with the post-Reconstruction accommodationist leadership of Booker T. Washington. The recent congress was generated from discourse criticizing post–civil rights liberal black leadership, whose perceived failure to effectively address current critical problems has, among other things, opened a way for equally misguided black conservative voices to gain stature and currency in public policy circles, and among the black masses.

African American Studies in a New Millennium

The conceptual diversity of African American Studies represented in programs that institutionalize its various schools of thought give hope for developing the kind of wide-ranging dialogue and critical discourse that will further solidify, refine, and strengthen the field. This would be timely, as there clearly are important roles and responsibilities for African American Studies as critical issues are resolved in public discourse and resolved into public policy. In context with the initiatives toward renewed activism, the full range of this array of institutional and intellectual resources will undoubtedly be put to use discerning and addressing the global and technological forces that shape the advent of a new century and a new millennium.

As that future approaches, with global changes reshaping economic, social, and political contours of the world, African Americans are experiencing their version of the crunch between local and global forces that has affected all the world's groups. On the one hand globalized economies and technologically enhanced communication modes increase the number of opportunities and ways of interacting across national, racial and cultural boundaries. On the other hand, the same forces circumscribe an "underclass" of urban maroons whose socioeconomic isolation is actually emphasized by the global impact of its culture impulses.

Our notions of black identity, or black identities, are reshaped by these processes as our similarities and connections with other blacks, peoples of colors, and other groups are illuminated even while new differences and forms of disjunction are simultaneously uncovered. On the continent of Africa, for example, events and circumstances in Nigeria, Kenya, South Africa, Rwanda, Zaire, and Eritrea tug at our senses of nationalism, Pan-Africanism, and Western acculturation in painfully complicated and contradictory ways. In this hemisphere, relations among African Americans, Afro-Caribbeans, and other black groups are similarly complicated. Among African Americans the ascendance of conservative voices, on the one hand, and the growing estrangement of persistent class division on the other further complicate the task of identifying or defining what the interests and objectives and goals of the "black community" are or should be.

Integration and Separation: Nonbinaries

For example, in the passage of history it has become gradually clear that black efforts to achieve integration have actually conflated two *different* goals: structural integration, and cultural assimilation. The former implies the ability to live, be educated, and be employed according to merit, not race. The latter means *both* adoption of mainstream cultural norms *and* loss of indigenous cultural distinctiveness. (It is important to note that these are different processes. In the compartmentalized reality of African American "double-consciousness" it should be possible to adopt mainstream cultural norms while nonetheless retaining at least certain key features of cultural distinctiveness.)

The tendency to conflate structural integration and cultural assimilation is a legacy of earlier periods in history when, as argued below, the distinction was not apparent or salient. Following from that legacy, current manifestations of the historic tension between integrationist and separatist tendencies among blacks seem to be locked in a language of discourse that has not kept pace with the changes history has brought.

Dating back to the antebellum nineteenth century and before, structural integration has always been a goal of the collective agendas and strategies that African Americans have developed to deal with the forms of racist oppression that various historical epochs have presented. Pursuit of this objective has entailed overcoming or striking down barriers of systematic discrimination and exclusion of blacks from institutions and social arenas. Originally, the objective was to live and to be accepted as "full" American citizens. Since differences in education, literacy, manner of speaking, dress, and other social markers reinforced the dominant mainstream perception of inferiority, blacks reasoned that by becoming literate and educated they would be more acceptable to whites and able to function and interact properly with them.

Their hope was that removing as much as possible those stigmatized differences—by speaking, dressing, and conducting themselves as much like the "respectable" mainstream as possible—would help prove that blacks were not inferior and (at least those "respectable" blacks) did not deserve stigmatized treatment. Thus, the goal of assimilation was inextricably embedded in the goal of integration.

These attempts to eliminate the stigma of cultural difference have been only marginally successful. Individually, some blacks become very accomplished and receive acceptance and recognition from some whites. However, as blacks keep discovering individually and collectively, there is virtually no escape from the social construction of racial difference. Nearly all blacks, no matter their level of success or accomplishment, have encounters at some point with the sting of racialized stigma that "remind" them that in the eyes of at least some whites they will always be despised—despite their accomplishment or their mainstream cultural assimilation.

Aside from, and in addition to, the economic, social, and physical oppression commonly experienced by blacks, this lack of recognition and affirmation from the wider culture constitutes a significant hardship in its own right. Namely, the persistence of racist stigma despite the degree of assimilation to mainstream cultural values, practices, and reference frames fundamentally confounds issues of black identity and culture. It is centrally involved in the dilemma of double-consciousness—described by Du Bois as the sense of always seeing oneself through the eyes of others that yields no true self-consciousness. The quest for true self-consciousness embodies the need for cultural affirmation in a framework where others see a person in ways that affirm rather than stigmatize and reject. It is this need for a framework of affirmation on which African American separatist tendencies are historically based.

In the nineteenth century, black literary and cultural organizations, black independent churches, and back-to-Africa and other emigration movements all reflected the high/elite leadership's turn to separatist tendencies in response to times and circumstances—the antebellum and Jim Crow periods, for example—when such affirmation was not forthcoming. Although present-day nationalists claim these predecessors, one could argue, as I did in chapter 5, that "failed assimilationism" might be a more accurate description of the sentiments guiding their separatist initiatives.

However, these assimilationist tendencies uncovered among the historical roots cf the traditional (high/elite) African American leadership class *must* be understood in terms of the particular historical context in which they emerged. Despite the view held by many in current times that such aggressive assimilationist tendencies represent "love of whites" and "rejection of their blackness," it seems clear, in the context of those times, that there were really no cultural choices for those historical elites. As "free" citizens in antebellum America, there simply were no alternative cultural models or frameworks that would affirm both their ethnicity (as blacks) and their status (as free, educated citizens). This condition illustrates a historical alignment that erased any functional distinction between what I now argue are two different issues: structural integration and cultural assimilation.

Frustrated by the failure of their assimilative efforts, the goal of structural integration was sometimes abandoned, or de-emphasized by antebellum free blacks. However, the assimilated cultural reference frame was largely retained. As a response to undiminished racism encountered in mainstream settings, separate institutions were created with "African" in the title. The practice, which continues today, of raising the memory of Egypt to the cause of race pride, was engaged. A general ethos, extremely important in freedom movements and organizational formations, of struggle and pursuit of social justice was collectively embraced in these alternative institutional formations. However, the basic, literate, Western, cultural and institutional framework embraced by antebellum free blacks in their pursuit of acceptance and assimilation was not fundamentally changed. Separatist cultural formations were thus created to affirm values and sensibilities fundamentally parallel to those of the cultural Westernized framework that rejected them. Very little in the way of African sensibilities was incorporated in these separatist efforts. Ironically, those transformed remnants of African sensibility that did survive in the oral culture of rural and southern blacks were, as already indicated, generally shunned and discouraged by those blacks attempting to create and live out a nonslave black identity.

The Soul of Black Folks

It is clear, when comparing black cultural orientations connected to African and slave experiences with those of the present day, that blacks have indeed largely assimilated. The high/elite leadership class has led the way, showing more disadvantaged blacks the ways of literacy, thrift, diligence, patience, morality, and virtue. Often passionate and selfless, this tradition has embodied self-help and racial uplift in movements as historically far-flung as the antebellum abolition and convention movements, the colored women's club movement of the 1890s, and the Civil Rights movement of the 1960s. Under this tutelage, blacks have made great collective strides toward assimilation in a framework that, as nationalists and others point out, does not recognize and affirm them.

Despite these assimilative tendencies, continuing social stigma and structural isolation perpetuates the existence of a cultural core that remains distinct from the mainstream. Organized around this core are a range of distinct sensibilities that involve aesthetics, expression, gesture, rhythm, movement, and attitude. In varying degrees and configurations for different black folks, these sensibilities truly affirm black identities and cultural reference frames against the storm of mainstream stigmatization and rejection. Though not always recognized or valued, the role of folk/popular tradition in creating this cultural home has been critical. It is this side of the African American duality that affirms most fundamentally the humanity of black individuals and validates the authenticity of their experiences. Consistently, critical sensibilities that enhance this framework of affirmation, buttressing black identity, esteem, and self-worth against the onslaught of mainstream stigma, have emerged from that folk/popular tradition, despite rejection and/or lack of recognition from the leadership class.

Again, the importance of music, that powerful voice of the folk/popular experience, in framing and cementing this alternate cultural space must be emphasized. With the barest of resources and in the most oppressive times African Americans have drawn from the musical traditions of their folk/popular tradition to fashion stunning affirmations of their own humanity that mitigate the scorn of the surrounding culture, and ultimately transform the wider culture itself. Among the multitude of musical forms blacks have created, mention of two should illustrate this point adequately.

The first is blues. Issuing from roots in the rural folk culture during the period described as the "nadir" of race relations in the late nineteenth century, the "secular spiritual" not only helped redeem the suffering of the rural masses but has become, arguably, the most influential music in the world. It is certainly the basis of all succeeding forms of black (and therefore American) popular music. The second form is blues' urban offshoot: rhythm and blues. R&B was also a product of bad times, germinating as part of a black "underground" culture that managed to flourish culturally in the 1930s and 1940s while the world at large was suffering in the throes of depression. Emerging from that underground after the Second World War, R&B became another form of black music that revolutionized the wider culture, becoming the basis for rock and roll and thus energizing an entire generation of world-changing baby boomers.

When dealing with aspects of black experiences such as the dynamics of cultural validation, it is indeed easy to undervalue the tremendous significance of what I have defined here as the African American folk/popular tradition. It is instructive, in that regard, to note how progress for the entire collective has been linked to the conditions of the most oppressed among them. The story of the Great Migration, for example, that demographically, culturally, socially, and politically transformed the African American collective along with the rest of America, is the story of the experiences of the folk/popular masses. (The more privileged class was largely urbanized already.) The cultivation of grassroots black communities in the urbanized, industrialized world of the twentieth century marked the beginning of wide-scale cultural interaction with and impact on the larger culture. The Civil Rights movement occurred because the grassroots masses became aroused and mobilized. Notwithstanding the integrationist goals fashioned by the middle-class leadership of that movement, the grassroots community's agenda embodied a great collective assertion of self-worth—celebrated in the soul music of that era—that transposed, as easily as a James Brown chord change, to being "black and proud" when called, in the later 1960s, to "say it loud."

The degree to which these folk/popular sensibilities become internalized and functional in the formation of a distinct, larger black culture is precisely the degree to which the differences between structural integration and cultural assimilation become functional. The story of the emergence of an aesthetically and socially distinct African American culture, therefore, is the story of the survival and transformation of the grassrooted folk/popular tradition. With the rich African American musical tradition as a soundtrack, it is the story of the "soul" of black folks.

Structural Integration *and* Cultural Transformation

With the emergence of complex but distinctly ethnic African American cultural reference frames, it becomes possible to conceive of pursuing integrationist (structural integration) goals without necessarily being integrationists (that is, cultural assimilationists). For example, blacks don't necessarily want to live with whites. They want access to housing of the same quality as middle-class whites. They don't necessarily want their children to sit next to white children. They want their children to have access to quality education, like middle-class white children. However, such distinctions are rarely acknowledged in discourse locked in those previous conceptions of black identity that continue to conflate structural integration and cultural assimilation, and that too often polarize the concept of integration as mutually exclusive to forms of black collectivity and separatism.

The notion that blacks could be, or that they even wished to be, *either* integrated into the wider culture *or* separated from it was always too simplistic. False dichotomies, polarization, and operational disunity, always products of this tension, are even more problematic given the complex trends currently affecting blacks' lives. In the globalized postmodern world African Americans need to affirm conceptions of black identity, culture, and community that leave them engaged with, rather than separated from, the rest of that globalized reality. Structural integration is a choice that cannot be readily abandoned given these modern complexities. The dream of constructing a nation-state, or a state of consciousness wherein it would be unnecessary to confront a global reality dominated by Westernism, racism, and (in the post-Soviet era) capitalism—cannot be realized. The idea of a nation, in the sense of a real, sovereign nation-state, which was the goal of the so-called "classical" black nationalists of the nineteenth century, is not achievable now, whether it was then or not. If, for argument's sake, the elusive land question was solved and all blacks voluntarily transported themselves there, they would still have to deal with the same internationalized global economy and so-called "world order" they confront now, and that Africa confronts now. The local particulars might be different, even very different, but the global reality would be exactly the same.

On the other hand, the notion of complete integration into the wider society seems equally unrealistic. Few, if any, of the most ardent integrationists believe it is possible or desirable—especially to the degree that it might require total assimilation. There is no doubt that blacks need separate spaces in their lives shaped by the "blackness" that nationalism hopes to organize and perpetuate. The negotiations with which they engage the wider world are psychologically draining, emotionally risky, and personally dangerous; blacks must have the collectivized home base to come back to, to anchor, to plug into for revitalization and affirmation. (On various levels, we all do it: come home and put on some Jodeci, Miles, Mahalia, James Brown, P-Funk, whatever. Then we go back out and, on some level, in some realm, "deal with white folks" somewhere in the wider global system. There are no choices in this regard. This is what we do.)

Thus, nationalist or collectivist tendencies continue to manifest themselves in the form of separate or independent black institutions, black caucuses and collectives within other organizational or institutional formations, black control or collective influence in neighborhoods, and cities where our strength is sufficient. The task for black studies professionals and black leaders is to find ways to focus and maximize this collective power of black heritage, history, and sense of community in ways appropriate to these various arenas of black life.

Class, Culture, and Globalism

Beyond these arenas, other serious issues related to global economic trends and class divisions within black communities will certainly claim the attention of black scholars and activists. Clearly, structural changes in the economy, favoring a more technologically literate workforce, have continued to deprive large portions of black youth of a viable future in the evolving global village. Such trends indicate that the economically marooned "underclass," first observed in the early 1970s, will be a long-term, if not permanent, problem for the black community as a whole. Indeed, the description of this group—characterized in terms of poor education; single-parent impoverished families; and violent, crime-ridden, and drug-infested communities—has changed little over the last two decades.

The internal class divisions reinforced by these trends create additional challenges to the notion of a "community" of African Americans who identity with a common destiny. To what degree do educated, relatively well-off African Americans see themselves as belonging to the same group as these maroons? From history we see that, prior to Emancipation, free blacks identified strongly with the plight of enslaved blacks, despite significant differences defined by education, economic resources, and cultural reference frames. Indeed free blacks played crucially important roles in the struggle against slavery. While compassion for their less fortunate kin undoubtedly played a role, their primary motivation was the clear understanding that their own oppression was linked to the existence of slavery; that their own well-being was firmly tied to that of enslaved blacks, regardless of what were essentially class-based differences.

Is it still possible to conceive definitions of blackness that link the interests of middle and stable working class blacks, many of whom are decidedly conservative in their outlooks, to those of the underclass maroons? Is it legitimate to question whether a similar sense of linkage and common destiny exists today between the educated, middle-class blacks and the so-called "underclass"? Can these underclass maroons be armed with power of the collective heritage, culture, sense of community, and destiny that other blacks value and cultivate? Remembering social power of the folk/popular tradition, can value and potential for empowerment be found in the cultural forms indigenous to this group? What constructive ways can be fashioned to engage the abundant energies that hip-hop culture has collectivized among much of our youth? Will the soul-transforming elements of that folk/popular tradition emerge once again to redeem their future?

These are a few of the questions African American Studies scholars, as carriers of a black intellectual tradition, could productively engage. Without suggesting that I have a definitive list of questions, much less answers, let me suggest in closing that the continuing evolution of Black Studies as an intellectual and social enterprise is located within a set of issues and factors that connect it to (post)modern manifestations of intellectual production, as well as of social mediation, struggle, and contestation. As the discourse continues among schools of thought in the field, it will be incumbent upon the participants to frame the discussion in terms of the challenges and opportunities that now confront us. It is this ground, inscribed with a catalog of critical issues facing black communities in the United States and elsewhere in the African diaspora at this critical historical juncture, upon which African American Studies now stands. And it is this ground over which it must tread on a road that leads through the end of this century and into the next millennium.

Appendix

The tables in this appendix offer further breakdowns of the data from the National Survey of Black Americans analyzed in chapter 6. These tables explore further possible correlations among age, region, and education in relation to the group identity measure.

Age Groups within Regions

Table A.1 below shows that the overall effect of the age variable noted in chapter 6 is generally consistent within regions. The study finds that wherever subsample sizes are adequate (greater than 30) the World War I group has the highest mean, slightly higher than the next older group. The only exception is the Northeast, where the subsample is still small, and where the pre-migration group (N = 32; mean = 3.45) has higher group identity than the World War I group (N = 55; mean = 3.40). Also, in most of the regions the means of the movement and post-movement groups are close.

Age Groups across Regions

Looking at age groups across regions (using the alternative age categorization) the study again finds strong regional correlations (table A.2). In every age group the means from the South are greater than those in the same age group from other regions. With the exceptions of the oldest (pre-migration) and youngest (post-movement) groups, the Midwest regional categories (census North Central and alternate industrial) have the next highest means. The difference nearly disappears but is still present in the postwar group. Among respondents in the pre-migration and post-movement age groups, those in the Northeast have higher racial group identity means than those in the Midwest. This could be the result of small sample sizes or other undetermined factors.

Comparing Education Levels within Age Groups

This study finds remarkable consistency in identity index variation among education levels within age categories (table A.3). Although this division of the data creates some small subsamples, both the general negative correlation of education and identity, as well as the rise among college graduates when separated from attendees, is seen within all age categories. A comparison of the alternative age categorization with that of the previous study also reveals another small consistent difference between the previous study's "protest years" birth year group and this study's "postwar (movement)" group. The mean group identity index of each education level in the postwar group is slightly but consistently higher than that of the same education level of the protest group.

Comparing Age Groups within Education Levels

Comparing different age groups while controlling for education level, the study again finds that older groups have higher means than younger groups with the same education level (table A.4). At the lowest education levels (11 years or less) the means of the World War I group are slightly higher than the older, pre-migration group. Among those who are high school graduates or better, the older group tends to have higher means than the younger one. This could be the result of small sample size or other undetermined influences. Among all other age groups, the depression group has the highest means, followed by the movement and post-movement groups in all education categories.

Comparing Education Levels across Regions

This study also finds consistency when looking at education levels across regions (table A.5). Education levels in the South show markedly higher racial group identity scores than other regions, with the exception of college graduates. Among college graduates, those in the Midwest (census "North Central" and alternate "industrial" regions) have means similar to those in the South. However, the subsamples of college graduates in the Midwest region categories are of barely adequate size.

Table A1. Age Groups within Regions

Northeast Region (Census)

Age Group	n	mean	Age Group	n	mean
Pre-Roosevelt	40	3.48	Pre-Migration	32	3.45
New Deal	119	3.31	World War I	55	3.40
Protest	111	3.16	Depr/WWII	99	3.32
Post-protest	66	3.08	Movement	109	3.06
			Post-movement	20	3.17

North Central Region (Census)

Age Group	n	mean	Age Group	n	mean
Pre-Roosevelt	45	3.41	Pre-Migration	37	3.40
New Deal	125	3.44	World War I	67	3.46
Protest	137	3.15	Depr/WWII	90	3.38
Post-protest	97	3.04	Movement	173	3.08
			Post-movement	37	3.08

South Region

Age Group	n	mean	Age Group	n	mean
Pre-Roosevelt	177	3.63	Pre-Migration	141	3.61
New Deal	255	3.60	World War I	179	3.66
Protest	320	3.37	Depr/WWII	190	3.51
Post-protest	213	3.27	Movement	376	3.33
			Post-movement	79	3.20

West Region

Age Group	n	mean	Age Group	n	mean
Pre-Roosevelt	13	3.57	Pre-Migration	8	3.49
New Deal	33	3.33	World War I	24	3.47
Protest	38	3.04	Depr/WWII	24	3.30
Post-protest	25	2.92	Movement	41	2.90
			Post-movement	12	2.98

Table A-2. Age Groups across Regions

Pre-Migration

Region	n	mean
Northeast	24	3.35
Indust	44	3.46
South	132	3.60
West	5	3.50

World War I

Region	n	mean
Northeast	33	3.38
Indust	86	3.45
South	175	3.66
West	22	3.54

Depr/WWII

Region	n	mean
Northeast	72	3.30
Indust	116	3.38
South	184	3.51
West	23	3.30

Movement

Region	n	mean
Northeast	87	3.07
Indust	116	3.08
South	364	3.33
West	36	2.97

Post-movement

Region	n	mean
Northeast	14	3.20
Indust	40	3.05
South	79	3.20
West	11	2.97

Table A-3. Education within Age Groups

Pre-Roosevelt

Education	n	mean
0–11 Yrs	216	3.60
H.S. Grads	36	3.46
Some College	13	3.38
College grads	10	3.55

Pre-migration

Education	n	mean
0–11 Yrs	171	3.57
H.S. Grads	27	3.49
Some College	12	3.33
College grads	8	3.59

World War II

Education	n	mean
0–11 Yrs	216	3.65
H.S. Grads	72	3.38
Some College	0	3.32
College grads	23	3.39

New Deal

Education	n	mean
0–8 YRS	152	3.63
9–11 YRS	142	3.52
H.S. Grads	139	3.41
College*	99	3.29
Attendees	52	3.27
Graduates	47	3.32

Depr/WWII

Education	n	mean
0–8 YRS	67	3.58
9–11 YRS	110	3.44
H.S. Grads	132	3.41
College*	102	3.28
Attendees	62	3.25
Graduates	40	3.32

Protest

Education	n	mean
0–8 YRS	25	3.43
9–11 YRS	126	3.30
H.S. Grads	290	3.22
College*	262	3.11
Attendees	170	3.08
Graduates	92	3.15

Movement

Education	n	mean
0–8 YRS	38	3.48
9–11 YRS	118	3.36
H.S. Grads	229	3.28
College*	221	3.15
Attendees	142	3.13
Graduates	79	3.19

Post-protest

Education	n	mean
0–8 YRS	9	3.50
9–11 YRS	87	3.20
H.S. Grads	183	3.17
College*	122	3.11
Attendees	93	3.07
Graduates	29	3.22

Post-movement

Education	n	mean
0–8 YRS	3	3.47
9–11 YRS	44	3.18
H.S. Grads	66	3.15
College*	38	3.12
Attendees	36	3.13
Graduates	2	3.38

Includes college attendees and graduates.

Table A-4. Age Group within Education Level

Grammar School or less (0–8 Yrs)

Age Group	n	mean
Pre-migration	138	3.56
World War I	137	3.66
Depr/WWII	67	3.58
Movement	25	3.43
Post-movement	3	3.67

Some High School (9–11 Yrs)

Age Group	n	mean
Pre-migration	33	3.64
World War I	79	3.62
Depr/WWII	110	3.43
Movement	126	3.30
Post-movement	44	3.18

College (Attendees and Graduates)

Age Group	n	mean
Pre-migration	20	3.44
World War I	43	3.35
Depr/WWII	102	3.28
Movement	262	3.11
Post-movement	38	3.12

College Graduates

Age Group	n	mean
Pre-migration	8	3.59
World War I	23	3.39
Depr/WWII	40	3.32
Movement	92	3.15
Post-movement	2	3.38

High School or Less (0–11 Yrs)

Age Group	n	mean
Pre-migration	171	3.57
World War I	216	3.65
Depr/WWII	177	3.49
Movement	151	3.32
Post-movement	47	3.19

High School Graduates

Age Group	n	mean
Pre-migration	27	3.49
World War I	72	3.38
Depr/WWII	132	3.41
Movement	290	3.22
Post-movement	66	3.15

College Attendees

Age Group	n	mean
Pre-migration	12	3.33
World War I	20	3.32
Depr/WWII	62	3.25
Movement	170	3.08
Post-movement	36	3.10

Table A-5. Education Levels across Regions

Grammar School (0–8 Yrs)

Region	*n*	mean
Northeast	31	3.37
Indust	63	3.43
South	249	3.65
West	8	3.69

Some High School (9–11 Yrs)

Region	*n*	mean
Northeast	51	3.28
Indust	112	3.40
South	195	3.48
West	17	3.44

H.S. Graduates

Region	*n*	mean
Northeast	85	3.23
Indust	166	3.19
South	270	3.38
West	42	3.18

College (Attendees and Graduates)

Region	*n*	mean
Northeast	63	3.10
Indust	131	3.12
South	225	3.29
West	38	2.98

College Attendees

Region	*n*	mean
Northeast	42	3.13
Indust	101	3.06
South	124	3.28
West	22	3.03

College Graduates

Region	*n*	mean
Northeast	21	3.02
Indust	30	3.31
South	96	3.30
West	8	2.76

Notes

Introduction

1. Nathan Huggins, *Afro-American Studies: Report to the Ford Foundation* (New York: Ford Foundation, 1985), 9.
2. Abdul Alkalimat and Associates, *Paradigms in Black Studies: Intellectual History, Cultural Meaning, and Political Ideology.* (Chicago: Twenty First Century Books, 1990); Talmadge Anderson, ed., *Black Studies: Theory, Method, and Cultural Perspectives* (Pullman: Washington State Univ. Press, 1990); James C. Conyers, *The Evolution of African American Studies* (Lanham, Md.: Univ. Press of America, 1995).
3. The terms *culturally deprived* and *culturally disadvantaged* were early forms of "political correctness" coined by social science liberals to describe and explain the circumstances of poor blacks. In their view, poor blacks, rather than being genetically "inferior," had been "deprived" of the advantages of "culture."
4. At the Yale Black Studies Symposium, discussed at length later, Nathan Hare said, "I used to tell my white colleagues that they were culturally deprived, because not a single one of them could tell me who Otis Redding was." Nathan Hare, "A Radical Perspective on Social Science Curricula," in *Black Studies in the University: A Symposium,* ed. Armstead L. Robinson, Craig C. Foster, and Donald H. Ogilvie (New Haven: Yale Univ. Press, 1969), 112.
5. Ralph Ellison, *Invisible Man* (New York: Random House, 1952).
6. See Paulo Freire, *Pedagogy of the Oppressed* (New York: Herder and Herder, 1970).

7. W. E. B. Du Bois, *The Souls of Black Folk* (New York: Signet Books, 1982), 54.

8. Gerald A. McWorter, "Deck the Ivy Racist Halls: The Case of Black Studies," in *Black Studies in the University*, ed. Robinson, Foster, and Ogilvie, 55–74.

9. See Paul Gilroy, *The Black Atlantic: Modernity and Black Consciousness* (Cambridge, Mass.: Harvard Univ. Press, 1993), 7–8. "The especially crude and reductive notions of culture that form the substance of racial politics today are clearly associated with an older discourse of racial and ethnic difference which is everywhere entangled in the history of the idea of culture in the modern West. This history has itself become hotly contested since debates about multiculturalism, cultural pluralism, and the responses to them that are sometimes dismissively called "political correctness" arrived to query the ease and speed with which European particularisms are still being translated into absolute, universal standards for human achievement, norms, and aspirations."

10. Robert L. Harris Jr., "The Intellectual and Institutional Development of Africana Studies," in *Black Studies in the United States: Three Essays*, ed. Robert L. Harris Jr., Darlene Clark Hine, and Nellie McKay (New York: Ford Foundation, 1990), 11.

11. See Huggins, *Afro-American Studies.*

12. Abdul Alkalimat and Associates, *Introduction to Afro-American Studies* (Chicago: Peoples College Press, 1977).

13. Maulana Karenga, *Introduction to Black Studies* (Los Angeles: Kawaida Publications, 1983).

14. Gloria T. Hull, Patricia Bell Scott, and Barbara Smith, eds., *All the Women Are White, All the Blacks Are Men, but Some of Us Are Brave: Black Women's Studies* (Old Westbury, N.Y.: Feminist Press, 1982).

15. Perry Hall et al., *National Council for Black Studies Report on Curriculum Standards.* (Bloomington, Ind.: National Council for Black Studies, 1981).

16. Harris, "The Intellectual and Institutional Development of Africana Studies," 13–14.

17. James B. Stewart, "Reaching for Higher Ground: Toward an Understanding of Black/Africana Studies," *Afrocentric Scholar* 1, no. 1 (May 1992): 1–63.

Chapter 1. Struggle Outward

1. See Mary Christine-Phillips, "25 Years of Black Studies," *Black Issues in Higher Education* 11, no. 5 (May 5, 1994): 14–19.

2. Darlene Clark Hine, "Black Studies: An Overview," in Robert L. Harris et al., *Black Studies in the United States*, 12.

3. *Black Studies in the University*, ed. Robinson, Foster, and Ogilvie.

4. Huggins, *Afro-American Studies*, 26.

5. Armstead L. Robinson, Preface to *Black Studies in the University*, ed. Robinson, Foster, and Ogilvie, vii.

6. A close examination of this conference, involving detailed consideration of all the papers and presentations and all the issues concerned, though important, is outside the scope of my purposes here. Thus, although what follows refers extensively to the proceedings of the symposium, it should not be perceived as an attempt at such an analysis.

7. Armstead L. Robinson, Preface to *Black Studies in the University*, ed. Robinson, Foster, and Ogilvie, x.

8. Yale President Kingman Brewster's preoccupation with the way the antiwar movement was shaking his campus, or perhaps the typical view that Black Studies was not a legitimate issue, or perhaps a combination of both of these apparently prevented Brewster from opening the conference himself.

9. Charles H. Taylor, "An Introduction to the Conference," in *Black Studies in the University*, ed. Robinson, Foster, and Ogilvie, 3.

10. Maulana Karenga, "The Black Community and the University: A Community Organizer's Perspective," in *Black Studies in the University*, ed. Robinson, Foster, and Ogilvie, 38.

11. McWorter, "Deck the Ivy Racist Halls," 59. "Brandishing of Leninist rhetoric" is a more accurate description of presentations like the one he gave nearly a decade later at the Annual Conference of the African Heritage Studies Association in Detroit, Michigan, in 1977. Here he accused nationalist/Pan-Africanists of views that "avoided the question of mass struggle in this country" and "advocated policies against the struggles that the masses of people were waging. . . . Any position that liquidates mass struggle in this country is providing assistance to imperialism."

12. Huggins, *Afro-American Studies*.

13. Unidentified questioner, "Question Period" (following first panel), in *Black Studies in the University*, ed. Robinson, Foster, and Ogilvie, 25.

14. Harold Cruse, "Question Period" (following first panel), in *Black Studies in the University*, ed. Robinson, Foster, and Ogilvie, 26–27.

15. Unidentified questioner, "Question Period" (following first panel), in *Black Studies in the University*, ed. Robinson, Foster, and Ogilvie, 29.

16. Ibid., 33.

17. McGeorge Bundy, "Some Thoughts on Afro-American Studies," in *Black Studies in the University*, ed. Robinson, Foster, and Ogilvie, 172–73.

18. Ibid.

19. Ibid., 174.

20. Huggins, *Afro-American Studies*, 21.
21. Robinson, Preface to *Black Studies in the University*, ed. Robinson, Foster, and Ogilvie, x.
22. David Brian Davis, "Reflections," in *Black Studies in the University*, ed. Robinson, Foster, and Ogilvie, 215.
23. Ibid., 217.
24. Ibid., 222.
25. Ibid., 219.
26. Ibid.
27. "Signifyn(g)," according to Henry Louis Gates Jr., means retelling "with a difference." See *Signifying Monkey: A Theory of African-American Literary Criticism* (New York: Oxford Univ. Press, 1988).
28. Unidentified questioner, "Question Period" (following first panel), in *Black Studies in the University*, ed. Robinson, Foster, and Ogilvie, 28.
29. For a thorough exploration of the issue of complicity regarding the Western intellectual tradition and the creation of racism and "racial terror," see Paul Gilroy, *The Black Atlantic*.
30. Donald H. Ogilvie, "A Student's Reflections," in *Black Studies in the University*, ed. Robinson, Foster, and Ogilvie, 80.
31. Ibid.
32. Addison Gayle, *The Black Aesthetic* (Garden City, N.Y.: Doubleday, 1971); Addison Gayle, *Black Expression: Essays by and about Black Americans in the Creative Arts* (New York: Weybright and Talley, 1969); Amistad Research Center, *Amistad*, 2 vols. (New York: Random House, 1970–71); LeRoi Jones and Larry Neal, eds., *Black Fire: An Anthology of Afro-American Writing* (New York: Morrow, 1968); Abraham Chapman, *Black Voices: An Anthology of Afro-American Literature* (New York: New American Library, 1968); W. E. B. Du Bois, *The Philadelphia Negro: A Social Study* (Pub. for the Univ. of Pennsylvania, 1899); St. Clair. Drake, *Black Metropolis: A Study of Negro Life in a Northern City* (New York: Harcourt, Brace, 1945); Charles S. Johnson, *Shadow of the Plantation* (Chicago: Univ. of Chicago Press, 1934).
33. For example, at my first university (Wayne State University, Detroit, Michigan) after I left that program in 1989.
34. Huggins, *Afro-American Studies*, 19.
35. Ibid., 42. "[I]ntegrationists . . . preferred to see Black Studies courses offered in the standard curriculum in conventional departments."
36. Wayne State Univ., Conference on Black Studies, Detroit, Mich., Feb. 3–5, 1973.
37. Huggins, *Afro-American Studies*, 58.
38. Ibid., 46.

39. Ibid., 43.

40. Ibid., 49.

41. Ibid., 24.

42. James Turner, ed., *The Next Decade: Theoretical and Research Issues in Africana Studies. Selected Papers from the Africana Studies and Research Center's Tenth Anniversary Conference, 1980* (Ithaca, N.Y.: Africana Studies and Research Center, 1984).

43. For example, the program where I am currently associated, at the University of North Carolina at Chapel Hill, was founded as a "curriculum" in 1968 and became the Department of African and Afro-American Studies in 1996.

Chapter 2. Struggle Inward

1. Robert. L Allen, "Politics of the Attack on Black Studies," *Black Scholar* 6, no. 1 (Sept. 1974): 2–7.

2. Ronald L. Taylor, "The Study of Black People: A Survey of Empirical and Theoretical Models," *Urban Research Review* 2, no. 2 (1987), rpt. in *Black Studies: Theory, Method, and Cultural Perspectives*, ed. Talmadge Anderson (Pullman: Washington State Univ. Press, 1990).

3. Davis, "Reflections," 222.

4. Russell Adams, "Intellectual Questions and Imperatives in the Development of Afro-American Studies," *Journal of Negro Education* 53, no. 3 (1984): 201.

5. Ibid., 206.

6. Ibid., 207.

7. James B. Stewart's reflection—in the same special issue of the *Journal of Negro Education*—on the importance of understanding the interdisciplinary and extra-academic dimensions of Du Bois's work is especially enlightening. Stewart, "The Legacy of W. E. B. Du Bois for Contemporary Black Studies," 296–311.

8. Carlos Brossard, "Classifying Black Studies Programs," *Journal of Negro Education* 53, no. 3 (Summer 1984): 286.

9. Maulana Ron Karenga, "Which Road: Nationalism, Pan-Africanism, Socialism?" *Black Scholar* 6, no. 2 (Oct. 1974): 24.

10. Ibid., 27.

11. Tony Thomas, "Black Nationalism and Confused Marxists," *Black Scholar* 4, no. 1 (Sept. 1972): 47.

12. See Imamu Amiri Baraka, "Black Nationalism: 1972," *Black Scholar* 4, no. 1 (Sept. 1972): 23–29.

13. "[T]he main basis for what Baraka has called 'a new era in our politics' can be traced to Newark itself where the experiences of Baraka with 'black' Mayor Kenneth Gibson have clearly shown the role of neocolonialism and the relationship of black front-men for monopoly capitalist and multinational corporations." Phil Hutchings, "Report on the ALSC National Conference," *Black Scholar* 5, no. 10 (July–Aug. 1974): 50.

14. Brossard, "Classifying Black Studies Programs," 286.

15. Stewart, "The Legacy of W. E. B. Du Bois for Contemporary Black Studies," 311.

16. Qtd. in Gerald A. McWorter and Ronald Bailey, "Black Studies Curriculum Development in the 1980s: Its Patterns and History," *Black Scholar* (Mar.–Apr. 1984): 18–31.

17. Hutchings, "Report on the ALSC National Conference," 51.

18. Robert Chrisman, "The Crisis of Harold Cruse," *Black Scholar* 1, no. 3 (Nov. 1969): 79.

19. Ibid., 80.

20. Harold Cruse, "The Integrationist Ethic as a Basis for Scholarly Endeavors," in *Black Studies in the University*, ed. Robinson, Foster, and Ogilvie, 4.

21. Molefi Kete Asante, "Systematic Nationalism," *Journal of Black Studies* 9, no. 1 (Sept. 1978): 118.

22. For example, see Mary Frances Berry and John W. Blassingame, *Long Memory: The Black Experience in America* (New York: Oxford Univ. Press, 1982), 382.

23. Asante, "Systematic Nationalism," 123.

24. Ronald Walters, "A Response to Haki Madhubuti," *Black Scholar* 6, no. 2 (Oct. 1974): 47.

25. Ibid., 48–49.

26. Darlene Clark Hine, "The Black Studies Movement: Afrocentrist-Traditionalist-Feminist Paradigms for the Next Stage," *Black Scholar* 22, no. 3 (Summer 1992): 11–18.

27. Harris, "The Intellectual and Institutional Development of Africana Studies," 11.

Chapter 3. Afrocentrism

1. Carlene Young , ed., *Black Experience: Analysis and Synthesis* (San Rafael, Calif.: Leswing Press, 1972).

2. Alkalimat et al., *Introduction to Afro-American Studies*.

3. Alfred L. Bright et al., *An Interdisciplinary Introduction to Black Studies:*

History, Sociology, Literature, Art, and Philosophy of Black Civilization (Dubuque, Iowa: Kendal/Hunt, 1977).

4. James B. Stewart, "Introducing Black Studies: A Critical Examination of Some Textual Materials," *Umoja* 3, no. 1 (1979): 113–17.

5. Karenga, *Introduction to Black Studies*.

6. Ibid., xiii.

7. Karenga, *Introduction to Black Studies*, 35.

8. James B. Stewart, "Book Review and Commentary: An Introduction to Black Studies." *Western Journal of Black Studies* 7. no. 3 (Fall 1983): 117.

9. Molefi Asante, *Afrocentricity* (Trenton, N.J.: Africa World Press, 1988), 103.

10. Molefi Asante, *The Afrocentric Idea* (Philadelphia: Temple Univ. Press, 1987), 175.

11. Asante, *Afrocentricity*, 45.

12. Ibid., 104.

13. Asante, *The Afrocentric Idea*, 9.

14. Molefi Asante, *Kemet, Afrocentricity, and Knowledge* (Trenton, N.J.: Africa World Press, 1990), 26.

15. Asante, *The Afrocentric Idea*, 32.

16. Ibid., 23.

17. Ibid., 165–67.

18. Asante, *Kemet, Afrocentricity, and Knowledge*, 35.

19. Ibid., 32.

20. Ibid., 35.

21. Asante, *The Afrocentric Idea*, 166.

22. Asante, *Kemet, Afrocentricity, and Knowledge*, 35.

23. Asante, *The Afrocentric Idea*, 165.

24. Ibid., 116.

25. Asante, *Afrocentricity*, 31.

26. Ibid., 31.

27. Asante, *The Afrocentric Idea*, 114.

28. Ibid., 21–22.

29. Asante, *Afrocentricity*, 106.

30. Asante, *The Afrocentric Idea*, 35.

31. Asante, *Afrocentricity*, 89.

32. Ibid., 90.

33. Asante, *Kemet, Afrocentricity, and Knowledge*, 61.

34. Ibid., 61.

35. Ibid., 92.

36. Ibid., 47.

37. Cheikh Anta Diop, *The African Origin of Civilization: Myth or Reality,* trans. Mercer Cook (New York: L. Hill, 1974).

38. Cheikh Anta Diop, *The Cultural Unity of Black Africa: Domains of Patriarchy and Matriarchy in Classical Antiquity* (Chicago: Third World Press, 1976).

39. See, for example, Anthony Kwame Appiah, *In My Father's House* (New York: Oxford Univ. Press, 1992), 101–2.

40. Martin Bernal, *Black Athena: The Afro-Asiatic Roots of Classical Civilization: Volume 1* (New Brunswick, N.J.: Rutgers Univ. Press, 1987).

41. Asante, *Kemet, Afrocentricity, and Knowledge,* 57.

42. Ibid., 67.

43. Ibid., 117.

44. W. E. B. Du Bois, *The World and Africa: An Inquiry into the Part Which Africa Has Played in World History* (New York: International Publishers, 1965), 21.

45. Asante, *Afrocentricity,* 58.

46. Stewart, "Reaching for Higher Ground," 45.

47. Asante, *The Afrocentric Idea,* 9.

48. Ibid., 172.

49. Asante, *Afrocentricity,* 42.

50. Asante, *Kemet, Afrocentricity, and Knowledge,* 12.

51. Ibid., 36.

52. Asante, *Afrocentric Idea,* 180.

53. Asante, *Afrocentricity,* 46.

54. Ibid., 5–6.

55. Asante, *Afrocentric Idea,* 170.

56. Ibid., 170.

57. Asante, *Afrocentricity,* 79.

58. Ibid., 80.

59. Stewart, "Reaching for Higher Ground," 35–36.

60. Asante, *Afrocentricity,* 80.

61. Ibid., 82.

62. Ibid., 18.

63. See Gilroy, *The Black Atlantic,* 188–93.

64. Asante, *Afrocentricity,* 40.

65. Ibid., 40.

66. Stewart, "Reaching for Higher Ground," 35–36.

67. Perry A. Hall, "Paradigms in Black Studies," in *Black Studies Handbook,* ed. Delores Aldridge and Carlene Young (Chicago: Third World Press, forthcoming). I also presented this conceptualization to the National Council for Black Studies Summer Institute, Columbus, Ohio, June 15, 1991.

Chapter 4. Alternative Approaches in African American Studies

1. Stewart, "Reaching for Higher Ground," 1–63.
2. Hall, "Paradigms in Black Studies."
3. Manning Marable, "The Divided Mind of Black America: Racial Ideologies and the Urban Crisis" (paper presented at the Race Matters: Black Americans, U.S. Terrain Conference [sponsored by the American Studies and Afro-American Studies Programs of Columbia Univ.], Apr. 30, 1994).
4. Stewart, "Reaching for Higher Ground," 1.
5. Ibid., 6.
6. See Marvin W. Peterson, Robert T. Blackburn et al., *Black Students on White Campuses: The Impacts of Increased Black Enrollments* (Ann Arbor: Institute for Social Research, Univ. of Michigan, 1978), 31–37.
7. Stewart, "Reaching for Higher Ground," 6.
8. Huggins, *Afro-American Studies*, 62.
9. Stewart, "Reaching for Higher Ground," 6.
10. Institute of the Black World, *Curriculum Development Project: Final Report* (Atlanta: Institute of the Black World, 1982).
11. Adams, "Intellectual Questions and Imperatives," 201.
12. Stewart, "Reaching for Higher Ground," 8.
13. Asante, *Kemet, Afrocentricity, and Knowledge*, 4.
14. Stewart, "Reaching for Higher Ground," 20.
15. Ibid., 12.
16. Ibid., 44–45.
17. Ibid., 21.
18. Ibid.
19. My thanks go to Ms. Chandra Guinn, doctoral candidate in sociology, University of North Carolina at Chapel Hill.
20. Deborah King, "Unraveling Fabric, Missing the Beat: Class and Gender in Afro-American Social Issues." Selected papers from the Wisconsin Conference on Afro-American Studies in the Twenty-first Century, April 18–20. 1991. *Black Scholar* 22, no. 3. (Summer 1992).
21. Deborah King, "Multiple Jeopardy, Multiple Consciousness: The Context of Black Feminist Ideology," *Signs: A Journal of Women in Culture and Society* 14, no. 1 (Fall 1988): 42–72.
22. Stewart, "Reaching for Higher Ground," 4.
23. See, for example, bell hooks, *Talking Back: Thinking Feminist, Thinking Black.* (Boston: South End Press, 1989).

24. Patricia Hill Collins, *Black Feminist Thought: Knowledge, Consciousness, and the Politics of Empowerment* (New York: Routledge, Chapman, 1991).

25. Deborah King, "Multiple Jeopardy, Multiple Consciousness."

26. Ibid.

27. King, "Class and Gender in Afro-American Social Issues."

28. Ibid.

29. Asante, *Afrocentricity*, 5.

30. Cheikh Anta Diop, *Civilization or Barbarism: An Authentic Anthropology*, trans. Yaa-Lengi Meema Mgemi, ed. Harold J. Salemson and Marjolin de Jager (Brooklyn, N.Y.: Lawrence Hill Books, 1991), 4.

31. The same terms are used in Manning Marable's recent paper, quoted earlier.

32. Henry Louis Gates Jr., "African American Studies in the 21st Century." Selected papers from the Wisconsin Conference on Afro-American Studies in the Twenty-first Century, April 18–20. 1991. *Black Scholar* 22, no. 3 (Summer 1992): 3.

33. Stewart, "Reaching for Higher Ground," 32.

34. Marable, "The Divided Mind of Black America."

35. This short list also overlaps the one offered by Marable as representatives of transformationism, which included feminists (Angela Y. Davis, bell hooks, Michelle Wallace, Patricia Hill Collins), historians (Nell Irvin Painter, Robin D. G. Kelley), theologian-philosophers (Cornel West, James M. Washington), political theorists (James Jennings and Clarence Lusane), and cultural critics (Michael Eric Dyson and Jan Carew).

36. See, for example, James B. Stewart, "Historical Patterns of Black-White Political-Economic Inequality in the United States and South Africa," *Review of Black Political Economy* (Summer 1977): 267–96.

37. Perry A. Hall, "Historical Transformation in African American Musical Cultural," *Word: A Black Culture Journal* 1, no. 1 (Spring 1991): 29–38; Perry A. Hall, "African-American Music: Dynamics of Appropriation and Innovation," in *Borrowed Power: Essays on Cultural Appropriation*, ed. Bruce Ziff and Pratima V. Rao (New Brunswick, N.J.: Rutgers Univ. Press, 1997), 31–51.

38. Du Bois, *The World and Africa*, 1–15.

39. A black person who grew up in London, England, Gilroy presents a provocative and controversial meditation on cultural, social, and historical issues that define the "Black Atlantic," where blacks have interacted within various theaters of Euro-American dominance, including a unique reflection on African-American "particularities."

40. Gilroy, *The Black Atlantic*, 42.

41. Ibid., 44.

42. Ibid.

43. Marable agrees that in the academic arena the pragmatic liberalism he associates with the "inclusionist" vision "is best expressed in the social science literature by William Julius Wilson; in the humanities its most prominent representative is . . . Henry Louis Gates." ("The Divided Mind of Black America.")

44. William J. Wilson, *The Declining Significance of Race* (Chicago: Univ. of Chicago Press, 1980).

45. William J. Wilson, *The Truly Disadvantaged* (Chicago: Univ. of Chicago Press, 1987).

46. Diop, *Civilization or Barbarism*, 212–13.

47. Ibid., 6.

Chapter 5. Systematic and Thematic Principles

1. Perry A. Hall, "Systematic and Thematic Principles for Black Studies," *Journal of Negro Education* 53 (Summer 1984): 351–58.

2. Asante, *The Afrocentric Idea.*

3. Collins, *Black Feminist Thought.*

4. Paula Giddings, *When and Where I Enter: The Impact of Black Women on Race and Sex In America* (New York: Morrow, 1984); Hull et al., *All the Women Are White, All the Blacks Are Men.*

5. Michael Eric Dyson, *Reflecting Black: African-American Cultural Criticism* (Minneapolis: Univ. of Minnesota Press, 1993).

6. Gates, *The Signifying Monkey.*

7. Stewart, "Reaching for Higher Ground.

8. Hine, "Black Studies: An Overview," 25.

9. Stewart, "Reaching for Higher Ground." 29.

10. Other indicators of synergistic linkages include the consistency maintained between artistic visions and social analyses, as well as the manner in which artistic and sociopolitical products were presented in the same media, such as the important Renaissance-era journals *Crisis* and *Opportunity.* (Stewart, "Reaching for Higher Ground," 29.)

11. This encounter group was a component of the "City Course," an experimental curricular module developed from a movement that included black and white students and professors at the University of Michigan, on the principle of "bringing the university to the community" and vice versa.

12. I distinguish *essence* from *essentialism* later in this chapter.

13. Gilroy, *The Black Atlantic,* 33.

14. Ibid., 190–91.

15. Du Bois, *The Souls of Black Folk,* 45.
16. Marable, "The Divided Mind of Black America."
17. Gilroy, *The Black Atlantic,* xi.
18. Perry. A. Hall, "Beyond Afrocentrism: Alternatives for African American Studies," *Western Journal of Black Studies* 15, no. 4 (Winter 1991), 209.
19. Gilroy, *The Black Atlantic,* 42.
20. Ibid.
21. Ibid.
22. Ibid.
23. Du Bois, *The World and Africa.*
24. Ibid., 18.
25. Ibid., 18–19.
26. Gilroy, *The Black Atlantic,* 8.
27. Du Bois, *The World and Africa,* 18.
28. Jean-Francois Lyotard, "Defining the Postmodern," in *Postmodernism,* ed. L. Appignanesi (London: ICA documents 4, 1986).
29. Robert Blauner, "Internal Colonialism and Ghetto Revolt," *Social Problems* 16 (1968): 393–408; Blauner, *Racial Oppression in America* (New York: Harper and Row, 1972).
30. Du Bois, *The World and Africa.*
31. Eric Williams, *Capitalism and Slavery* (Chapel Hill: Univ. of North Carolina Press, 1944).
32. William A. Darity Jr., "British Industry and the West Indies Plantations," in *The Atlantic Slave Trade: Effects on Economies, Societies, and Peoples in Africa, the Americas, and Europe,* ed. Joseph E. Inikori and Stanley L. Engerman, 247–79 (Durham, N.C.: Duke Univ. Press, 1992).
33. Darity, "British Industry and the West Indies Plantations," 251.
34. Qtd. in Mark Twain, *Autobiography,* ed. Charles Neider (New York: Harper, 1959), chap. 29.
35. Darity, "British Industry and the West Indies Plantations," 248.
36. Du Bois, *The World and Africa,* 20.
37. Darity, "British Industry and the West Indies Plantations," 273.
38. Du Bois, *The World and Africa,* 12.
39. Alkalimat et al., *Introduction to Afro-American Studies.*
40. Du Bois, *The World and Africa,* 13.
41. Hall, "Beyond Afrocentrism."
42. Ortiz Walton, "A Comparative Analysis of the African and the Western Aesthetic," in *The Black Aesthetic,* ed. Addison Gayle (Garden City, N.Y.: Anchor/Doubleday, 1971).

43. Richard W. Thomas, "Working-Class and Lower-Class Origins of Black Culture: Class Formation and the Division of Black Cultural Labor," *Minority Voices* (Fall 1977): 81–103.

44. Thomas, "Working-Class and Lower-Class Origins of Black Culture."

45. Ibid.

46. Ibid.

47. Giddings, *When and Where I Enter*; Hull et al., *All the Women Are White, All the Blacks Are Men*; bell hooks, *Breaking Bread: Insurgent Black Intellectual Life* (Boston: South End Press, 1981).

48. Thomas, "Working-Class and Lower-Class Origins of Black Culture."

49. Ibid.

50. Marable, "The Divided Mind of Black America."

51. Asante, *The Afrocentric Idea*, 165–67.

52. Marable, "The Divided Mind of Black America."

53. Thomas, "Working-Class and Lower-Class Origins of Black Culture."

54. Ibid.

55. Gilroy, *The Black Atlantic*, 20.

56. Ibid., 23.

57. Asante. *The Afrocentric Idea*, 153.

58. Geneva Smitherman, *Talkin and Testifyin* (Boston: Houghton-Mifflin, 1977); see also, Smitherman, *Black Talk* (Boston: Houghton-Mifflin, 1994).

59. LeRoi Jones, *Blues People* (New York: William Morrow, 1963).

60. Norman Harris, *Connecting Times: The Sixties in Afro-American Fiction* (Jackson: Univ. Press of Mississippi, 1988).

61. Alice Walker, *In Search of Our Mothers' Gardens: Feminist Prose* (New York: Harcourt Brace, 1983).

62. Harris, *Connecting Times*, 5.

63. Ibid., 9.

64. Hall, "Systematic and Thematic Principles."

Chapter 6. Conceptualizing Black Identity

1. Wade Nobles, "African Philosophy: Foundations for Black Psychology," in *Black Psychology*, ed. Reginald L. Jones (New York: Harper & Row, 1972), 18–32. According to William Cross Jr., this essay "would mark for many the origin of the Afrocentric movement, although technically the concept of Afrocentricity is usually credited to Molefi Asante." *Shades of Black: Diversity in African-American Identity* (Temple Univ. Press, 1991), 222.

2. William Cross Jr., "Negro-to-Black Conversion Experience," *Black World* 20, no. 13 (1972): 13–27.

3. Stewart, "Reaching for Higher Ground," 31.

4. Kenneth B. Clark and Mamie P. Clark, "Racial Identification and Preference in Negro Children," in *Readings in Social Psychology,* ed. Theodore M. Newcomb and Eugene L. Hartley (New York: Holt, 1947), 169–78.

5. William L. Yancey, Leo Rigsby, and John D. McCarthy, "Social Position and Self Evaluation: The Relative Importance of Race," *American Journal of Sociology* 78 (1972): 338–59; William E. Cross Jr., "Black Identity: Rediscovering the Distinction between Personal Identity and Reference Group Orientation," in *Beginnings: The Social and Affective Development of Black Children,* ed. Margaret B. Spencer, Geraldine K. Brookins, and Walter R. Allen (Hillsdale, N.J.: Erlbaum, 1985), 155–71; Jerold Heiss and Susan Owens, "Self-evaluation of Blacks and Whites," *American Journal of Sociology* 78 (1972): 360–70.

6. Currently at Penn State University, Cross spent more than two decades at Cornell, where his model was developed and refined.

7. Cross, *Shades of Black.*

8. Ibid., 10.

9. E. J. Barnes, "The Black Community as the Source of Positive Self-concept for Black Children: A Theoretical Perspective," in *Black Psychology,* ed. Reginald L. Jones (New York: Harper and Row, 1972).

10. Cross, *Shades of Black,* 73.

11. Ibid., x.

12. Ibid., 152.

13. Sidney Kronus, *The Black Middle Class* (Columbus, Ohio: Charles E. Merrill Publishing, 1971); William A. Sampson and Vera Milam, "The Intraracial Attitudes of the Black Middle Class: Have They Changed?" *Social Problems* 23 (1975): 153–65.

14. Lee Rainwater, "Crucible of Identity: The Negro Lower-Class Family," in *Black Psyche,* ed. Stanley S. Guterman (Berkeley, Calif.: Glendessary Press, 1972), 31–64; Elaine Brand, Rene A. Ruiz, and Amado M. Padilla, "Ethnic Identification and Preference: A Review," *Psychological Bulletin* 81 (1974): 860–90.

15. William Cross Jr., "The Black Experience Viewed as a Process: A Crude Model for Black Self-Actualization" (paper presented at the thirty-fourth annual meeting of the Association of Social and Behavioral Scientists, Tallahassee, Fla., Apr. 23–24, 1970).

16. Cross, *Shades of Black,* 173.

17. Ibid., 181.

18. Ibid., xi.

19. Clifford L. Broman, Harold W. Neighbors, and James S. Jackson, "Racial Group Identification among Black Adults," *Social Forces* 67, no. 1 (1988): 146–58.

20. James S. Jackson, Wayne R. McCullough, and Gerald Gurin, "Group Identity Development within Black Families," in *Black Families*, ed. Harriet P. McAdoo (Beverly Hills, Calif.: Sage, 1981), 252–63; Wayne R. McCullough, "The Development of Group Identification in Black Americans" (Ph.D. diss., Univ. of Michigan, 1982); Deborah M. Robinson, "The Effect of Multiple Group Identity among Black Women on Race Consciousness" (Ph.D. diss., Univ. of Michigan, 1987); Clifford L. Broman et al., "Racial Group Identification among Black Adults."

21. James S. Jackson, Belinda Tucker, and Philip J. Bowman, "Conceptual and Methodological Problems in Survey Research on Black Americans," in *Methodological Problems in Minority Research*, ed. William T. Liu (Chicago: Pacific/Asian American Mental Health Research Center, 1982), 5–29.

22. P. A. Gurin, A. H. Miller, and G. Gurin, "Stratum Identification and Consciousness," *Social Psychology Quarterly* 43 (1980): 30–47.

23. Janet E. Helms, "Considering Some Methodological Issues in Racial Identity Counseling Research (Psychological Nigrescence)," *Counseling Psychologist* 17, no. 2 (Apr. 1989): 227–52.

24. Helms gives a complex rendition of how instruments appropriate to the Cross multistage theory of black identity might be developed and validated, while Daudi Ajani Ya Azibo has formulated instruments consistent with a more Afrocentric approach ("Personality, Clinical, and Social Psychological Research on Blacks: Appropriate and Inappropriate Research Frameworks," in *Black Studies: Theory, Method, and Cultural Perspectives*, ed. Talmadge Anderson (Pullman: Washington State Univ. Press, 1990).

25. Broman et al., "Racial Group Identification among Black Adults"; Ronald Brown, James S. Jackson, and Philip J. Bowman, "Racial Conscious and Political Mobilization of Black Americans" (paper presented at the American Political Science Association meeting, Denver, 1982).

26. Jackson et al., "Group Identity Development within Black Families."

27. Leachim Tufani Semaj, "Afrikanity, Cognition, and Extended Self-Identity," in *Beginnings: The Social and Affective Development of Black Children*, ed. Geraldine K. Brookins Spencer and Walter R. Allen, 173–84 (Hillsdale, N.J.: Erlbaum, 1985).

28. This group is clearly associated with the black movements of the 1960s; but not because they were socialized during that time. Rather, because their prior socialization helped create the movements. Their sense of group identity was not caused by the movement, but in fact helped to cause it. The

cause, in this framework, was socioeconomic changes affecting blacks beginning in World War II, when this group was born.

29. The author's analytical framework would have created a new region out of the census North-Central states west of the Mississippi River (except Missouri). However, it turns out that there were no respondents from those states (Nebraska, Iowa, North Dakota, South Dakota.)

30. While some of the subsamples of the New York area respondents (by age group and educational level) are too small for valid statistical comparison, there is a consistent similarity between New York and the West across educational groups. (Most educated groups in those places are less closely identified than those of the rest of the sample. Variation in historical sociodemographic influences can explain this "bicoastal" effect, and would be the focus of a separate study).

31. Cross, *Shades of Black*, 174.

32. Ibid.,. xii.

Chapter 7. The Songs of Black Folks

1. As expressed by Richard W. Thomas: "If the core cultural products of Black culture have been music, songs, dance and folklore, then the sole responsibility for producing and reproducing must go to the Southern slaves and their social class heirs." Thomas, "Working-Class and Lower-Class Origins of Black Culture: Class Formation and the Division of Black Cultural Labor," *Minority Voices* 1 (Fall 1977): 81–103.

2. Ortiz Walton, "A Comparative Analysis of the African and Western Aesthetic," in *The Black Aesthetic*, ed. Addison Gayle (Garden City, N.Y.: Anchor/Doubleday, 1971).

3. Ben Sidran, *Black Talk: How the Music of Black America Created a Radical Alternative to the Values of Western Literary Tradition* (New York: Da Capo Press, 1971), chap. 2.

4. Kris Kristoferson, "Me and Bobby McGee." Most popular version recorded by Janis Joplin, Columbia Records 45314, 1971.

5. LeRoi Jones, *Blues People: The Negro Experience in White America and the Music that Developed from It* (New York: Morrow, 1963), chap. 3.

6. Portia Maultsby, "West African Influences and Retentions in U.S. Black Music: A Sociocultural Study," in *More than Dancing: Essays on Afro-American Music and Musicians*, ed. Irene Jackson (Westport, Conn.: Greenwood Press, 1987), 34.

7. Irene V. Jackson, "Music among Blacks in the Episcopal Church: Some Preliminary Considerations," in *More than Dancing*, ed. Irene Jackson, 111.

8. Asante, *The Afrocentric Idea*, 91.

9. Maulana Karenga, *Introduction to Black Studies. Second Edition* (Los Angeles: Univ. of Sankore Press, 1993), 233.

10. "The high point of the Northern strand's cultural production was between 1920 and about 1933, during the Harlem Renaissance. . . . All of the novelist of the Harlem Renaissance came from middle-class backgrounds, and most of them received college and graduate school educations at prominent universities." Thomas, "Working-Class and Lower-Class Origins of Black Culture."

11. Such a "de-centered" conception of black cultural transformation in the urban context was recently initiated by Darlene Clark-Hine in "A History of Black Chicago," a paper presented at the 81st Annual Meeting of the Association for the Study of Afro-American Life and History, Charleston, S.C., Oct. 2–6, 1996.

12. "As early as elsewhere there was a school of piano ragtimers in New Orleans. Back so far indeed that the black, itinerant John the Baptist of that city, who roamed the mid-American red-light districts from the late seventies into the nineties, is almost a legend. . . . Piano and band developed separately in New Orleans, but grew side by side into the same sort of music." Rudi Blesh and Harriet Janis, *They All Played Ragtime* (1950; rpt. New York: Oak Publications, 1971), 165.

13. Donald M. Marquis, *In Search of Buddy Bolden: First Man of Jazz* (Baton Rouge: Louisiana State Univ. Press, 1978), 33.

14. Sidran, *Black Talk*, 37.

15. Marquis, *In Search of Buddy Bolden*, 37.

16. Blesh and Janis, *They All Played Ragtime*, 168.

17. Charles "Buddy" Bolden—a musical ancestor claimed by virtually every one of the early New Orleans innovators—was trying his new sound as early as 1895. Apparently it took a few years to catch on, but by 1900 this "First Man of Jazz" had achieved citywide popularity, not to mention the title "King Bolden." Generally his popularity "did not, however, extend into white New Orleans." Marquis, *In Search of Buddy Bolden*, 72.

18. Marquis, *In Search of Buddy Bolden*, 43.

19. Ibid.

20. Ibid.

21. Ibid., 74.

22. Martin W. Laforse and James A. Drake, *Popular Culture and American Life: Se-*

lected Topics in the Study of American Popular Culture (Chicago: Nelson Hall, 1981), 75.

23. Qtd. in William D. Pierson, *Black Legacy: America's Hidden Heritage* (Amherst: Univ. of Massachusetts Press, 1993), 173.

24. Donald A. Donaldson, "A Window on Slave Culture: Dances at Congo Square in New Orleans, 1800–1862," *Journal of Negro Education* 69, no. 1 (Spring 1984): 61–72.

25. *New Orleans Times-Picayune,* June 20, 1918.

26. William J. Schafer and Johaness Riedel, *The Art of Ragtime* (1973; rpt., New York: Da Capo Press, 1977), xi.

27. E. Belfield Spriggins, "Excavating Local Jazz," *Louisiana Weekly,* Apr. 22, 1933, qtd. in Marquis, *In Search of Buddy Bolden,* 2.

28. As depicted by Nathan Huggins: "Harlem intellectuals promoted Negro art, but one thing is very curious, except for Langston Hughes, none of them took jazz—the new music [which had artistic and cultural roots in the folk culture] seriously. Of course, they all mentioned it as background, as descriptive of Harlem life. But none thought enough of it to try and figure out what was happening. They tended to view it as folk art—like the spirituals and the dance—the unrefined source for the new art. Men like James Weldon Johnson and Alain Locke expected some race genius to appear who would transform that source into high culture." Huggins, *Harlem Renaissance* (New York: Galaxy Books, 1971), 10.

29. Laforse, *Popular Culture in American Life,* 43.

30. Ibid., 82; Blesh and Janis, *They All Played Ragtime,* 168.

31. Laforse, *Popular Culture in American Life,* 89.

32. Paul Goodman and Frank Otto Gatell, *America in the Twenties: The Beginnings of Contemporary America* (New York: Holt, Rinehart and Winston, 1972), 87.

33. Sidran, *Black Talk,* 68.

34. Laforse, *Popular Culture in American Life,* 89.

35. Ibid., 91.

36. Blesh and Janis, *They All Played Ragtime,* 176.

37. Laforse, *Popular Culture in American Life,* 45.

38. Beiderbecke certainly does share at least one fact in common with several important African American innovators, a tragically short life. A familiar gang of suspects—alcohol, disaffection, alienation, and economic ruin—lurk suggestively around his death at age twenty-eight in 1931.

39. Thomas Hennessey, *From Jazz to Swing: African-American Jazz Musicians and Their Music, 1890–1935* (Detroit: Wayne State Univ. Press, 1993), chaps. 5, 6, and 7.

40. Sidran, *Black Talk,* 78.

41. Perry A. Hall, "Toward a Dramaturgical Analysis of Historical Transformation in African-American Musical Culture," *Word: A Black Culture Journal* 1, no. 1 (Spring 1991), 29–38.

42. Sidran, *Black Talk*, 59.

43. LeRoi Jones, *Blues People*, 167.

44. Ibid., 182.

45. Nelson George, *The Death of Rhythm and Blues* (New York: E. P. Dutton, 1988), 26.

46. Ibid., 61–69.

47. By 1960, however, it seems that "the state of popular music in America was a sorry one, with the initial wave of rock 'n' roll having been replaced by the plastic posturings of the Fabians and Frankie Avalons." Ian Hoare, Tony Cummings, Clive Anderson, and Simon Frith, *The Soul Book* (New York: Dell Publishing, 1975), 25.

48. Peter Guralnick, *Sweet Soul Music: Rhythm and Blues and the Southern Dream of Freedom* (New York: Harper and Row, 1986), chap. 1.

49. George, *Death of Rhythm and Blues*, 86–89.

50. Ibid., 188–94.

51. Ibid., chap. 5, "Redemption Songs in the Age of Corporations (1971–1975)," and chap. 6, "Crossover: The Death of Rhythm and Blues."

52. Sidran, *Black Talk*, 67.

53. George, *Death of Rhythm and Blues*, 154.

54. Faruk Z. Bey, leader and lead sax for the Detroit jazz group Griot Galaxy, personal communication, 1984.

55. Tommie Lee Lott, "Marooned in America: Black Urban Youth Culture and Social Pathology," unpublished paper, 1990.

56. *Detroit Metro Times*, Feb. 19, 1990.

57. Tricia Rose, *Black Noise: Rap Music and Black Culture in Contemporary America* (Hanover, N.H.: Univ. Press of New England, 1994). See chapter 1, "Voices from the Margins: Rap Music and Contemporary Black Cultural Production," and chapter 2, "'All Aboard the Night Train': Flow, Layering, and Rupture in Postindustrial New York," for discussion that links the eruption of hip-hop culture in the South Bronx with deteriorating economic conditions affecting that community in the late 1970s.

58. Presaging by a decade the movie "New Jack City," an early 1980s Detroit youth gang, named quite appropriately "Young Boys, Inc.," had institutionalized hierarchy, a systematized distribution process, and an accounting system. They ran promotions and sales. Their sales staff was made more productive with incentives, bonuses, trips to Las Vegas, chauffeur-driven limousine outings to concerts, and the like.

Chapter 8. Crisis, Culture, and Literacy in the Community

1. Miguel Escobar et al., eds., *Paulo Freire on Higher Education: A Dialogue at the University of Mexico* (Albany: State Univ. of New York Press, 1994), 37.
2. Wilson, *The Declining Significance of Race*, 95.
3. Lott, "Marooned in America: Black Urban Culture and Social Pathology."
4. Wilson, *The Truly Disadvantaged*, 82.
5. Charisse Jones, William J Eaton, and David G. Savage, "1 in 4 Young Blacks in Jail or in Court Control, Study Says," *Los Angeles Times*, Feb. 27, 1990.
6. Ronald J. Ostrow, "U.S. Imprisons Black Men at 4 Times S. Africa Rate," *Los Angeles Times*, Jan 5, 1991.
7. Nora S. Gustavsson, "The War Metaphor: A Threat to Vulnerable Populations. (The State of the War on Drugs) War on Drugs Spending for Law Enforcement, Prevention and Rehabilitation," *Social Work* 36, no. 4 (July 1991): 277.
8. Carolyn Schurr, "Crime and Punishment," *ABA Journal* 77 (May 1991): 23; David C. Anderson, "A World Leader, in Prisons: What Does The U.S. Get for Its $16 Billion?" *New York Times*, Mar. 2, 1991.
9. On the other hand, Stewart notes, there are few concrete linkages *within academia* between black/Africana Studies programs and "practitioner" fields like communications, education, and helping and policy-making professions. "The absence of these linkages means that even given the limited extent to which academe is directly connected to the process of social change, Black/Africana Studies is not making use of the available options. It also means that Black/Africana Studies is neither actively involved in serious policy discussions nor well connected to important social change initiatives." (Stewart, "Reaching for Higher Ground.") Lack of formal linkages notwithstanding, ideas, paradigms, and sensibilities generated by Black Studies activists had moved inexorably to influence practitioners and programs in many of these areas.
10. Smitherman, *Talkin and Testifyn*.
11. Charles J. Fillmore, "A Linguist Looks at Ebonics Debate," Center for Applied Linguistics Ebonics Information Page (http://www.cal.org/ebonics/), Center for Applied Linguistics, Oct. 1, 1997.
12. Elliot Diringer and Lori Olzewski, "Critics May Not Understand Oakland Ebonics Plan Goal Is to Teach Standard English," *San Francisco Chronicle*, Dec. 21, 1996.
13. Lori Olzewski, "Oakland Schools OK Black English: Ebonics Considered Different, Not Wrong," *San Francisco Chronicle*, Dec. 19, 1996.
14. Robert Rosenthal, *Pygmalion in the Classroom: Teacher Expectations and Pupil's Intellectual Development* (New York: Holt, Rinehart, and Winston, 1968).

15. Fillmore, "Linguist Looks at Ebonics Debate."

16. Freire, *Pedagogy of the Oppressed*.

17. Marcio D'Olne Campos, "Reading the World (Interview with Brazilian Educator Paulo Freire)," *UNESCO Courier* (Dec. 1990): 4–9.

18. Freire, *Pedagogy of the Oppressed*.

19. Perry A. Hall, "Commentary," in *Black English and the Education of Black Children and Youth: Proceedings of the National Invitational Symposium on the King Decision*, ed. Geneva Smitherman (Detroit: Center for Black Studies, Wayne State Univ., 1981), 32.

20. Campos, "Reading the World."

21. Norman Harris, *Connecting Times: The Sixties in Afro-American Fiction.* (Oxford: Univ. Press of Mississippi, 1988), 9.

22. Jonothan Kozol, *Illiterate America* (New York: Anchor Press/Doubleday, 1985); N. Elasser and V. John-Steiner, "An Interactionist Approach to Advancing Literacy," *Harvard Educational Review* 47, no. 3 (1977).

23. Nina Wallerstein and Edward Bernstein, "Empowerment Education: Freire's Ideas Adapted to Health Education," *Health Education Quarterly* 15, no. 4 (Winter 1988): 370–94.

24. P. Moriarty, "Codifications in Freire's Pedagogy: A North American Application" (master's thesis, San Francisco State Univ., 1984).

25. Deborah Prothrow-Stith, M.D., with Michaele Weissman, *Deadly Consequences: How Violence Is Destroying Our Teenage Population and a Plan to Begin Solving the Problem* (New York: HarperCollins, 1991); see chap. 11, "Helping Schools Prevent Violence."

26. Elasser and John-Steiner, "An Interactionist Approach to Advancing Literacy."

27. Campos, "Reading the World."

28. Lott, "Marooned in America."

29. Escobar et al., *Paulo Freire on Higher Education*.

30. Lott, "Marooned in America."

31. Youth Violence: A Public Health Issue. Conference sponsored by the Centers for Disease Control. "Working Group Report." Atlanta, Ga., Dec. 12–14, 1990.

Epilogue

1. See, for example, Wahneema Lubiano, "Mapping the Interstices between Afro-American Cultural Discourse and Cultural Studies: A Prolegomenon," *Callaloo* 19, no. 1 (Winter 1996): 68–77.

2. Mae G. Henderson, "Where, by the Way, Is This Train Going?": A Case for Black (Cultural) Studies," *Callaloo* 19, no. 1 (Winter 1996), 60–67.

3. Gilroy, *The Black Atlantic*, 8.

4. Michael West, "Like a River: The Million Man March and the Black Nationalist Tradition in the United States," unpublished paper, 1996.

5. The Future of African-American Studies: A Conference on Theory, Pedagogy, and Research. Institute for Research in African-American Studies, Columbia Univ., New York, Oct. 18–19, 1998.

6. Ronald Daniels, "In Defense of Black Nationalism," *The Black World Today* (online publication: http://twtb.com), Mar. 16, 1998; Ronald Walters, "The Black Radical Congress," *The Black World Today* (http://twtb.com), June 21, 1998.

7. Clarence Lang and Jennifer Hamer, "A Response to Ron Daniels," online discussion accessible through the Web page of the Black Radical Congress (http://blackradicalcongress.com), Mar. 29, 1998.

8. Gerald C. Horne, "Letter to the Editor," *Black World Today* (http://www.twbwt.com), undated.

9. Lang and Hamer, "A Response to Ron Daniels."

Bibliography

Adams, Russell. "Intellectual Questions and Imperatives in the Development of Afro-American Studies." *Journal of Negro Education* 53, no. 3 (1984): 201–25.

Alkalimat, Abdul, and Associates. *Introduction to Afro-American Studies.* Chicago: Peoples College Press, 1977.

———. *Paradigms in Black Studies: Intellectual History, Cultural Meaning and Political Ideology.* Chicago: Twenty First Century Books, 1990.

Allen, Robert. L. "Politics of the Attack on Black Studies." *Black Scholar* 6, no. 1 (Sept. 1974): 2–7.

Amistad Research Center. *Amistad.* 2 vols. New York : Random House, 1970–71.

Anderson, Talmadge, ed. *Black Studies: Theory, Method, and Cultural Perspectives.* Pullman Washington: Washington State Univ. Press, 1990.

Appiah, Anthony Kwame. *In My Father's House.* New York: Oxford Univ. Press, 1992.

Asante, Molefi Kete. "Systematic Nationalism." *Journal of Black Studies* 9, no. 1 (Sept. 1978).

———. *Afrocentricity: The Theory of Social Change.* Buffalo, N.Y.: Amulefi, 1980.

———. *The Afrocentric Idea.* Philadelphia: Temple Univ. Press, 1987.

———. *Afrocentricity.* Trenton, N.J.: Africa World Press, 1988.

———. *Kemet, Afrocentricity, and Knowledge.* Trenton, N.J.: Africa World Press, 1990.

Azibo, Daudi Ajani Ya. "Personality, Clinical, and Social Psychological Research on Blacks: Appropriate and Inappropriate Research Frameworks." In *Black Studies: Theory, Method, and Cultural Perspectives,* ed. Talmadge Anderson. Pullman: Washington State Univ. Press, 1990.

Baraka, Imamu Amiri. "Black Nationalism: 1972." *Black Scholar* 4, no. 1 (Sept. 1972): 23–29.

Barnes, E. J. "The Black Community as the Source of Positive Self-concept for Black Children: A Theoretical Perspective." In *Black Psychology,* ed. Reginald L. Jones. New York: Harper and Row, 1972.

Bernal, Martin. *Black Athena: The Afro-Asiatic Roots of Classical Civilization: Volume 1.* New Brunswick, N.J.: Rutgers Univ. Press, 1987.

Berry, Mary Frances, and John W. Blassingame. *Long Memory: The Black Experience in America.* New York: Oxford Univ. Press, 1982.

Blauner, Robert. "Internal Colonialism and Ghetto Revolt." *Social Problems* 16 (1968): 393–408.

———. *Racial Oppression in America.* New York: Harper and Row, 1972.

Blesh, Rudi, and Harriet Janis. *They All Played Ragtime.* 1950. Rpt. New York: Oak Publications, 1971.

Brand, Elaine, Rene A. Ruiz, and Amado M. Padilla. "Ethnic Identification and Preference: A Review." *Psychological Bulletin* 81 (1974): 860–90.

Bright, Alfred L., et al. *An Interdisciplinary Introduction to Black Studies: History, Sociology, Literature, Art, and Philosophy of Black Civilization.* Dubuque, Iowa: Kendal/ Hunt, 1977.

Broman, Clifford L., Harold W. Neighbors, and James S. Jackson. "Racial Group Identification among Black Adults." *Social Forces* 67, no. 1 (1988): 146–58.

Brossard, Carlos. "Classifying Black Studies Programs." *The Journal of Negro Education* 53, no. 3 (1984).

Brown, Ronald, James S. Jackson, and Philip J. Bowman. "Racial Conscious and Political Mobilization of Black Americans." Presented at the American Political Science Association meeting, Denver, 1982.

Campos, Marcio D'Olne. "Reading the World (Interview with Brazilian Educator Paulo Freire)." *UNESCO Courier* (Dec. 1990): 4–9.

Chapman, Abraham. *Black Voices: An Anthology of Afro-American Literature.* New York: New American Library, 1968.

Chrisman, Robert. "The Crisis of Harold Cruse." *The Black Scholar* 1, no. 3 (Nov. 1969): 77–84.

Christine-Phillips, Mary. "25 Years of Black Studies." *Black Issues in Higher Education* 11, no. 5 (May 5, 1994): 14–19.

Clark, Kenneth B., and Mamie P. Clark. "Racial Identification and Preference in Negro Children." In *Readings in Social Psychology,* ed. Theodore M. Newcomb and Eugene L. Hartley, 169–78. New York: Holt, 1947.

Collins, Patricia Hill. *Black Feminist Thought: Knowledge, Consciousness, and the Politics of Empowerment.* New York: Routledge, Chapman, 1991.

Conyers, James C. *The Evolution of African American Studies.* Lanham, Md.: Univ. Press of America, 1995.

Cross, William E., Jr. "The Black Experience Viewed as a Process: A Crude Model for Black Self-Actualization." Presented at the thirty-fourth annual meeting of the Association of Social and Behavioral Scientists, Tallahassee, Fla., Apr. 23–24, 1970.

———. "Negro-to-Black Conversion Experience." *Black World* 20, no. 13 (1972): 13–27.

———. "Black Identity: Rediscovering the Distinction between Personal Identity and Reference Group Orientation." In *Beginnings: The Social and Affective Development of Black Children,* ed. Margaret B. Spencer, Geraldine K. Brookins, and Walter R. Allen, 155–71. Hillsdale, N.J.: Erlbaum, 1985.

———. *Shades of Black: Diversity in African-American Identity.* Temple Univ. Press, 1991.

Darity, William A., Jr. "British Industry and the West Indies Plantations." In *The At-*

lantic Slave Trade: Effects on Economies, Societies, and Peoples in Africa, the Americas, and Europe, ed. Joseph E. Inikori and Stanley L. Engerman, 247–79. Durham, N.C.: Duke Univ. Press, 1992.

Diop, Cheikh Anta. *The African Origin of Civilization: Myth or Reality.* Trans. Mercer Cook. New York: L. Hill, 1974.

———. *The Cultural Unity of Black Africa: Domains of Patriarchy and Matriarchy in Classical Antiquity.* Chicago: Third World Press, 1976.

———. *Civilization or Barbarism: An Authentic Anthropology.* Trans. Yaa-Lengi Meema Mgemi. Ed. Harold J. Salemson and Marjolin de Jager. Brooklyn: Lawrence Hill Books, 1991.

Donaldson, Donald A. "A Window on Slave Culture: Dances at Congo Square in New Orleans, 1800–1862." *The Journal of Negro Education* 69, no. 1 (Spring 1984): 61–72.

Drake, St. Clair. *Black Metropolis: A Study of Negro Life in a Northern City.* New York: Harcourt, Brace, 1945.

Du Bois, W. E. B. *The Philadelphia Negro: A Social Study.* Pub. for the Univ. of Pennsylvania, 1899.

———. *The World and Africa: An Inquiry into the Part Which Africa Has Played in World History.* New York: International Publishers, 1965.

———. *The Souls of Black Folk.* New York: Signet Books, 1982.

Dyson, Michael Eric. *Reflecting Black: African-American Cultural Criticism.* Minneapolis: Univ. of Minnesota Press, 1993.

Elasser, N., and V. John-Steiner. "An Interactionist Approach to Advancing Literacy." *Harvard Educational Review* 47, no. 3 (1977).

Ellison, Ralph. *Invisible Man.* New York: Random House, 1952.

Escobar, Miguel, et al., eds. *Paulo Freire on Higher Education: A Dialogue at the University of Mexico.* Albany: State Univ. of New York Press, 1994.

Fillmore, Charles J. "A Linguist Looks at Ebonics Debate." *Center for Applied Linguistics Ebonics Information Page* (http://www.cal.org/ebonics/) Center for Applied Linguistics, Oct. 1, 1997.

Freire, Paulo. *Pedagogy of the Oppressed.* New York: Herder and Herder, 1970.

Gates, Henry Louis, Jr. *Signifying Monkey: A Theory of African-American Literary Criticism.* New York: Oxford Univ. Press, 1988.

———. "African American Studies in the 21st Century." Selected papers from the Wisconsin Conference on Afro-American Studies in the Twenty-first Century, April 18–20, 1991. *The Black Scholar* 22, no. 3 (Summer 1992).

Gayle, Addison. *Black Expression: Essays by and about Black Americans in the Creative Arts.* New York: Weybright and Talley, 1969.

———. *The Black Aesthetic.* Garden City, N.Y.: Doubleday, 1971.

George, Nelson. *The Death of Rhythm and Blues.* New York: E. P. Dutton, 1988.

Giddings, Paula. *When and Where I Enter: The Impact of Black Women on Race and Sex in America.* New York: Morrow, 1984.

Gilroy, Paul. *The Black Atlantic: Modernity and Black Consciousness.* Cambridge, Mass.: Harvard Univ. Press, 1993.

Goodman, Paul, and Frank Otto Gatell. *America in the Twenties: The Beginnings of Contemporary America.* New York: Holt, Rinehart and Winston, 1972.

Guralnick, Peter. *Sweet Soul Music: Rhythm and Blues and the Southern Dream of Freedom.* New York: Harper and Row, 1986.

Gurin, P. A., A. H. Miller, and G. Gurin. "Stratum Identification and Consciousness." *Social Psychology Quarterly* 43 (1980): 30–47.

Gustavsson, Nora S. "The War Metaphor: A Threat to Vulnerable Populations. (The State of the War on Drugs) War on Drugs Spending for Law Enforcement, Prevention, and Rehabilitation." *Social Work* 36, no. 4 (July 1991): 277.

Hall, Perry A. "Commentary." In *Black English and the Education of Black Children and Youth: Proceedings of the National Invitational Symposium on the King Decision,* ed. Geneva Smitherman. Detroit: Center for Black Studies, Wayne State Univ., 1981.

———. "Systematic and Thematic Principles for Black Studies." *Journal of Negro Education* 53, no. 4 (Summer 1984): 351–58.

———. "Toward a Dramaturgical Analysis of Historical Transformation in African-American Musical Culture." *Word: A Black Culture Journal* 1, no. 1 (Spring 1991): 29–38.

———. "Beyond Afrocentrism: Alternatives for African American Studies." *Western Journal of Black Studies* 15, no. 4 (Winter 1991): 207–12.

———. "Historical Transformation in African American Musical Cultural." *Word: A Black Culture Journal* 1, no. 1 (Spring 1991): 29–38.

———. "African-American Music: Dynamics of Appropriation and Innovation." In *Borrowed Power: Essays on Cultural Appropriation,* ed. Bruce Ziff and Pratima V. Rao, 31–51. New Brunswick, N.J.: Rutgers Univ. Press, 1997.

Hall, Perry, et al. *National Council for Black Studies Report on Curriculum Standards.* Bloomington, Ind.: National Council for Black Studies, 1981.

Harris, Norman. *Connecting Times: The Sixties in Afro-American Fiction.* Jackson: Univ. Press of Mississippi, 1988.

Harris, Robert L., Jr., Darlene Clark Hine, and Nellie McKay. *Black Studies in the United States: Three Essays.* New York: Ford Foundation, 1990.

Heiss, Jerold, and Susan Owens. "Self-evaluation of Blacks and Whites." *American Journal of Sociology* 78 (1972): 360–70.

Helms, Janet E. "Considering Some Methodological Issues in Racial Identity Counseling Research (Psychological Nigrescence)." *The Counseling Psychologist* 17, no. 2 (Apr. 1989): 227–52.

Henderson, Mae G. "Where, By the Way, Is This Train Going? A Case for Black (Cultural) Studies." *Callaloo* 19, no. 1 (Winter 1996): 60–67.

Hennessey, Thomas. *From Jazz to Swing: African-American Jazz Musicians and Their Music, 1890–1935.* Detroit: Wayne State Univ. Press, 1993.

Hine, Darlene Clark. "The Black Studies Movement: Afrocentrist-Traditionalist-Feminist Paradigms for the Next Stage." *The Black Scholar* 22, no. 3 (Summer 1992): 11–18.

Hoare, Ian, Tony Cummings, Clive Anderson, and Simon Frith. *The Soul Book.* New York: Dell Publishing Co., 1975.

hooks, bell. *Breaking Bread: Insurgent Black Intellectual Life.* Boston: South End Press, 1981.

———. *Talking Back: Thinking Feminist, Thinking Black.* Boston: South End Press, 1989.

Huggins, Nathan. *Harlem Renaissance.* New York: Galaxy Books, 1971.

———. *Afro-American Studies: Report to the Ford Foundation.* New York: Ford Foundation, 1985.

Hull, Gloria T., Patricia Bell Scott, and Barbara Smith, eds. *All the Women Are White,*

All the Blacks Are Men, but Some of Us Are Brave: Black Women's Studies. Old Westbury, N.Y.: Feminist Press, 1982.

Hutchings, Phil. "Report on the ALSC National Conference." *Black Scholar* 5, no. 10 (July–Aug. 1974): 48–53.

Institute of the Black World. *Curriculum Development Project: Final Report.* Atlanta: Institute of the Black World, 1982.

Jackson, Irene, ed. *More than Dancing: Essays on Afro-American Music and Musicians.* Westport, Conn.: Greenwood Press, 1987.

Jackson, James S., Belinda Tucker, and Philip J. Bowman. "Conceptual and Methodological Problems in Survey Research on Black Americans." In *Methodological Problems in Minority Research,* ed. William T. Liu, 5–29. Chicago: Pacific/Asian American Mental Health Research Center, 1982.

Jackson, James S., Wayne R. McCullough, and Gerald Gurin. "Group Identity Development within Black Families." In *Black Families,* ed. Harriet P. McAdoo, 252–63. Beverly Hills, Calif.: Sage, 1981.

Johnson, Charles S. *Shadow of the Plantation.* Chicago: Univ. of Chicago Press, 1934.

Jones, LeRoi (Amiri Baraka). *Blues People: The Negro Experience in White America and the Music that Developed from It.* New York: William Morrow, 1963.

Jones, LeRoi, and Larry Neal, eds. *Black Fire: An Anthology of Afro-American Writing.* New York: Morrow, 1968.

Karenga, Maulana Ron. "Which Road: Nationalism, Pan-Africanism, Socialism?" *Black Scholar* 6, no. 2 (Oct. 1974): 21–30.

———. *Introduction to Black Studies.* Los Angeles: Kawaida Publications, 1983.

———. *Introduction to Black Studies. Second Edition.* Los Angeles: The Univ. of Sankore Press, 1993.

King, Deborah. "Multiple Jeopardy, Multiple Consciousness: The Context of Black Feminist Ideology." *Signs: A Journal of Women in Culture and Society* 14, no. 1 (Fall 1988): 42–72.

———. "Unraveling Fabric, Missing the Beat: Class and Gender in Afro-American Social Issues." Selected papers from the Wisconsin Conference on Afro-American Studies in the Twenty-first Century, April 18–20, 1991. *The Black Scholar* 22, no. 3. (Summer 1992).

Kozol, Jonothan. *Illiterate America.* New York: Anchor Press/Doubleday, 1985.

Kronus, Sidney. *The Black Middle Class.* Columbus, Ohio: Charles E. Merrill Publishing, 1971.

Laforse, Martin W., and James A. Drake. *Popular Culture and American Life: Selected Topics in the Study of American Popular Culture.* Chicago: Nelson Hall, 1981.

Lott, Tommie Lee. "Marooned in America: Black Urban Youth Culture and Social Pathology." Unpublished paper, 1990.

Lubiano, Wahneema. "Mapping the Interstices between Afro-American Cultural Discourse and Cultural Studies: A Prolegomenon." *Callaloo* 19, no. 1 (Winter 1996): 68–77.

Lyotard, Jean-Francois. "Defining the Postmodern." In *Postmodernism,* ed. L. Appignanesi. London: ICA documents 4, 1986.

Marable, Manning. "The Divided Mind of Black America: Racial Ideologies and the Urban Crisis." Paper presented at the Race Matters: Black Americans, U.S. Terrain Conference (sponsored by the American Studies and Afro-American Studies Programs of Columbia Univ.), Apr. 30, 1994.

Marquis, Donald M. *In Search of Buddy Bolden: First Man of Jazz.* Baton Rouge: Louisiana State Univ. Press, 1978.

McCullough, Wayne R. "The Development of Group Identification in Black Americans." Ph.D. diss., Univ. of Michigan, 1982.

McWorter, Gerald A., and Ronald Bailey. "Black Studies Curriculum Development in the 1980s: Its Patterns and History." *Black Scholar* (Mar.–Apr. 1984): 18–31.

Moriarty, P. "Codifications in Freire's Pedagogy: A North American Application." Master's thesis, San Francisco State Univ., 1984.

Nobles, Wade. "African Philosophy: Foundations for Black Psychology." In *Black Psychology,* ed. Reginald L. Jones, 18–32. New York: Harper & Row, 1972.

Peterson, Marvin W., Robert T. Blackburn et al. *Black Students on White Campuses: The Impacts of Increased Black Enrollments.* Ann Arbor: Institute for Social Research, Univ. of Michigan, 1978.

Pierson, William D. *Black Legacy: America's Hidden Heritage.* Amherst: Univ. of Massachusetts Press, 1993.

Prowthrow-Stith, Deborah, M.D., with Michaele Weissman. *Deadly Consequences: How Violence Is Destroying Our Teenage Population and a Plan to Begin Solving the Problem.* New York: HarperCollins, 1991.

Rainwater, Lee. "Crucible of Identity: The Negro Lower-Class Family." In *Black Psyche,* ed. Stanley S. Guterman, 31–64. Berkeley, Calif.: Glendessary Press, 1972.

Robinson, Armstead L., Craig C. Foster, and Donald H. Ogilvie, eds. *Black Studies in the University: A Symposium.* New Haven: Yale Univ. Press, 1969.

Robinson, Deborah M. "The Effect of Multiple Group Identity among Black Women on Race Consciousness." Ph.D. diss., Univ. of Michigan, 1987.

Rose, Tricia. *Black Noise: Rap Music and Black Culture in Contemporary America.* Hanover, N.H.: Univ. Press of New England, 1994.

Rosenthal, Robert. *Pygmalion in the Classroom: Teacher Expectations and Pupil's Intellectual Development.* New York: Holt, Rinehart, and Winston, 1968.

Sampson, William A., and Vera Milam. "The Intraracial Attitudes of the Black Middle Class: Have They Changed?" *Social Problems* 23 (1975): 153–65.

Schafer, William J., and Johaness Riedel. *The Art of Ragtime.* 1973. Rpt. New York: Da Capo Press, 1977.

Semaj Leachim Tufani. "Afrikanity, Cognition and Extended Self-Identity." In *Beginnings: The Social and Affective Development of Black Children,* ed. Geraldine K. Brookins Spencer and Walter R. Allen, 173–84. Hillsdale, N.J.: Erlbaum, 1985.

Sidran, Ben. *Black Talk: How the Music of Black America Created a Radical Alternative to the Values of Western Literary Tradition.* New York: Da Capo Press, 1971.

Smitherman, Geneva. *Talkin and Testifyin: The Language of Black America.* Boston: Houghton-Mifflin, 1977.

———. *Black Talk: Words and Phrases from the Hood to the Amen Corner.* Boston: Houghton-Mifflin, 1994.

Stewart, James B. "Historical Patterns of Black-White Political-Economic Inequality in the United States and South Africa." *The Review of Black Political Economy* (Summer 1977): 267–96.

———. "Introducing Black Studies: A Critical Examination of Some Textual Materials." *Umoja* 3, no. 1 (1979): 113–17.

———. "Book Review and Commentary: An Introduction to Black Studies." *The Western Journal of Black Studies* 7. no. 3 (Fall 1983): 113–17.

———. "The Legacy of W. E. B. Du Bois for Contemporary Black Studies." *Journal of Negro Education* 53, no. 3 (1984): 296–311.

———. "Reaching for Higher Ground: Toward an Understanding of Black/Africana Studies." *The Afrocentric Scholar* 1, no. 1 (May 1992): 1–63.

Taylor, Ronald L. "The Study of Black People: A Survey of Empirical and Theoretical Models." *Urban Research Review* 2, no. 2 (1987), rpt. in *Black Studies: Theory, Method, and Cultural Perspectives,* ed. Talmadge Anderson (Pullman: Washington State Univ. Press, 1990).

Thomas, Richard W. "Working-Class and Lower-Class Origins of Black Culture: Class Formation and the Division of Black Cultural Labor." *Minority Voices* (Fall 1977): 81–103.

Thomas, Tony. "Black Nationalism and Confused Marxists." *Black Scholar* 4, no. 1 (Sept. 1972): 47–52.

Turner, James, ed. *The Next Decade: Theoretical and Research Issues in Africana Studies; Selected Papers from the Africana Studies and Research Center's Tenth Anniversary Conference, 1980.* Ithaca, N.Y.: Africana Studies and Research Center, 1984.

Walker, Alice. *In Search of Our Mothers' Gardens: Feminist Prose.* New York: Harcourt Brace, 1983.

Wallerstein, Nina, and Edward Bernstein. "Empowerment Education: Freire's Ideas Adapted to Health Education." *Health Education Quarterly* 15, no. 4 (Winter 1988): 370–94.

Walters, Ronald. "A Response to Haki Madhubuti." *The Black Scholar* 6, no. 2 (Oct. 1974): 47–49.

Walton, Ortiz. "A Comparative Analysis of the African and the Western Aesthetic." In *The Black Aesthetic,* ed. Addison Gayle. Garden City, N.Y.: Anchor/Doubleday, 1971.

West, Michael. "Like a River: The Million Man March and the Black Nationalist Tradition in the United States." Unpublished paper, 1996.

Williams, Eric. *Capitalism and Slavery.* Chapel Hill: Univ. of North Carolina Press, 1944.

Wilson, William J. *The Declining Significance of Race.* Chicago: Univ. of Chicago Press, 1980.

———. *The Truly Disadvantaged.* Chicago: Univ. of Chicago Press, 1987.

Yancey, William L., Leo Rigsby, and John D. McCarthy. "Social Position and Self-Evaluation: The Relative Importance of Race." *American Journal of Sociology* 78 (1972): 338–59.

Young , Carlene, ed. *Black Experience: Analysis and Synthesis.* San Rafael, Calif.: Leswing Press, 1972.

Index

Bechet, Sidney, 156

Beiderbecke, Bix, 157, 158

ben-Jochannan, Yosef, 43

Bennett, Lerone, Jr., 28

Bernal, Martin, 57

Berry, Chuck, 162

Black Arts movement, 3

Black Atlantic, The, 79

Black culture, 3, 23–24, 40–41, 101–13, 194–200 (*see also* assimilation; black identity; literature; music); African influence, 44, 51, 77, 79, 102–3, 105–8, 151, 165, 173 (*see also* Afrocentrism); class influence, 106, 108–10; cultural literacy, 174–85; folk/popular reference frame, 12, 44, 84, 88, 103–8, 109, 138–41, 142–55, 160–67, 185, 196–97, 199–200; high/elite reference frame, 103–8, 110–13, 144–48, 152, 194–95; and mainstream culture: influence of, 127, 139, 142, 189; and mainstream culture: influence on, 90, 142, 151–53, 156–57, 164, 167, 193; systematic (external) influences, 11–12, 88–90, 91–98, 109, 110, 113, 140; thematic (internal) influences, 11–12, 88–90, 110–13, 140

black identity: African influence, 102, 125, 193; and group identity studies: age influence, 24, 123–25, 127–32, 135, 137, 138, 141; education level influence, 123, 126, 134–35, 137, 139–40; historical period influence, 120, 125, 127–33, 138–39, 140; personal vs. group, 120; psychology of, 117; regional influence, 123–24, 125,

127–28, 133–35, 137, 139, 141; *see also* duality; nigrescence

black militancy, 87, 120, 122, 125

black music, 12, 105, 109, 142–68, 182, 196–97 (*see also* bebop; black culture: mainstream culture; blues; disco; funk; hip-hop; jazz; ragtime; rap; rhythm and blues; rock and roll; soul music; swing); African influence on, 103, 110, 143, 144–45, 146, 147, 149–51, 153, 160–61, 164, 165–67; characteristics of, 126; 143; 150; 165; and radio, 162, 165, 166; influence of Reconstruction, 145, 148–49, 160; and technology, 154, 164, 165, 166–67

Black Power, 3, 31, 87

Black Radical Congress, 191

Black Scholar, The, 20, 37, 43

Black Studies: conceptual frameworks, 8–9, 33–34, 41, 70, 76, 83, 110 (*see also* Afrocentrism; integrationist perspective; transformative perspective); curricula, 4, 7–9, 17, 21–23, 28–30, 38, 67, 72, 84–85, 189, 173–74; disciplinary matrix, 11, 67, 70–72, 74–76, 78, 84–86, 117, 138; interdisciplinary aspects, 17, 30, 50, 68–69, 81, 84–86, 189; legitimacy of, 3, 7–8, 10, 17–18, 27, 29, 67, 187–88; and literature, 4, 28–29, 66–68, 75–76, 81, 84–86, 110, 188; mission of, 169; primary and secondary education, 109, 170–76; and psychology, 44, 49, 50; and sociology, 75, 86, 123–24, 167; texts, 4, 9, 27–29, 47–50, 51, 52, 110; within conventional disci-

plines, 10, 33–35, 65–69, 71, 74–
75, 77, 81, 84, 120, 125; *see also*
integrationist perspective;
multiculturalism
Black Studies Curriculum Project,
38, 72
black women's studies, 9, 72–76, 79,
84, 105, 112, 188
Blassingame, John, 28
blues, 105, 145, 148, 149–50, 153, 154,
160, 161, 167, 196; *see also*
rhythm and blues
blues continuum, 110, 139, 148
Blyden, Edward, 55, 107–8
Bolden, Charles ("Buddy"), 150
Boston University, 181
British Birmingham School, 189
British industrialization, 97–98
British (music) Invasion, 189
Broman, Clifford L., 129–33, 137, 139
Brown vs. Board of Education, 129
Brown, James, 164, 197, 199
Bundy, McGeorge, 19, 22–23, 27

Cabral, Amical, 39
Calhoun, John, 25, 26
call-response, 143, 147, 163, 165
Cambridge University, 187
Carruthers, Jacob, 55, 57
Center for Applied Linguists, 176
Charles, Ray, 162
chitlin circuit, 160
Chrisman, Robert, 40–41
civil uprisings: Detroit, 3; Miami, 19;
Watts, 3
Clinton, George, 164
codifications, 180–84
Collins, Patricia Hill, 75, 78, 84, 188
colonialism, 39, 62, 79, 94–96, 98–
100, 146, 170

Columbia University, 19, 30, 188, 191
Congo Square, 143, 148, 151, 160
Cooke, Sam, 162
Cornell University, 30, 31, 119
Creoles, 148, 150, 160
Crescent City, 148
crime, 81, 113, 172, 179, 199
Cross, Jr., William, 117–18, 119, 121–
23, 137–39
Cruse, Harold, 20–21, 33, 38, 40–41

Darity, Jr., William A., 97–98
Davis, David Brion, 24, 26, 35
Delany, Martin, 28, 55, 107–8
demographics, 85, 89, 120, 123–24,
126–27, 129, 135, 140, 197
Dent, Gina, 188
dialogical pedagogy, 179–86
Diddley, Bo, 162
Diop, Cheik Anta, 43, 57, 77, 81–82
disciplinary matrix, 11, 67, 70–72,
74–76, 78, 84–86, 117, 138
disco, 162, 163–64, 165, 166
Disraeli, Benjamin, 97
Dodson, Howard, 72
double consciousness, 3–8, 78, 90,
100, 112, 141, 193
Douglass, Frederick, 28, 110–11, 112,
189
Drake, St. Clair, 29
drug abuse, 6, 11, 12, 81, 113, 167–68,
172, 179–80, 199
Du Bois, W. E. B., 58, 94–100, 194
(*see also* double consciousness);
author's discovery of, 3–6; and
black studies text materials, 28–
29, 35; capitalism and slavery,
97–98; color line, 5, 98; and
discplinary matrix, 71; and duality, 90–91, 101, 102, 141;

Du Bois, W. E. B., *cont.*
  Enlightenment rationalism, 95–96, 189; and Harlem Renaissance, 85; historical interpretations: racism and slavery, 94–95; and transformationist perspective, 78, 79
duality, 12, 87, 100, 117–19, 121–22, 124–27, 137–38, 161, 193; in author's educational experiences, 3–8; and class vs. cultural reference frame, 108–9; and cultural literacy, 113; and folk/popular vs. high/elite reference frame, 103–5, 106; as form vs. essence 102–3; in historical perspectives, 146; in musical forms, 145; and nineteenth century nationalism, 106, 108; and racial group identity studies, 140–41; and structural integration vs. cultural assimilation, 194–96, 198; as thematic principle, 90–91, 101–2, 155; in transformationist approach, 11, 77–80
Duke University, 188
dysfunction, 12, 81, 113, 171–72, 179–80
Dyson, Michael Eric, 78, 84, 188

early parenthood, 12, 81, 171, 180
ebonics, 109, 168, 170–71, 174–79, 186
Egypt, 43, 51–52, 55–57, 59–60, 62, 70–71, 77, 195; *see also* Afrocentrism; Kemet
Ellington, Duke (Edward Kennedy), 158
Ellison, Ralph, 5, 28
Engerman, Stanley, 97

Enlightenment, 53, 79–80, 93–96
European Renaissance, 94

Fanon, Franz, 54, 78
Farrakhan, Louis, 190
Fillmore, Charles J., 176
Ford Foundation, 2, 7, 19, 21–22, 30–31, 68
Franklin, John Hope, 28
freedom and literacy: in folk/popular reference frame, 112; in high/elite reference frame, 111; pregeneric quest/myth of, 28, 110–14; and program implications 169, 178–81; *see also* literacy
Freire, Paulo, 170–71, 178–79, 182, 184
funk, 163–64, 166

Genovese, Eugene, 28
Giddings, Paula, 188
Gilroy, Paul, 79–80, 88, 92–94, 107–8, 189
globalization, 191–92, 198
Goodman, Benny, 158–59
graduate programs, 44
Great Migration, 1, 89, 109, 139, 148, 152–53, 197
Gutman, Herbert, 28

Habermas, Jurgen, 94
Haley, Bill, 162
Harding, Vincent, 72
Hare, Nathan, 20, 33
Harlem Renaissance, 85–86, 89, 148, 152
Harris, Norman, 111–12, 180, 183
Harris, Robert L., 10, 68
Harvard University, 21, 30, 68, 81, 181, 187–88, 191

Hegel, Georg, 53
Helms, Janet E., 122, 126
Henderson, Fletcher, 158–59
Henderson, Mae G., 189
Henderson, Stephen, 112
Hine, Darlene Clark, 18, 43, 68, 84
hip-hop, 90, 154, 164–68, 183, 200
historical periodization, 110; in introductory texts, 47, 50; and People's College, 99–100; in racial group identity studies, 125, 129–30, 132–33, 138; in transformationist approach, 99–101, 113
Hogan, Lloyd, 38
Holloway, Karla, 188
hooks, bell, 75–76, 78
Horne, Gerald, 191
Horowitz, Eugene, 118–19
Horowitz, Ruth, 118–19
Howard University, 35, 42, 68
Huggins, Nathan, 2, 21, 23, 25, 30–31, 50, 67–68
Hughes, Langston, 152
Hurston, Zora Neal, 111
Hutchings, Phil, 39

Ice Cube, 155
inclusionism, 11, 34–35, 44, 66–69, 76–77, 88, 107, 187
Indiana University, 30
Industrial Revolution, 93, 96, 98
industrialization, 93, 95–100; and Enlightenment philosophy, 93; and folk/popular reference frame, 106, 153–54, 197; and Great Migration, 89, 100; and group identity studies, 133–35, 139; and slavery, 96–98, 100; as systematic (external) force, 89,

96–98; and Western culture, 79, 95; and underclass, 171
Institute of the Black World (IBW), 38, 72, 74
integrationist perspective, 11, 21, 24, 66–67; in disciplinary matrix, 71, 75–78, 82, 85–87; and epistemological issues, 33–35; at Harvard, 187; influence in, African American studies, 67–68, 187–88; institutionalization of, 187; and program approach, 30–31, 33; rejection of, 35, 40–43; and "weak" multidisciplinary rationale, 69

Jackson, James, 126, 128–29, 133, 140
Jackson, Jesse, 42
James, C. L. R., 78, 97
jazz, 148–53, 156–62, 166; *see also* bebop; swing
Jeffries, Leonard, 190
Johnson, Charles, 29
Johnson, Lyndon Baines, 19
Joiner, Charles, 174
Jones, LeRoi, 37, 110, 145, 148, 166; *see also* Baraka, Imamu Amiri
Jones, Reginald, 117
Journal of Black Studies, 36–37
Journal of Negro Education, 35, 68, 83
jump blues, 161

Karenga, Maulana, 9, 20–23, 37, 48–51, 55, 57, 69, 117, 147, 190–91
Kawaida theory, 49–59; *see also* Afrocentrism
Kelley, Robin, D. G., 78, 90
Kemet, 51–52, 55–57, 59–60, 71; *see also* Egypt
Kennedy, John F., 22

40–41; in disciplinary matrix, 66, 75, 78, 87–88; and feminism, 75, 76; and globalization, 193, 198–99; and high/elite reference frame, 106–8, 111, 144, 194; in introductory texts, 48; Marxism, debate with, 9, 36–43, 191–92; Marxism, influence on, 38; and Million Man March, 190; in the nineteenth century, 106–8, 111, 194; and Yale Symposium, 20–23, 31

New Deal, the, 129

nigrescence, 117, 121–27, 137–39; *see also* black identity

Nobles, Wade, 117

Ogilvie, Donald H., 27

Ohio State University, 30

Oliver, King, 156

oral tradition: in Africa, 56; and Afrocentrism, 56, 107, 147; and black language, 109, 179; and black music, 159; in folk/popular reference frame, 12, 104–7, 143, 195–96; and jazz, 149–50; and (pre-generic quest/myth of) freedom and literacy, 112; and rap music, 165, 167

Otis, Johnny, 158

Pan-Africanism, 36–37, 41–42, 170, 193

Parham, Thomas A., 122

Parker, Charlie, 41, 160

Parks, Rosa, 26–27

Peoples College, 47, 99

Philadelphia International Records, 163

Presley, Elvis, 158

primary and secondary education, 109, 170–76; teacher expectations, 177

Prince, 155

problem-posing, 179

Prothrow-Stith, Deborah, 181, 183, 185

Quarles, Benjamin, 28

racial inequality, 89, 158, 172

racism: in academia, 24; in Afrocentrism, 61; as culture/identity determinant 87, 104–5, 120, 143, 194; in Enlightenment philosophy, 79–80, 95–96; factors defining legacy of, 79; and gender issues, 75; and globalization, 198; and language 54; Marxist explanation of, 40; and music, effects on, 158; nationalist explanation of, 42; and perception of black culture, 146–47, 151; role in institutional separatism, 195; and slavery, and capitalism, 37–40, 96; and Western progress 92

ragtime, 149–50, 151–53, 156, 157, 166

ragtime piano music, 149–50, 152, 166

Rainey, "Ma," 163

rap music, 164–67, 182, 183

Reconstruction, 85, 100, 108, 112, 145, 148, 160, 192

Redman, Don, 158

religion, 50, 82, 104, 147

rhythm and blues (R&B), 153, 161–63, 166, 196

rhythmic syncopation, 143, 149–50, 156

rock and roll, 162, 164, 197
Rodney, Walter, 78, 97
Rolling Stones, 189

sampling, 126, 166
San Francisco State University, 20, 25, 30
scratching, 165
Sentencing Alternative Project, 171
separatism: in Black Studies movement, 23, 31; for cultural validation, 142–44, 194; and globalization, 198–99; and high/elite reference frame, 194, 195; integration and, 193; as response to racism, 41, 87, 107, 144, 190
Shakur, Tupak, 183
slavery, 92–100, 146–47; Afrocentric view of, 62; and capitalism, 38, 92, 94–98, 100; Du Bois's views of effects of, 96; and folk/popular reference frame, 103–6, 143, 145–48, 160, 195; and freedom and literacy, 112, 114; historical period of, 99, 100, 113, 148; and industrialization, 96–97, 100; justification of, 24; Marxist explanation of, 92; revision of history of, 28; struggles against, 105, 111, 146, 195, 196, 199; and transformationist perspective, 79, 146
Smith, Adam, 96
Smith, Bessie, 163
Smitherman, Geneva, 109, 174, 175
social activism: and African American Studies' instrumental mission, 169–70; and African liberation, 37; and Afrocentrism, 44; and black identity, 117; in Black

Studies movement, 9, 17–19, 23, 25, 26, 30, 34, 39–40, 47–48, 59, 67–68, 70; and globalization, 199–200; resurgence of, 187, 188, 189, 190–92; as role of black intellectual, 5–6; student, 7, 8, 17, 21, 23, 25, 87
social crisis, 6, 12, 81; *see also* crime; drug abuse; early parenthood; marginalization; unemployment
socialism, 36–37, 39, 41–42; *see also* Marxism
soul music, 162, 197
Stax-Volt, 163
Stepto, Robert, 110
Stewart, James B., 11, 38, 48, 50–61, 66–71, 75–78, 84–86, 118
Stuckey, Sterling, 28
Sumner, William Graham, 25–26
swing, 157–61

Taylor, Charles, 20
Taylor, Ronald, 33
technologization: and Black Radical Congress, 191; and freedom and literacy, 113; and globalization, 192, 199; and industrialization, 96; and liberation pedagogy, 181; in popular music, 154, 164–66; as systematic (external) force), 79, 93–94; in transformationist perspective, 109
Temple University, 49, 188
Tet offensive, 19, 99
Thomas, Richard, 103, 107, 146
Thomas, Tony, 37, 67
transformationist perspective, 11–12, 66, 77–79, 82, 91–99, 108–9, 127–28, 141, 146, 188, 191, 197

In the Vineyard was designed and typeset on a Macintosh computer system using PageMaker software. The text is set in Palatino and the titles in Bickley Script and Stone Sans. This book was designed by Kay Jursik, composed by Kimberly Scarbrough, and manufactured in the United States by Thomson-Shore, Inc. The recycled paper used in this book is designed for an effective life of at least three hundred years.